Essentials of WMS®-III Assessment

Essentials of Psychological Assessment Series
Series Editors, Alan S. Kaufman and Nadeen L. Kaufman

Essentials

of WMS®-III

Assessment

Elizabeth O. Lichtenberger,
Alan S. Kaufman, and Zona C. Lai

Foreword by Joseph J. Ryan, Professor of Psychology
Central Missouri State University

 John Wiley & Sons, Inc.

WMS®-*III*, *WMS*®-*R*, *WAIS*®-*R, and WAIS*®-*III* are registered trademarks of The Psychological Corporation.
WJ III™ is a trademark of Riverside Publishing.

Library of Congress Cataloging-in-Publication Data:
Lichtenberger, Elizabeth O.
    Essentials of WMS-III assessment / Elizabeth O. Lichtenberger, Alan S. Kaufman, and Zona C. Lai.
      p. cm. — (Essentials of psychological assessment series)
    Includes bibliographical references and index.
    ISBN 0-471-38080-6 (pbk. : alk. paper)
    1. Wechsler Memory Scale—Handbooks, manuals, etc.   I. Title: Essentials of Wechsler Memory Scale, Third Edition assessment.   II. Kaufman, Alan S., 1944–   III. Lai, Zona C.
IV. Title.   V. Series.

RC394.M46 L53 2001
616.8′4—dc21

                                                  2001026445

Printed in the United States of America.

10 9 8 7 6 5 4 3 2 1

In loving memory of
My Uncle, Vernon Allen Smoots,
and others who can no longer remember;
We will never forget you.

Forget not those who cannot remember.

E.O.L.

To my son,
James Corey Kaufman,
In honor of his recent PhD in Cognitive Psychology from Yale University
and his engagement to a wonderful young woman, Allison;
With enormous respect for his creativity, intelligence, and compassion;
With great pride in watching his plays be performed around the world;
And with appreciation for his value as my colleague in our joint research and
writing ventures (in psychology and baseball), and for the invaluable research
assistance he has unselfishly given me for years in my own work.
With love always from a grateful Dad.

A.S.K.

This book is dedicated to my parents, Dr. and Mrs. Grace Lai,
who remind me about the pursuit of dreams;
my mentor in the clinical neuropsychology of memory, Roberta F. White, PhD;
and, of course, I cannot forget the loving presence of Michael.

Z.C.L.

CONTENTS

FOREWORD

I was flattered when the authors of *Essentials of WMS®-III Assessment* invited me to write this foreword. As a practicing clinical neuropsychologist for over 25 years, I have examined countless patients with documented or suspected mnestic dysfunctions. Until publication of the Wechsler Memory Scale-Third Edition (WMS-III), I relied upon a flexible approach to memory assessment that used a variety of instruments selected on the basis of clinical judgment, referral questions, and the presenting problems of each examinee. The limitations of this approach are well known and often include (a) unavailability of comparable norms across instruments, (b) use of a relatively unique compilation of tests for each patient, and (c) lack of information concerning the interrelationships of memory measures with each other and with scores from tests of psychometric intelligence. In 1997, I gave up the flexible assessment approach and began administering the WMS-III as my standard memory battery. I made this decision because the WMS-III is a state-of-the-art assessment device that measures working, immediate, and delayed memory across the auditory and visual modalities using both free recall and recognition formats. In addition, the scale has an excellent normative sample, the interrelationships among subtests are known, and it was co-normed with the Wechsler Adult Intelligence Scale-Third Edition (WAIS®-III). The last characteristic makes it possible for examiners to evaluate IQ-memory discrepancies in a psychometrically defensible manner.

Drs. Lichtenberger, Kaufman, and Lai have written a useful and timely book. *Essentials of WMS® - III Assessment* will appeal to practicing psychologists, psychology technicians, researchers, and other professionals who assess the memory functions of patients, students, or study participants. Graduate programs in clinical, counseling, and school psychology should be interested in this book because it will ease the task of introducing graduate students to the

WMS-III and to many of the principles of dealing with patients during the assessment process. It will also help students examine, score, organize, and interpret the plethora of information provided by a WMS-III examination. Finally, it should be useful to attorneys who practice personal injury law. Two components that are likely to be of interest to attorneys are the (a) detailed presentation of scale strengths and weaknesses and (b) the utilization of a down-to-earth practical presentation of how one goes about a complex task—the valid and reliable assessment of memory disorders using the WMS-III.

The volume is organized into seven chapters; each of the first six is followed by a brief quiz to help the reader solidify what she or he has read. Most chapters are filled with handy tables and figures that allow the reader to quickly locate clinically relevant tips, reminders, facts, or guidelines. Appendix A provides a detailed checklist for WMS-III administration and scoring. This document is useful for training novice examiners and for conducting quality assurance studies of experienced practitioners. An interpretation worksheet appears in Appendix B. If properly used, this worksheet can help examiners organize the plethora of scores yielded by the WMS-III and also prevent them from overlooking potentially important results.

The first chapter traces the history and background of the Wechsler Memory Scale family. The WMS-III is then described in terms of structure, changes and improvements relative to previous editions, theoretical underpinnings, standardization, and psychometric properties. The second chapter is devoted to scale administration. In addition to discussions on the testing environment, examiner-examinee relationship, time requirements, common examiner errors, and administration tips for each of the subtests, the authors provide helpful suggestions for constructing abbreviated WMS-III batteries. They present a series of decision trees to help examiners select subtest combinations that not only reduce administration time but also provide sufficient information to effectively handle three types of clinical memory referrals. In Chapter 3 the authors take the reader through a step-by-step process for scoring the standard and supplementary subtests and obtaining the various WMS-III indexes. The material dealing with scale administration and scoring (and Appendix A) should be useful to both the novice and experienced examiner, as one can never be too competent or skillful when using a clinical instrument like the WMS-III. As we all know, mistakes in administration or scoring may easily compromise the validity of the WMS-III scores.

The remaining sections of the text, with the exception of Chapter 5, provide the "meat and potatoes" of WMS-III interpretation. Chapter 5, on the other hand, contains a listing of the strengths and weaknesses that characterize the scale based not only on a review of the WMS-III manuals and published literature, but also on the personal communications of a group of seasoned clinical practitioners. This chapter should be especially valuable to clinicians working in the forensic area. During pretrial deposition or actual court testimony, the expert witness may be asked by an opposing attorney to defend her or his selection of the WMS-III to evaluate the memory functions of a plaintiff or defendant. Knowledge of the strengths and weaknesses of the WMS-III will help the expert witness anticipate possible challenges to the validity and clinical utility of the scale.

Chapters 4, 6, and 7 are the essence of the volume. Chapter 4 gives the reader a step-by-step blueprint for WMS-III interpretation. This is a sophisticated approach that places each subtest within the Cattell-Horn-Carroll Gf-Gc model of human ability and stresses hypothesis testing based on integration of theory, clinical experience, and information gleaned from behavioral observations and pertinent history. This chapter is filled with hints about the possible meaning of individual responses, how to test specific interpretative hypotheses, and clinically relevant base rate information. The interpretability and practical meaningfulness of the various indexes is covered in depth, as is the most efficacious approach to evaluating differences between and among the eight summary values. Interpretive suggestions abound and a series of highly useful tables provide the reader with information that is both clinically useful and unique to this text. For instance, the authors provide both a table of shared abilities for the primary and optional subtests based on the Cattell-Horn-Carroll Gf-Gc model and a table of differences between individual supplemental subtest scaled scores and the mean scaled score for the 13 supplemental subtests.

Chapter 6 focuses on the clinical application of the WMS-III. The authors review the relevant literature dealing with the previous and current versions of the scale and provide information concerning the distinctive patterns of performance (across the Indexes and subtests) that are likely to characterize a variety of disorders. The conditions covered include traumatic brain injury, temporal lobe epilepsy, dementia syndromes (e.g., Parkinson's disease and Alzheimer's disease), schizophrenia, and substance abuse disorders. Space is also devoted to discussions of normal aging and the detection of malingered memory impairment. A series of tables summarizes the anticipated WMS-III findings for each disorder and for patients whose performance suggests malingering. These tables should prove useful to clinicians and researchers alike as they are constructed in a manner reminiscent of the research diagnostic criteria for psychiatric disorders that were widely used prior to the publication of the *DSM-III* in 1980. The final chapter consists of two case studies that illustrate the principles presented in the first six chapters (e.g., hypothesis testing and integrating test results with extra-test behaviors) as well as an approach for integrating the WMS-III into a comprehensive neuropsychological battery. Careful reading of the case studies also provides numerous examples of how clinicians may effectively communicate complex information (e.g., description of individual tests and the meaning of specific scores or patterns of scores) via the written report.

This book represents a cogent effort to create a practical, up-to-date reference for the clinical use of the WMS-III. It is my contention that the authors have accomplished their goal, especially as it pertains to the organization and interpretation of the seemingly overwhelming array of scores and summary values yielded by this instrument. This book will not solve the advanced student's or the seasoned practitioner's task of extracting meaningful and accurate interpretations from the WMS-III, but it will make interpretation seem less imposing. It is the considered opinion of the undersigned that *Essentials of WMS®-III Assessment* fills a significant void in the literature on memory assessment and that it will become a widely used resource.

Joseph J. Ryan, PhD, ABPP-CN
Professor of Psychology
Central Missouri State University

SERIES PREFACE

n the *Essentials of Psychological Assessment* series, we have attempted to provide the reader with books that will deliver key practical information in the most efficient and accessible style. The series features instruments in a variety of domains, such as cognition, personality, education, and neuropsychology. For the experienced clinician, books in the series will offer a concise, yet thorough way to master utilization of the continuously evolving supply of new and revised instruments, as well as a convenient method for keeping up to date on the tried-and-true measures. The novice will find here a prioritized assembly of all the information and techniques that must be at one's fingertips to begin the complicated process of individual psychological diagnosis.

Wherever feasible, visual shortcuts to highlight key points are utilized alongside systematic, step-by-step guidelines. Chapters are focused and succinct. Topics are targeted for an easy understanding of the essentials of administration, scoring, interpretation, and clinical application. Theory and research are continually woven into the fabric of each book, but always to enhance clinical inference, never to sidetrack or overwhelm. We have long been advocates of "intelligent" testing—the notion that a profile of test scores is meaningless unless it is brought to life by the clinical observations and astute detective work of knowledgeable examiners. Test profiles must be used to make a difference in the child's or adult's life, or why bother to test? We want this series to help our readers become the best intelligent testers they can be.

In *Essentials of WMS®-III Assessment,* the authors have provided readers with a solid informational base for administering, scoring, and interpreting the most recent version of the highly popular Wechsler Memory Scale. The information on interpretation is enriched with highlights from the expansive literature on neuropsychological and clinical uses of the WMS-III and its previous versions. Thus, this book integrates research and information steeped in good clinical practice to provide sets of guidelines that enable psychologists and neuropsychologists to administer and then systematically interpret this thoroughly revised and restandardized measure of memory functioning.

Alan S. Kaufman, PhD, and Nadeen L. Kaufman, EdD, Series Editors
Yale University School of Medicine

One

OVERVIEW

INTRODUCTION

The assessment of the diverse aspects of memory functioning is an essential part of clinical and neuropsychological evaluation, especially for adults. Because many adult neuropsychiatric disorders involve disruption of certain memory functions (The Psychological Corporation, 1997), as does the normal aging process, comprehensive measurement of short- and long-term memory often plays a key role in assessment. One of the goals of this book is to provide an easy reference source for those who wish to learn the essentials of the Wechsler Memory Scale®–Third Edition (WMS®-III) in a direct, nononsense, systematic manner. In addition, we, the authors, intend to provide an administrative and interpretive guide for those who administer a complete or partial WMS-III battery and want to integrate it with other neuropsychological tests. This book also brings clinicians up to date on the latest WMS-III and related research that is directly applicable to clinical practice.

Essentials of WMS®-III Assessment was developed with an easy-to-read format in mind. The topics covered in the book emphasize administration, scoring, interpretation, and application of the WMS-III. Each chapter includes several "Rapid Reference," "Caution," and "Don't Forget" boxes, which highlight important points for easy reference. At the end of each chapter, questions are provided to help clinicians solidify what they have read. The information provided in this book helps clinicians to understand, in depth, the latest of the measures in the Wechsler family of memory tests and helps them become a competent WMS-III examiner and clinician.

HISTORY AND DEVELOPMENT

Researchers have examined the topic of adult memory assessment in considerable depth, from both clinical (Kaufman, 1990) and neuropsychological (Squire & Butters, 1992) perspectives, and they have given much attention to memory disorders of the elderly within both of these disciplines (Nixon, 1996a; 1996b). Research on memory has been summarized and integrated, including research on the original Wechsler Memory Scale (WMS), the Wechsler Memory Scale–Revised (WMS-R) (Wechsler, 1987; The Psychological Corporation, 1997), and Russell's (1975, 1988) "revision" of Wechsler's (1945) original memory battery (Mitrushina, Boone, & D'Elia, 1999). This section provides a brief history of the tests in the family of Wechsler Memory Scales, and Chapter 6 reviews research pertinent to the global topic of memory as well as research specific to the WMS-III and WMS-R.

VARIOUS EDITIONS OF THE WECHSLER MEMORY SCALE

The Original Wechsler Memory Scale

Seven subtests comprised Wechsler's (1945) version of the WMS: Personal and Current Information, Orientation, Mental Control, Logical Memory, Digits Forward and Backward, Visual Reproduction, and Associate Learning. Although the WMS came in two forms, only Form I was adequately normed for clinical use (Mitrushina et al., 1999). Thus, clinicians have used the global Memory Quotient yielded by Form I most often to obtain information about a person's memory function. The WMS emphasized short-term memory of verbal material and did not offer verbal and visual memory distinctions nor short- and long-term memory contrasts. These dichotomies have proved to be of diagnostic relevance for clinical and neuropsychological assessment (Groth-Marnat, 2000). In addition, the global treatment of memory was antithetical to the results of laboratory experiments with normal individuals and the findings from brain-related studies of disordered adults (Kaufman, 1990). The norms for the WMS were based on a small, restricted sample of 200 patients at Bellevue Hospital in New York, ages 25 to 50 years, with norms simply extrapolated for younger and older individuals. The WMS was sometimes found to be diagnostically useful, but was typically criticized (Kaufman, 1990). Despite its shortcomings, the WMS persisted as one of the most popular clinical assessment tools (Brinkman, Largen, Gerganoff, & Pomara, 1983).

Russell's Wechsler Memory Scale–Revised

Russell (1975, 1988) attempted to eliminate some of the problems with the WMS by adapting and renorming Wechsler's scale. He selected the Logical Memory subtest and the Visual Reproduction subtest to administer to participants. He incorporated two conditions: immediate and delayed response (30-min delay filled with interference activities). Russell's 1975 adaptation of the WMS was titled the Wechsler Memory Scale–Revised (WMS-R), and this instrument became "the first choice of a growing number of clinicians for general, all-purpose memory assessment" (Gregory, 1987, pp. 27–28). Because of it's increasing popularity, Russell's WMS-R generated a number of research studies.

Despite its use for clinical and research purposes, the psychometric properties of Russell's WMS-R were weak; it was poorly standardized by any reasonable criterion and had been developed in an unsystematic manner. Although left hemisphere/right hemisphere comparisons and short-term/long-term contrasts were possible to some extent with Russell's WMS-R, the battery, nonetheless, was a weak link in the clinical evaluation process.

Wechsler Memory Scale–Revised (WMS-R)

In 1987, The Psychological Corporation revised and restandardized the old WMS, creating a stronger psychometric instrument, the WMS-R. Unfortunately, the name chosen for The Psychological Corporation's revision of the battery (though a logical choice) was identical to the name Russell (1975, 1988) assigned to his popular clinical tool. The result was confusion for anyone examining the clinical literature in memory, because the title "WMS-R" referred to two entirely different instruments. From this point on, this book refers to The Psychological Corporation's (1987) revision of the original Wechsler Memory Scale as the "WMS-R" and Russell's (1975) version as "Russell's WMS-R."

The WMS-R was normed in 1985–86 on individuals aged 16 to 74 years, matching the WAIS-R age range. Normative scores for three of the WMS-R age groups (18–19 years, 25–34 years, and 45–54 years) were interpolated on the basis of the scores of the adjacent sampled age groups. The battery contains eight short-term memory tasks plus four delayed recall trials. In addition, there is a brief test of mental status (information and orientation questions) to determine a person's general alertness to the environment and ability to be tested validly on cognitive tests. The eight subtests are grouped in various ways to provide the following standard scores, known as Indexes, which have a mean of 100 and SD of 15: Verbal Memory, Visual Memory, General Memory (Verbal + Visual), Attention/Concentration, and Delayed Recall. The 14 questions that comprise the information and orientation section are not calculated as part of the indexes.

Overall, the WMS-R made significant improvements in the measurement of memory functions (Mitrushina et al., 1999). However, reviews of the test suggested that there was further room for improvement (Elwood, 1991; Franzen & Iverson, 2000; Kaufman, 1990; Lezak, 1995; Loring, 1989; Spreen & Strauss, 1998). The most noteworthy criticisms of the WMS-R were as follows:

- The WMS-R has low subtest and index reliability (Elwood, 1991; Kaufman, 1990).
- The WMS-R was not developed from an integrated theoretical foundation (Kaufman, 1990).
- Scores were interpolated for three WMS-R age groups (18–19 years, 25–34 years, and 45–54 years), and the overall sample is small (Franzen & Iverson, 2000; Kaufman, 1990).
- The WMS-R does not separate delayed memory into verbal and visual components (Loring, 1989).
- Factor-analytic studies do not lend confidence in the ability to state which aspects of memory may be reflected in the WMS-R index scores (Franzen & Iverson, 2000; Kaufman, 1990).
- The limited factor-analytic support for some scales and their low reliability and stability coefficients, taken together "render them almost useless for individual diagnosis" (Kaufman, 1990, p. 597).

OVERVIEW AND ORGANIZATION OF THE WMS-III

During the development of the WMS-III, The Psychological Corporation reviewed all WMS-R subtests for cultural and gender bias, appropriateness of content, theoretical basis, and clinical utility. The Psychological Corporation also solicited and integrated reviews from clinical psychologists and neuro-psychologists to determine the ways in which the WMS-R could be improved. The *WAIS-III-WMS-III Technical Manual* (The Psychological Corporation, 1997), summarizes the improvements to content, the psychometric proper-ties, and the score configuration of the newest version of the test (see Rapid Reference 1.1).

≡Rapid Reference 1.1

Improvements in the WMS-III over the WMS-R

- **Increased the sample size** from 500 to 1,250.
- **Broadened the age range** from 6 age groups (ages 16–74) to 13 age groups (ages 16–89).
- **Ensured representativeness of the general population's ability level** by randomly administering the WMS-III to one-half of the WAIS-III standardization sample, within each stratification variable.
- **Sampled each age group** in the WMS-III standardization sample rather than interpolating norms, as was done for some age groups on the WMS-R.
- **Improved the reliability coefficients** so that average internal reliability coefficients of the WMS-III Primary Indexes ranged from .74 (Auditory Recognition Delayed—the single subtest index) to .93 (Auditory Immedi-ate) with a median value of .87; the mean average split-half reliability coeffi-cients for the WMS-R Indexes ranged from .70 (Visual Memory) to .90 (Attention-Concentration) with a median value of .77.
- **Changed the visual memory stimuli** and no longer purports to assess a verbal or visual memory system exclusively because there was little empir-ical evidence that the WMS-R visual memory subtests adequately mea-sured the "pure" visual memory system, or that they discriminated between individuals with unilateral hemispheric lesions.
- **Improved internal validity** by constructing WMS-III indexes on the ba-sis of clinically meaningful aspects of clinical memory assessment rather than on the basis of factor analysis.
- **Added recognition measures** to the WMS-III, as the WMS-R only pro-vided standardized recall measures, limiting the test as a means of identifying specific retrieval problems.

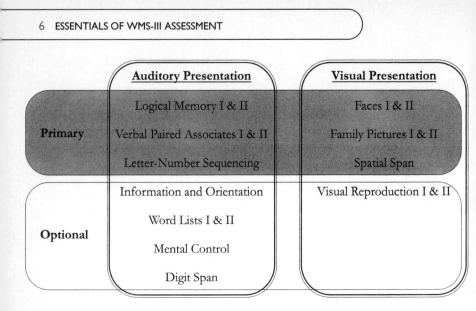

Figure 1.1 WMS-III Primary and Optional Subtests

The 11 subtests of the WMS-III include 7 that were retained from the WMS-R plus 4 new subtests (Faces, Family Pictures, Word Lists, and Letter-Number Sequencing). Six of the subtests have both an immediate recall condition and a delayed recall condition (administered 25 to 35 min after the immediate condition). Two of the WMS-R subtests were dropped in the revision: Figural Memory and Visual Paired Associates. The *WMS-III Administration and Scoring Manual* describes each of the subtests in the introduction section (Wechsler, 1997). Of the 11 subtests, 6 are considered part of the primary battery and 5 are considered optional (see Figure 1.1). The index scores cannot be calculated unless the 6 primary subtests are administered.

The WMS-III produces eight Primary Indexes, each of which comprises two to five subtests. Figure 1.2 depicts how the subtests are organized into the eight Primary Indexes. The WMS-III includes three more indexes than the WMS-R, and many of the WMS-R global scales have been renamed (see Rapid Reference 1.2 for WMS-R to WMS-III Index changes). The most confusing change for clinicians well-versed in the WMS-R concerns the label "General Memory Scale." On the WMS-R, this label refers to a global measure of *immediate* memory; on the WMS-III, the General Memory Scale is a global measure of *delayed* memory. Also, note that, except for the scale that includes the word

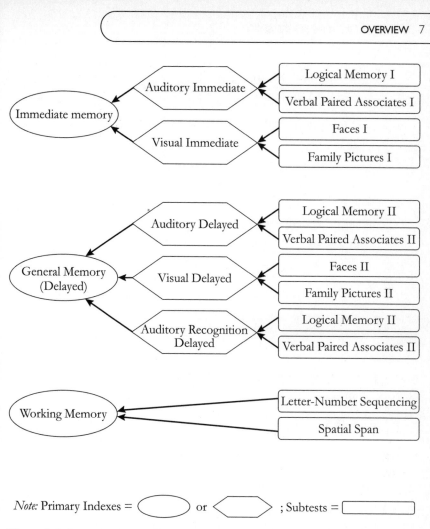

Figure 1.2 Organization of Primary Indexes and the Subtests Comprising Them

"recognition" (Auditory Recognition Delayed), all WMS-III "delayed" scales, including General Memory, measure delayed *recall*.

Values obtained for the WMS-III Primary Indexes are standard scores with mean = 100 and SD = 15; subtests yield scaled scores with mean = 10 and SD = 3. As is noted in Figure 1.2, three of the Primary Indexes are derived only from the orally presented subtests, two are derived only from the visually presented subtests, and the remaining three are composed of both orally and

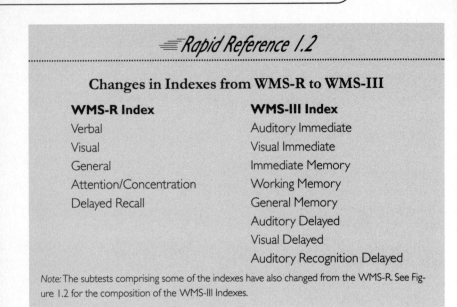

$\equiv$*Rapid Reference 1.2*

Changes in Indexes from WMS-R to WMS-III

WMS-R Index	WMS-III Index
Verbal	Auditory Immediate
Visual	Visual Immediate
General	Immediate Memory
Attention/Concentration	Working Memory
Delayed Recall	General Memory
	Auditory Delayed
	Visual Delayed
	Auditory Recognition Delayed

Note: The subtests comprising some of the indexes have also changed from the WMS-R. See Figure 1.2 for the composition of the WMS-III Indexes.

visually presented subtests. The Indexes measure three different types of memory (immediate, delayed, and working). Also, as indicated, the WMS-III assesses memory both visually and auditorally, permitting meaningful comparisons across modalities, as well as providing information on delayed recall versus delayed recognition.

Clinicians may also obtain supplemental data on the WMS-III from the Auditory Process Composites: Single-Trial Learning, Learning Slope, Retention, and Retrieval. Scores from the auditorally presented subtests, Logical Memory I and II and Verbal Paired Associates I and II, contribute to the four Auditory Process Composites.

- *Single-Trial Learning* measures the examinee's ability to immediately recall auditory information after a single exposure to the material.
- *Learning Slope* measures the examinee's ability to recall auditory information after repeated exposures (by comparing the relative increase in recall ability from the first to the last trial).
- *Retention* indicates the examinee's delayed recall ability in relation to the immediate recall ability over a 25 to 35 min delay.
- *Retrieval* measures the strength of an examinee's recall ability in comparison to his or her recognition memory.

THEORETICAL AND RESEARCH FOUNDATION

The concept of memory is broadly defined and often linked with learning. When you learn, you are also committing new information to memory. While the *process* of acquiring new information is learning, the *persistence* of that learning is memory (Squire, 1987).

The concept of memory is most often divided into two systems: long-term and short-term. *Short-term memory* is most commonly recognized as information held on the order of minutes; *long-term memory* is information that is stored on the order of hours, days, weeks, or permanently. *Encoding* is the process by which new information enters memory systems, and *retrieval* is the process by which stored information is recalled.

Memory is conceptualized according to the type of information stored. There are at least two qualitatively different types of memory: procedural and declarative. *Procedural memories* include those that are, by and large, acquired at an unconscious level. These memories typically involve skills and complex motor actions, such as riding a bike, playing a musical instrument, or swinging a golf club. *Declarative memories* are stored material that can be encoded in symbols and expressed by language, such as recalling a phone number, a shopping list, or a movie. Unlike procedural memory, declarative memory is available to the conscious mind. Declarative memory is subdivided into episodic memory (information that is tied to specific time and place events) and semantic memory (facts and general information gathered in the course of specific experiences) (Squire, 1987), a distinction perhaps most clearly made by Tulving (1983, 2000). *Episodic memory* is defined as personally experienced events or episodes that can be experimentally assessed with immediate or delayed recall of word lists, geometric designs, text, faces, and similar tasks (as well as with more personally relevant tasks that require individuals to recall things that occurred to them at a particular time or within a specific context). *Semantic memory,* in contrast, reflects general word knowledge and is often assessed with tests of information, naming ability, or vocabulary. Within this framework, the WMS-III primarily assesses declarative, episodic memory. The information presented in the test is "contextually bound by the testing situation and requires the examinee to learn and retrieve information" (The Psychological Corporation, 1997, p. 3).

Working memory is a process that most people are scarcely aware of; it allows people to hold information in mind long enough to carry out sequential actions. Examples include holding a phone number in mind so that you can dial it, or searching for a lost object while being able to remember which places you have already inspected. Some view working memory as "a scratch pad" or as "a blackboard of the mind" (Baddeley, 1986). On the WMS-III and WAIS-III, subtests such as Arithmetic (doing mental arithmetic), Digits Backward (mentally reordering number sequences), Spatial Span (mentally retaining and reversing the order in which blocks are touched), and Letter-Number Sequencing (separating and recalling sequences of letters and numbers) all assess working memory, among other capabilities (Kaufman & Lichtenberger, 1999). In addition to these tasks, factor-analytic studies of the WAIS-III have shown that specific visual tasks traditionally viewed as processing speed measures, such as Symbol Search and Digit Symbol-Coding, may also measure working memory (Kaufman, Lichtenberger, & McLean, 2001). Such studies support the theory that executive functioning and working memory are related concepts in terms of how information is processed (e.g., Logie, 1996). Theorists such as Logie (1996) propose that some working memory systems have a central executive processor and two "slave systems," one that stores and processes verbal material and the other that processes visual-spatial stimuli. Thus, the WMS-III's Working Memory Index assesses both of the "slave systems": the visual-spatial system by Spatial Span and the verbal system by Letter-Number Sequencing. While some theorists have deemphasized the verbal-visual distinction in working memory (e.g., Richardson, 1996), most researchers studying working memory agree that working memory involves the temporary storage of active information.

One new theory of working memory posits that working memory capacity is synonymous with g, or general intellectual ability (Kyllonen, in press). This theory is supported by the fact that numerous measures of working memory capacity correlate highly with measures of g (e.g., Kyllonen, 1993; Kyllonen & Christal, 1990).

Brain Basis for Memory

Over the past few decades, research has elucidated many of the neurobiological bases of memory. This is not a text on neuroanatomy, so this section offers some of the highlights of research on the neuroanatomic correlates of memory. No single neural region houses all memories in the brain. Several parts of the brain participate in the storage of memories, although specific regions are specialized for memory storage. The main structures implicated in memory functioning include the cortical and subcortical limbic structures of the medial temporal lobes, namely, the hippocampus, amygdala, and related diencephalic areas (Squire, 1992; Squire & Butters, 1992). Other areas such as the medial-dorsal nuclei of the thalamus and the frontal lobe have also been linked to some memory dysfunction (Squire & Butters, 1992).

More specifically, *explicit* (declarative) *memory* depends on the limbic-diencephalic system and the prefrontal cortex (Raz, 2000). The hippocampal formation and associated structures (such as the fornix, the entorhinal cortex, the medial-dorsal thalamus, and the mammillary bodies) contribute to the formation and maintenance of memories. According to Nyberg and colleagues' (1996) hemispheric encoding-retrieval asymmetry model, the left prefrontal cortex is preferentially involved in encoding episodic memories, whereas the right prefrontal cortex is dominant in retrieving episodically acquired information (Nyberg, Cabeza, & Tulving, 1996). The right and left hemispheres transfer information across the corpus callosum to facilitate retrieval of memories stored in modality-specific cortices (Hasegawa, Fukuishma, Ihara, & Miyashita, 1998).

In contrast to explicit memory, *implicit memory* depends on multiple cortical and subcortical systems rather than limbic-diencephalic systems (Prull, Gabrieli, & Bunge, 2000). Learning and remembering skills (nondeclarative skills) are subserved by the basal ganglia and in some cases, the cerebellum (Prull et al., 2000). Other nondeclarative tasks such as repetition priming, are attributed to the cerebral neocortex (Squire, 1992). Research has associated working memory with prefrontal association areas, and modality-specific secondary association cortices appear to play a supporting role (Cabeza & Nyberg, 1997). Klingberg, O'Sullivan, and Roland (1997) posit that coactivation of anterior and posterior association cortices is critical for maintaining performances during an increased load on working memory.

Study of the clinical presentations of different types of memory deficits have helped neurobiologists discern the neuroanotomic substrates of memory (Purves et al., 1997). Examples of widely studied populations that have elucidated our understanding of the brain basis for mnemonic systems include patients with Alzheimer's Dementia, Parkinson's disease, Huntington's disease, focal lesions, and amnesia (Prull et al., 2000).

Standardization and Psychometric Properties

The standardization sample for the WMS-III ($N = 1,250$) was selected according to 1995 U.S. Census data and was stratified according to age, gender, race/ethnicity, geographic region, and education level. Thirteen age groups were created from a large sample of adolescents and adults; each age group between ages 16 and 79 years contained 100 participants, and each age group between ages 80 and 89 contained 75 participants. An additional 437 individuals were tested so that 20 participants would be included in each educational level within each group. These data were treated as oversampling data and were not included in the basic standardization samples.

The average split-half reliability coefficients for the Indexes across the 13 age groups were relatively strong, ranging from .93 for Auditory Immediate to .74 for Auditory Recognition Delayed (median = .87) (see Rapid Reference 1.3 for split-half and test-retest reliability for all scales and subtests). Individual subtest reliabilities ranged from an average of .93 for Verbal Paired Associates I to .74 for Faces I, Faces II, and Auditory Recognition Delayed (median = .81). A subset of the standardization sample (297 adults) provided test-retest data, with an average of five weeks between testings. The results of the test-retest study showed that for the two subsamples (16–54 and 55–89 years), reliability coefficients ranged from .62 to .82 (median = .71) for the Primary subtest scores, and .70 to .88 (median = .82) for the Primary Indexes. The mean subtest scaled scores and mean Index scores increased by roughly 0.33 SD to 1 SD from the first to second testings. Thus, on Indexes such as Immediate and General (Delayed) Memory, which both had close to 1 SD difference between the first and second testing, the practice effect appears significant. Anastasi and Urbina (1997) suggest that the desirable level for reliability coefficients is at least .80. Thus, we suggest using caution when interpreting subtests or indexes whose reliability coefficients are below this desirable level, paying careful attention to those below .75 or .70.

COMPREHENSIVE REFERENCES ON TEST

The *WMS-III Administration and Scoring Manual* (Wechsler, 1997) and the *WAIS-III and WMS-III Technical Manual* (The Psychological Corporation, 1997) currently provide the most detailed information about the WMS-III. These

≡Rapid Reference 1.3

Average WMS-III Primary Subtest and Primary Index Split-Half Internal Consistency and Test-Retest Reliability Coefficients

	Average Split-Half r_{xx}	Average Test-Retest r_{12}
Primary Index		
Auditory Immediate	.93	.85
Visual Immediate	.82	.75
Immediate Memory	.91	.84
Auditory Delayed	.87	.84
Visual Delayed	.83	.76
Auditory Recognition Delayed	.74	.70
General Memory	.91	.88
Working Memory	.86	.80
Primary Subtest		
Logical Memory I	.88	.77
Faces I	.74	.67
Verbal Paired Associates I	.93	.82
Family Pictures I	.81	.66
Letter-Number Sequencing	.82	.74
Spatial Span	.79	.71
Logical Memory II	.79	.76
Faces II	.74	.62
Verbal Paired Associates II	.83	.78
Family Pictures II	.84	.71
Auditory Recognition	.74	.70

Note: Reliability coefficients for the Primary Subtests are based on Total Scores.

manuals review the development of the test, give descriptions of each of the subtests and Indexes, and summarize their standardization, reliability, and validity. A chapter in the *Handbook of Normative data for Neuropsychological Assessment* (Mitrushina et al., 1999), titled "Wechsler Memory Scale," provides an excellent review of the research on the WMS, WMS-R, and the WMS-III. "The Wechsler

Rapid Reference 1.4

Publication Information for the Wechsler Memory Scale– Third Edition

Author: David Wechsler

Publication Date: 1997

What the test measures: Verbal and auditory memory, and recent and delayed memory

Age Range: 16–89 years

Administration Time: Primary subtests = 30–35 min; administration of optional subtests adds approximately 15–20 min to the testing time

Qualification of Examiners: Graduate- or professional-level training in psychological assessment

Publisher: The Psychological Corporation
555 Academic Court
San Antonio, TX 78204-2498
Ordering phone number: 800-211-8378
www.PsychCorp.com

Price: WMS-III Complete kit test price = $399.00 (as of November 2000)

Memory Scales" (Franzen & Iverson, 2000) provides a review of this history of the Wechsler Memory Scales, the assets and limitations of each of the test's versions, and case examples using the tests. Tulsky and Ledbetter (2000) review several points to consider when switching from the WMS-R to the WMS-III, and Hawkins (1998) provides data from the WMS-III standardization sample that help to delineate the clinical utility of the WMS-III indexes. Rapid Reference 1.4 provides basic information on the WMS-III and its publisher.

🖋 TEST YOURSELF 🖋

....

1. **One of the more confusing changes made from the WMS-R to the WMS-III was in the "General Memory Index." On the WMS-R it refers to a measure of global immediate memory, but on the WMS-III it is a measure of**

    (a) global auditory memory.

    (b) global visual memory.

    (c) global delayed memory.

    (d) global recognition memory.

2. **The Auditory Recognition Delayed total score is composed of the recognition total scores of what two subtests?**

    (a) Logical Memory I and Logical Memory II

    (b) Logical Memory II and Verbal Paired Associates II

    (c) Verbal Paired Associates I and Verbal Paired Associates II

    (d) Letter-Number Sequencing and Spatial Span

3. **Single-Trial Learning, Learning Slope, Retention, and Retrieval are all part of the**

    (a) Visual Process Composites.

    (b) Auditory Process Composites.

    (c) Recognition Composites.

    (d) WMS-R Composite.

4. **The WMS-III may be best viewed as assessing what type of memory?**

    (a) Declarative episodic memory

    (b) Procedural memory

    (c) Semantic memory

    (d) Working memory

5. **All memory functions have been explicitly linked to the hippocampus.** True or False?

6. **Most of the WMS-III Indexes have internal reliability coefficients that are below the desirable .80 level.** True or False?

7. **In addition to measuring auditory delayed and visual delayed memory abilities, the General Memory Index captures what other aspect of memory functioning?**

    (a) Immediate memory

    (b) Learning slope

    (c) Auditory recognition delayed

    (d) Working memory

Answers: 1. c; 2. b; 3. b; 4. a; 5. False; 6. False; 7. c

Two

HOW TO ADMINISTER THE WMS-III

As with any standardized test, administrators should carefully adhere to WMS-III administration procedures and scoring rules to allow comparison of results to the test's national norms. Deviance from these prescribed procedures can invalidate comparison to normative groups. The test provides clear instructions for reliable and precise administration, and these instructions are designed to reduce across-experimenter error. However, administration should proceed smoothly and without a rigid or stilted presentation. Familiarity with standardized procedures and all of the cues to be provided by the examiner help promote a comfortable, natural test session. "Testing of the limits," by modifying a subtest's directions in creative ways, in order to follow up clinical hypotheses and hunches is good clinical practice, *as long as it is done after the subtest has been administered under standardized conditions.* Otherwise, the person's derived score on the subtest might be invalidated.

APPROPRIATE TESTING CONDITIONS

Testing Environment

As with any neuropsychological testing, the context in which the WMS-III is administered varies, and examiners may administer the test in a clinic, office, school, or hospital, among other settings. Regardless of the setting, the most important feature of the testing is a table or desk that allows the client to be seated across from the examiner. Use a testing surface that is large enough to support the testing easel and has enough room to fill out the protocol as testing is conducted. A reserved space nearby (ideally off the table surface) can be used to place test items that are not currently in use, so that they are within easy reach of the examiner. Placing items outside of the client's view will reduce distraction and the need to field questions about what is coming next; it will also eliminate potential anxiety related to test length or specific materials that examinees may recognize from previous testing. Use a quiet room that is set to a comfortable temperature and does not have visual distractions. If there is a window, place the client with his or her back toward it. If the client is being tested while sitting at a regular desk, orient the desk for maximum comfort, providing optimal leg-room. A chair without wheels helps to keep the client from moving excessively if hyperactivity is a concern.

> ## CAUTION
>
> ### Additional Materials Needed for WMS-III Administration
>
> - Stopwatch
> - At least two No. 2 Pencils with erasers for *both* the examiner and client
> - Extra lined paper for note taking and verbatim response recording of Logical Memory I and II

Testing Materials

During testing, the examiner should place only the stimulus booklet directly in the client's view. The *Manual* is not required for test administration because all relevant directions are found in the stimulus booklets for the WMS-III. To keep the protocol form from the client's view, the examiner should use the stimulus booklet as a shield and write on the form, but avoid invoking a secretive stance. Almost everything needed to perform the assessment is included in the WMS-III kit, with the exception of a stopwatch, pencils, and extra paper for note taking.

ORDER OF TEST ADMINISTRATION

If possible, administer the WMS-III after first administering other, less difficult, measures. Ideally, an intelligence test such as the WAIS-III, the Kaufman Adolescent and Adult Intelligence Test (KAIT) (Kaufman & Kaufman, 1993), the Woodcock-Johnson Tests of Cognitive Ability–Third Edition (WJ III) (Woodcock, McGrew, & Mather, 2000), or a brief IQ measure is administered with the WMS-III. This dual administration of intelligence and memory measures is important for the most in-depth interpretation of WMS-III results. The WAIS-III and WMS-III were co-normed, so that the same individuals comprise the norms for both tests. Therefore, the WAIS-III (or selected portions of it) has an advantage over other IQ tests because the WMS-III/WAIS-III combination takes best advantage of the joint norms. If the examiner has sufficient experience and, therefore, speed, he or she can administer the WAIS-III first, followed by a break, and then the WMS-III.

ADMINISTERING A PARTIAL WMS-III BATTERY

Many clinical psychologists, neuropsychologists, or other WMS-III examiners choose not to administer the WMS-III battery in its entirety, and instead select particular WMS-III subtests and administer a partial WMS-III battery. When selecting the subtests to create a partial battery, examiners must choose carefully to ensure the maximum amount of information is obtained and the referral questions can be answered from the data that are gathered. One factor that may impel neuropsychologists and other examiners to administer a partial WMS-III battery is the limited time available for testing. The time variable may also help delineate what subtests to select for a partial battery. Rapid Reference 2.1 provides a list of the approximate time required to administer each of the WMS-III subtests, developed from our clinical experience with the instrument. However, whenever examiners are administering a partial WMS-III battery, it is essential to ensure that they do not alter the interval between an immediate subtest and the delayed recall version of the subtest (see the section on specific subtests that follow in the chapter). Although there are many combinations of subtests that can be chosen to create a partial battery, some choices are more logical than others. In Figure 2.1 we provide a series of decision trees, which map out possible partial batteries that best meet three types of clinical memory referral concerns. This figure is not intended to be all-inclusive, but may provide guidance for clinicians who cannot, or do not wish to, administer the entire WMS-III.

The three general referral complaints highlighted in Figure 2.1 may be directly presented to the examiner, but most of the time, the examiner must discern the nature of a memory complaint from the symptoms that the client describes. Very often, patients experience an attentional problem as a memory problem, or do not differentiate between memory for verbal and visual material. An astute clinician considers the following presentations, which provide

Rapid Reference 2.1

Approximate Time Required to Administer Each Subtest

Subtests (and Their Delay and Recognition Conditions)	Time in Minutes
Information and Orientation	2–5
Logical Memory I and II and Recognition	10–12
Faces I and II	4–10
Verbal Paired Associates I and II	5–10
Family Pictures I and II	10–12
Word Lists I and II (Optional)	10–15
Visual Reproduction I and II (Optional)	8–15
Letter-Number Sequencing	4–6
Spatial Span	5–8
Mental Control (Optional)	3–4
Digit Span (Optional)	3–5
Digit Span (Optional)	3–5
Total Primary	40–63
Total Optional	24–39
Total Primary + Optional	64–102

Note: These time estimates are based on our clinical experience with the instrument in addition to the global time estimates that are provided in the Manual.

insight into specific diagnoses, and lead to suggestions with respect to rehabilitation.

I. Attentional problem versus memory loss problem. This clinical presentation includes attentional difficulties that disrupt efficient encoding and storage of new information into memories that are readily retrievable. If a clinician is administering a partial battery to assess such problems, suggested indexes to obtain include Auditory Immediate, Visual Immediate (for comparison to Auditory Delayed Index), and Visual Delayed Index. The examiner can expect to see significantly low scores on measures of attention including Auditory Immediate Index subtests (Logical Memory I, Verbal Paired Associates I), and Visual Immediate Index subtests (Faces I and Family Pictures I) (Chapter 4 addresses these scores in more detail). Because the immediate scores are low, the delayed scores are likely to be low as well, including Auditory Delayed In-

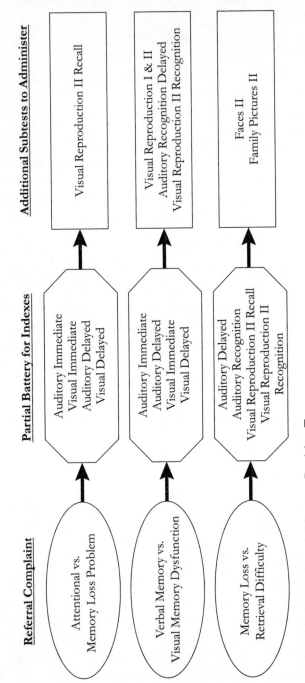

Figure 2.1 WMS-III Partial Battery Decision Trees

dex (Logical Memory II, Verbal Paired Associates II) and Visual Delayed Index subtests (Faces II and Family Pictures II). This pattern suggests problems in arousal or attention, subserved by brainstem and frontal lobes. Mesial temporal structure integrity may be described as intact if the information that is encoded is not forgotten over a delay.

II. Verbal memory versus visual memory dysfunction. This clinical presentation includes a significantly stronger ability to encode and store information in either the verbal or visual domain. If a clinician is administering a partial battery to assess such problems, suggested indexes to obtain are Auditory (Immediate and Delayed), and Visual (Immediate and Delayed) indexes. Clinicians can obtain further information through administration of the Visual Reproduction (I and II). To rule out a retrieval problem versus memory loss, clinicians should also administer the recognition paradigms for the aforementioned subtests, including Auditory Recognition Delayed and Visual Reproduction Recognition.

If an examinee's verbal memory is weaker relative to visual memory, expect to find that the Visual Delayed scores are lower than the Auditory Delayed scores, and that immediate scores are approximately the same for verbal and visual information. Such patterns suggest that verbal information is lost (i.e., forgotten) over time, and clinicians can support this by considering the Auditory Recognition Delayed Total Score. If this score is lower than the Auditory Delayed score, then the paradigm did not significantly assist performance in the verbal realm, and the pattern represents that of abnormal forgetting rather than a retrieval deficit.

Conversely, if visual memory is weaker relative to verbal memory in an examinee's profile, the examiner should expect to find the opposite pattern. Visual Delayed score should be significantly lower than the Auditory Delayed score, while immediate scores are approximately the same. Here again, examiners can establish a visual memory deficit versus a visual memory retrieval problem by administering the Visual Reproduction (I and II) Recall and Recognition measures, which help to rule-out a retrieval problem and provide support for a memory issue (i.e., abnormal forgetting over time).

As addressed in Chapter 4, a lateralization pattern can be inferred, particularly in the case that the patient is right-hand (conventionally) dominant. In this usual case, auditory/verbal memory problems suggest left-hemisphere dysfunction, whereas visual-memory problems suggest right-hemisphere dysfunction, specifically with respect to mesial temporal structures. If there is an additional differential in the immediate recall conditions for verbal-versus-visual information conforming to delayed recall results, then an attentional or primary processing deficit can be hypothesized for the weaker score (i.e., auditory verbal or visual-processing). This pattern suggests that regions other than mesial temporal structures are dysfunctional, within that respective hemisphere.

III. Memory loss versus a memory retrieval problem. This clinical presentation is characterized by adequate encoding and storage of information, but difficulty in self-organization for retrieving the stored information. Recognition paradigms provide significant assistance (over and above what is considered normal), suggesting that the examinee can choose the correct answer because he or she has encoded it, but cannot spontaneously produce the information in delayed conditions. A retrieval deficit can be material specific (i.e., observed only for auditory, or only for visual information). If the clinician is administering an abbreviated battery, suggested indexes to obtain include Auditory Delayed and Auditory Recognition Delayed for the auditory domain, and the Visual Reproduction Recall and Visual Reproduction Recognition Total Scores for the visual domain. Within the visual modality, examiners can obtain more information by comparing visual reproduction discrepancy scores with other visual tasks (e.g., comparing Visual Reproduction Recognition Total score *in addition* to Faces II versus Family Pictures II).

Within the auditory domain, the Auditory Recognition Delayed score is likely to be significantly higher than the Auditory Delayed, suggesting that the recognition paradigms of Logical Memory and Verbal Paired Associates subtests provide more help than would be expected in a normal sample (see Chapter 4 for more detail). That is, most people are assisted by recognition format unless they have recalled so much at spontaneous recall conditions that recognition does not provide extra points. If an examiner discerns this pattern, he or she could interpret it as an auditory *retrieval* deficit, versus an *encoding and storage* deficit. The examinee is not able to produce information spontaneously at delayed recall conditions but can recognize a significant amount of the presented stimuli, suggesting that the examinee has encoded and stored the information but cannot readily retrieve it.

The same reasoning can be applied to the visual domain. There is not an analogous "recognition" index for the visual memory tasks. However, if comparison of Visual Reproduction II Recall (Age-Adjusted) score versus the Recognition Total (Age-Adjusted) score reveals a relatively better recognition than spontaneous retrieval score, then the clinician should entertain a hypothesis of a retrieval deficit in the visual domain.

To further test the hypothesis for a visual retrieval deficit, clinicians can examine other scores. As visual memory subtests vary inherently with respect to their design, scores can be compared with respect to whether memory is assessed through recognition or spontaneous recall procedures. Specifically, Faces II uses a recognition format in testing recall of facial information. Conversely, Family Pictures II uses a free recall format, without recognition paradigm. Consideration of whether an individual does better on the Facial II and Visual Reproduction II Recognition (Age-Adjusted) score than the Family Pictures and Visual Reproduction Recall Total (Age-Adjusted) score may provide even stronger evidence for a retrieval-versus-encoding deficit for visual information. However, it is also possible to have a memory loss specific to faces, to spatial elements of scenes, or abstract figures. Additionally, a clinician could observe a retrieval deficit that is specific to either of these domains.

Consider a hypothesis that frontal/executive brain regions or basal ganglia structures (in the case of subcortical conditions such as Parkinson's and Huntington's disease) are dysfunctional, versus mesial temporal structures if a retrieval, versus a memory deficit, is observed. Additional mesial temporal structure dysfunction could be indicated if there is rapid forgetting of information that has been encoded at immediate conditions.

DEVELOPING RAPPORT WITH EXAMINEE

Interacting comfortably with the client is important, particularly for memory testing, which may elicit anxiety and is unusually susceptible to distractibility. Throughout the test session, make a conscious effort to establish positive rapport, such as conversing with the client in a professional, but pleasant and engaging, manner. Familiarity with the test materials and where to find the subtests on the protocol (they are listed in the order to be administered), helps the examiner focus on establishing rapport rather than finding and organizing test materials. Also, familiarity is required to transition naturally from one subtest to the next. While it is not necessary to memorize all instructions, being thoroughly familiar with task demands makes the administration as smooth as possible and reduces the possibility that data will be omitted. There are few stop/start criteria throughout the WMS-III; all items are administered in each subtest except in Letter-Number Sequencing, Spatial Span, and Digit Span.

Establishing Rapport

Building positive rapport begins with the initial telephone contact and scheduling of the appointment. This process of building positive rapport continues at the start of the test session. Inform the examinee of the nature of all test procedures. With respect to the memory testing, provide an overview of what aspects of memory the test assesses. Discuss at the outset questions or concerns that the examinee may have. As in the case for WAIS-III instructions, it is useful to inform the examinee that some portions of the testing will be easy and some will be more challenging, but that the examinee is expected only to try his or her best on all tasks. Provide reassurance by indicating that the test is not designed so that people can obtain perfect scores. Examiners can inform clients that their performances will be compared to those of other people in their age group. This may be a particular issue among older patients who are being assessed, in large part, to determine whether there is benign or significant memory loss. Concerns about test performance may provoke anxiety for individuals who have attention or concentration difficulties.

Maintaining Rapport

Examiners should minimize small talk during testing; however, if reassuring statements are needed to keep the client motivated, then provide judiciously placed statements, preferably between subtests. Observe the client's verbal and nonverbal cues, and when he or she shows significant discomfort, provide reassuring statements that commend the individual's effort rather than performance ("You're really working hard"). The examiner should remind him or her that the test was designed so that almost no one attains complete success ("Those were meant to be tough"). The examiner should note in the protocol the client's sensitivity to fatigue, frustration, or other changes in motivation, and should say or do what is necessary to reduce these potentially interfering variables. The goal is to obtain the highest level of performance possible, and such extra test factors often undermine an individual's capabilities. The examiner can convey this fact, if needed, to help the client regain composure or motivation. The examiner can do quite a bit to alleviate and remove some of these adverse factors, through appropriately timed supportive statements and reassuring comments. However, avoid specific feedback about individual item performances, as this raises the expectation that feedback will occur regularly, when it should not. The examiner can also decide whether the client needs a few moments to get back into test-taking mode. Avoid breaks within subtests, almost at all costs, as returning to a task may well require repeated instructions that are not part of standardized testing, or it may interrupt information retrieval. Once testing has commenced, adhere to standardized procedures and give only instructions provided. If the client indicates that he or she can not or will not continue testing, provide encouragement with statements such as, "Just try your best," or "Give it your best effort," or "Sometimes your guess will be a good one," particularly because the client may unknowingly remember correct responses, even when he or she is not sure of the answer.

TESTING INDIVIDUALS WITH SPECIAL NEEDS

Examples of adolescents or adults who have special testing needs may include those who have hearing impairment, visual problems, motor difficulties, or are not fluent in English. When testing such individuals, examiners should take special consideration to accommodate the particular examinee while maintaining standardized procedures to the degree possible. Clinicians should conduct a thorough history about the individual's impairment prior to the assessment, which should include the examinee's vision, hearing, physical condition, or any other limitations. Such limitations may require modification of test procedures. When making decisions about subtests to administer, the examiner should take into account whether the examinee will be penalized because of sensory or motor deficits, or lack of exposure to the English language. Sometimes, subtests must be administered despite these conditions, if having some data is better than having none. In this situation, the examiner can write a caveat into the test report to emphasize that the results may represent an underestimate and why (Chapter 4 addresses this topic at greater length). Major modification of the standardized procedure may, of course, impact test scores or invalidate the use of the norms. Examiners must

≡ *Rapid Reference 2.2*

Accommodations for a Client's Special Needs

- Add printed words to facilitate comprehension of directions for hard-of-hearing individuals (note that this will result in potential problems in the use of the norms, which are obtained under standardized procedures, and this must be addressed in the report text), administer the test in closer proximity to the client than usual, and deliver instructions in a loud tone.

- Administer only auditorily delivered subtests for blind or low-vision individuals.

- Extend the testing over more than one session for individuals who require it. If this decision is made, it must not interfere with the timing conditions required for Delayed Recall and Recognition testing. In other words, decisions to divide the test into two sessions require divisions that allow specific tests and their recall/recognition paradigms to be administered within a single session.

- Translate verbal items into another language for individuals not fluent in English. (This modification will definitely result in problematic use of the norms, and it must be addressed in the report text.)

use clinical judgment to determine whether the examinee's impairment prohibits obtaining valid scores on a portion of test, or the entire test. Test modifications for accommodating an examinee's special needs include those listed in Rapid Reference 2.2. When any modification is done, problems in interpreting the scores may arise. Examiners should carefully consider whether using modifications are better than administering fewer subtests, choosing another instrument, or choosing supplemental instruments. The goal is to obtain the most meaningful and useful information possible from the examinee's scores.

Testing the Elderly

Specific concerns arise in the case of testing older individuals. Most importantly, these include underestimates of capabilities due to fatigue, particularly when the WMS-III comprises only a portion of planned testing. To help minimize such effects, pay attention to nonverbal signs of fatigue such as yawning, heavy sighing, or a desire to converse rather than continue testing. Providing adequate breaks for a drink of water or use of the restroom facilitates validity of test scores. When scheduling any examinee, but especially when testing older examinees, the examiner should suggest a good night's rest the evening before, and remind the client to bring glasses if he or she wears them. Suggest that the client bring a favorite beverage or snack for a refreshment, because dietary issues may be of relevance for the elderly.

Recording Responses

In most standardized testing, it is critical to write down responses verbatim. The WMS-III and the WMS-III Record Form were designed to minimize this requirement. While there are subtests, such as Family Pictures, that do require careful notation, the rest are less reliant on the examiner's writing. However, we do suggest writing down responses where possible. For example, on Letter-Number Sequencing and Spatial Span, notation of responses allows for error-analysis. While there is no place to write down exact verbalization for Logical Memory I and II, verbatim notation of the verbal output on these subtests allows analysis about retrieval strategies, order of elements presented, which elements are present versus omitted, and their syntactical form. For efficiency, examiners should use the abbreviations that testers use for other standardized instruments (such as the WAIS-III); abbreviations allow the examiner to keep pace with the client's response delivery, without slowing down the client. This also supports maintenance of positive rapport. In summary, we believe that examiners should record all utterances, as well as relevant gestures, to the extent that it is possible. Due to the presentation of the items, and responses required, some tasks are not amenable to recording more than what is required by the protocol. For example, Faces I and II provide two choice-response possibilities, and a marking of what the client chooses is adequate. For most subtests, correct responses are noted in bold green ink, so that the examiner only needs to circle that response. For even greater clarity in response recording, we recommend circling the correct responses and using a slash mark to denote error responses. Many subtests have a score column immediately adjacent to the circled response column, and a 1 or 0 can be assigned during testing. Examiners should always double-check raw scores before calculating standard scores.

Discontinue Rules, Querying, and Repeating Presentation

Administration of the WMS-III is straightforward in terms of starting and stopping subtests, as most subtests are administered in their entirety. However, three subtests do have discontinue rules: Letter-Number Sequence, Spatial Span, and Digit Span.

Occasionally during test administration, an examinee refuses to respond to an item or hesitates while responding. In such instances, there are specific instructions for how to proceed. The examiner may prompt the examinee by saying, "Just try it once more," or "Try it a little longer," or "I think you can do it." Where useful, repeat a question after providing encouragement. If the examinee asks for help or clues, the examiner should say, "It is important for me to see how well you can do it yourself." When an item is queried, record Q followed by the examinee's response to make it clear that the additional response was not spontaneous. If, after a prompt or query, the examinee does not respond or continues to hesitate, say, "Let's go on," and move to the next subtest or item.

To maintain standardized administration, read the instructions to the examinee verbatim. To ease smooth administration and to promote rapport, examiners should thoroughly familiarize themselves with the instructions before administering the test, and be clear on what can or cannot be repeated. If an examinee does not understand the directions, clinicians may reread the *instructions*. Note when the examinee needs repetition of directions, so that test behavior can be incorporated into the report; attentional and concentration difficulties can be more readily discerned. Repeating *test items* is generally not permissible. Most items are *not* meant to be repeated after their initial presentation, so the examiner should be sure that the client is attending before he or she proceeds, and should read the items audibly and clearly for any subtest or trial where listening and processing is a task demand. Auditory memory subtests such as Logical Memory, Verbal Paired Associates, and Word Lists have restrictions regarding what can be repeated. While the *Manual* does not explicitly address what to do if an examinee indicates that he or she did not hear the item, examiners should try to avoid this problem by checking for nonverbal behavior that indicates the examinee is paying attention and ready. Remind the examinee to concentrate as best as he or she can before proceeding, and mark the item according to the best re-

DON'T FORGET

Repetition in WMS-III

May Repeat	May Not Repeat
• Instructions on all subtests	• Logical Memory I
• Recognition Items for Logical Memory II, Verbal Paired Associates II, and Word Lists II	• Verbal Paired Associates I
	• Word Lists (per trial)
• Information and Orientation Items	• Faces I stimuli
	• Family Pictures I stimuli
	• Visual Reproduction I Items
	• Letter-Number Sequencing Items
	• Spatial Span Items (Forward and Backward)
	• Digit Span Items (Forward and Backward)

sponse given. As a general rule, repetition of test items is not allowed; however, there are exceptions.

For some subtests, querying and prompting of responses is appropriate. Except where noted, the examiner may repeat questions or instructions when the examinee requests it or when he or she does not appear to understand the directions (e.g., while repetition of the passages in the recall portions of Logical Memory is not allowed, repetition of recognition items is permitted).

SUBTEST-BY-SUBTEST RULES OF ADMINISTRATION

The WMS-III stimulus booklet provides detailed rules for subtest-by-subtest administration (The Psychological Corporation, 1997). This section offers some important reminders for competent administration of each subtest, and it may be used as a guide or as a refresher if examiners have already learned details for test administration. The subtests are listed in order of administration. In addition, the Don't Forget box on the next page presents some general tips for competent administration. During administration of the WMS-III, record astute observations of the examinee's behaviors. These can provide insight into how an examinee approaches a particular subtest, which subtests the examinee perceives to be most difficult, and which the examinee perceives as relatively easy. Such information is valuable when examiners begin test interpretation. After the WMS-III gives the rules of each subtest, it suggests key behaviors to note. Appendix A of this book offers a checklist of WAIS-III administrative procedures, and this checklist may be especially useful for professors and teaching assistants who are instructing graduate students on WMS-III administration and scoring procedures, as well as for clinicians who want to fine-tune their administration and scoring.

DON'T FORGET

General Administration Tips for any Subtests

- Ask if the client is near- or far-sighted to ensure that he or she can see the stimuli properly during the assessment. Remind the client to bring his or her glasses if necessary. Also ask about color-blindness, other visual problems (e.g., double vision), or hearing difficulties.

- Plan to take breaks in between subtests rather than in the middle of administering a subtest (i.e., try to avoid interruptions while delivering the prose passages in Logical Memory I, exposing the Faces I target stimuli, exposing the items in Visual Reproduction, or providing multiple trials for the Word Lists).

- Remember to check whether the client is attending to the subtest before proceeding.

- Observe personality variables, such as anxiety or a desire not to guess if the client is unsure. Encourage clients to respond if they seem hesitant to guess.

- Familiarize yourself completely with the test materials before administering the test.

- You may do "testing limits" procedures if they are administered in a manner that does not invalidate the test score.

- When giving an abbreviated form of the test, try to alternate the administration order of the subtests to avoid several verbal memory subtests or visual memory subtests in a row.

- For visual subtests, remember to note whether errors tend to be on one side of the page or one quadrant of the visual field. Designs may be drawn in one visual field only.

Information and Orientation (Optional)

This subtest requires the test protocol only and is easy to administer, as it is composed of questions read verbatim. If the examinee's response is unclear, the clinician may ask for clarification, but use open-ended, *not* leading or hinted, queries that provide structure for retrieval (e.g., an inappropriate prompt to obtain more information about the name of the President is, "He was just in the news today, his name is . . . ,"; and a poor prompt for more information about what day of the week it is, "Yesterday was __ so today is __").

Our recommendation is that, in order to obtain a valid score, examiners should ask all of the questions, and that they should administer Questions 15 through 18, even though these questions are not included in the scoring. These last items query handedness and hearing or vision problems that are relevant to the assessment. Handedness is important with respect to conventional brain lateralization of cognitive functions. Left-handedness or ambidexterity presents the question of whether left hemisphere is organized for language and analytic function and right hemisphere for gestalt, visual-spatial processing; therefore, this has implications for whether memory structures in these hemispheres are specialized to subserve verbal or visual material (Lezak, 1995).

Behaviors to Observe
- Hesitations, or restarts on responses. For example, the client may say, "Janu__(pause) February" for the month. Inflections at the end of the response, indicating uncertainty are likely to be clinically relevant.
- Nonverbal gestures of exasperation, or facial expressions that demonstrate the responses are a guess.
- Record defensive statements or attempts to make light of questions in reaction to them. For example, responses such as, "Why would I want to remember who the President is?" or "I'm old enough to try to forget my age" are notable.
- Clearly note errors since they provide clues to the degree of disorientation. For example, someone who states that the date is October 17 when it is October 19 is probably better oriented than someone who indicates that the month is July. Response on who the President is may indicate the degree of anteriorgrade amnesia, in the case that a client is "stuck in time" and has not encoded new information

since that President's term. The same can be said about the stated year.

Logical Memory I

This subtest requires the stimulus booklet; it is also a good idea to use additional paper for recording responses verbatim, which can then be analyzed with respect to scoring later. The *Manual* also allows the examinee's responses to be audiotaped. In this case, the examiner tells the client, "For this task, I am going to use a tape recorder so that I can write down your exact words later on." Logical Memory I consists of two paragraphs that are read out loud. The first describes a woman who is robbed, her strained family context, and the policemen's charitable response. The second describes a man who was about to go out but hears a weather bulletin that predicts impending stormy weather, so he decides to stay home and watch old movies instead. Both paragraphs include many details. Because they are delivered once within a trial, examiners should familiarize themselves with the paragraphs and read them aloud before their first administration. Read the stories at a conversational pace, with natural pauses between sentences. For both paragraphs, the examiner instructs the examinee to start at the beginning of the story and repeat what is remembered about each story. The second story is given twice, without warning ahead of time. After these items are given, the examiner tells the examinee to remember as much of the stories as possible because he or she will be asked to tell the stories again later. Note the time that the examinee completes this subtest because it is important to know how many minutes have elapsed prior to administration of Logical Memory II.

Queries

The examiner should gently deny requests for repetition but encourage the client to go ahead and try his or her best. If the client attempts to interrupt in the middle of the story, request that the client wait until the examiner is finished before he or she asks questions. Sometimes, a nonverbal gesture, such as holding up a hand, is sufficient to signal the examinee to wait and continue listening.

If the client offers very little in his or her response, the examiner can encourage the client to provide more information (e.g., "What other details can you give me?"). Before moving on to the next item, the clinician should be sure that the examinee has exhausted his or her recall of the paragraphs.

Behaviors to Observe

- Make note of any statements the examinee made before giving a response, such as, "Oh man, I am really bad at this kind of thing!" or, "You have to be kidding me!" Gently encourage the client to go ahead and start.
- Use abbreviations, but if the examinee proceeds at a rate that is far too fast to record, the examiner should slow him or her down so that the entire response can be recorded.
- Note repetition of output and underline any added (confabulated) material. Underline instances where there is contamination from one story to another. This contamination suggests source memory difficulty, which has clinical relevance.
- During response analysis, note whether the examinee recalled the gist of the story or irrelevant details.

Faces I

Administration of this subtest requires the stimulus booklet and the protocol sheet. The subtest shows a set of 24 unique faces, presenting 1 face per page, and exposing each for only 2 s (use of stopwatch for timing is not recommended; rather, counting seconds mentally will suffice). The examinee is instructed to remember what each face looks like. This stimulus set is immediately followed by a recognition paradigm, which displays 48 faces for as long as the examinee wants to view them (but not so long that the viewing significantly lengthens test administration time). The examinee indicates (with a *Yes* or *No* response) whether the face was one of the faces he or she was asked to remember from the first set, and the examiner records this response. It is advised that examiners circle correct responses (provided in bold green ink) and indicate wrong responses with a slash mark. On-line scoring of 1 or 0 points can be done after each item is displayed. After completing the recognition paradigm, the examiner should instruct the examinee to try to remember the first group of faces because he or she will be asked to pick them out of another group of faces later.

Behaviors to Observe

- Note responses such as, "I remember her because she's so cute," or "scary looking."
- Comments on the cultural group or race of the faces can be revealing (e.g., "I know there was an Asian person in the group").
- Make note of items to which the client takes an excessive amount of time to respond. There may be an identifiable pattern of facial types that are more challenging for the client.

Verbal Paired Associates I

Administration of this subtest requires the stimulus booklet and the protocol sheet. Stimuli include eight auditorily delivered word pairs that are not semantically related. After the examiner reads the list of word pairs, the client hears one word from a pair and is instructed to provide the word that went with it. Two sample items are given in the instruction, with the correct responses provided. If the examinee is confused about the task requirements, the examiner may read the instructions again or paraphrase them. The word pairs are read at a rate of one pair every 3 s, with each word separated by 1 s, and each pair separated by 2 s. The examiner should read the pairs audibly and clearly, as they cannot be repeated in this first exposure, and should record the response that the client gives (although recording is not required for scoring purposes). When a client makes an error, the examiner provides the correct response and then proceeds to the next item. Only 5 s are allowed for the response. The examiner reads the list again, four times in total with four test opportunities for the client to provide the second word. The client is told to try to remember these pairs as the pairs will be tested again later in the session.

Behaviors to Observe

- Individuals with serious memory disturbance can experience confusion about task demands. Slow delivery of instructions can circumvent the confusion. The examinee may say, "Those words do not go together at all!" or some comment that suggests that the examinee is not certain that he or she is to impose some kind of learning structure on the words, such as a visual strategy that pairs the two, or a verbal "hook" to link the two.

- A record of exact responses can provide clues about whether there is confusion between items and whether errors are semantically (similar in meaning) or literally (similar in phonemes) related to the correct response. The examiner can score items (0 or 1 point) on-line as he or she administers them. If the client raises the inflection at the end of the word, indicate the client's uncertainty on the record form with a question mark.

Family Pictures I

Four scenes with characters in them are shown for 10 s each. Before beginning this subtest, the examiner shows a "Group Photo" drawing to familiarize the client with the seven characters that appear in the four scenes. The client is instructed to remember as much as possible about each scene in order to answer questions about them. The examiner presents each scene after an introductory statement is made about it (i.e., "I'm going to show you the picnic scene, the department store scene, etc."). Testing begins with a question about who was in the first scene and is followed by displaying a page divided into four numbered quadrants. The client is instructed to pretend that the grid is a particular scene and to indicate where the character named was in that scene. The client is then asked a question about what the character was doing in the scene. In this subtest the examiner records responses verbatim. If the client adds other, erroneous, characters to the scene, the examiner also asks location and activity questions for those erroneous characters.

Behaviors to Observe
- Take note of any pattern of errors. For example, the examinee may identify who is in the scene correctly, but place them incorrectly. The client may misattribute actions to different people. If a particular person or character has salience for the client the character may be correctly recalled across the items (e.g., the dog, a grandparent, or grandchild).
- The examiner should notice if the client needs to be re-cued as to

what to do with the numbered grid quarters. This is an indicator of "loss of set."

- Look for perseverative responses (e.g., the same person in the same locations across scenes, or the same activity within or across scenes).

Word Lists I (Optional)

Administration of this subtest requires the stimulus booklet and the protocol sheet. The examiner reads a list of words and asks the client to repeat as many of the words as he or she can remember; the order does not need to be preserved. The examiner reads each word at the rate of one word per 1.5 s. The examiner reads the list a total of four times, and the client is given opportunity to recite the list verbally after each presentation. The examiner then administers a completely new list and again asks the client to recall as many words as possible from that new list. The test concludes when the client is asked to recall words on the first list, although they are *not* provided again.

Behaviors to Observe

- Record the order of the words produced by the client by numbering the cell for that word. While this is not required in test instructions, it allows the examiner to see whether the client used a strategy for production (this can be deduced by the meanings and whether the words are always presented together in sequence). Recording helps the examiner hypothesize how the information is learned.
- Circle errors that represent intrusions from the word-pair list. This represents source confusion that is of clinical significance. The examiner should write confabulations (words that do not appear on the list) on the protocol where allowed. Perseveration of the same errors is also of clinical significance, indicating that, despite the client's repetition of the list, he or she cannot inhibit the same error.

Visual Reproduction I (Optional)

Administration of this subtest requires the stimulus booklet, the Visual Reproduction Response Booklet, and the protocol sheet. This task includes presentation of a total of seven figural designs, four of them in pairs. After an exposure time of 10 s, the examiner removes the target item from view and asks the client to draw it from memory. If the client expresses concerns about artistic ability, the examiner should instruct the client not to worry about artistic ability, but to try to draw the figure as best as he or she can remember. The examiner provides a warning prior to exposure of the items that consist of two designs. The client is told that he or she only has 10 s to look at both and to draw them on the sides of the page on which the designs were originally displayed. At the conclusion of the subtest, the client is told to remember these designs because, later in the test, she or he will be asked to draw them again from memory.

Behaviors to Observe

- Note any waviness of lines, unusual pressure (light or heavy), and proportions (very small or very large). If the drawings crowd one side of the page, the examiner should note this, as they may indicate neglect, visual-spatial dysfunction, or poor spatial planning.
- Note confusion of elements or a consistent emphasis on the overall structure versus the inner details or vice versa. Also note rotations of items or misplacements with respect to side.
- An examiner should observe a client's unusual pencil grasp, such as holding the pencil very close to the tip or using more fingers in front of the pencil. Any changing from hand to hand in drawing should be noted.
- Note overdrawing (repeated efforts to draw a particular element) and erasing.

Letter-Number Sequencing

Administration of this subtest requires the stimulus booklet and the protocol sheet. The examiner reads test items from the protocol form. The stimuli for this task consist of combinations of numbers and letters, which increase in length over trials. The examinee repeats the numbers and letters back in an order, reciting first the lowest numbers and then reciting the letters in alphabetical order. The examinee receives two examples and five practice items from the stimulus booklet. The examiner reads the items at a rate of 1 number or letter per second. If the client makes any errors on practice trials, the examiner corrects them immediately. After the examiner administers the five practice items, he or she does not provide further feedback. This task is discontinued when the client incorrectly answers all three trials within an item. While not required, it is suggested that the examiner record erroneous responses so that error analysis can be conducted.

Behaviors to Observe

- Confusion about task demands may suggest that the client does not know the order of the numbers or the alphabet (or has forgotten it). If the examiner suspects this, after the subtest is concluded, he or she should ask the client to recite the numbers in increasing order from 1 to 10 or the complete alphabet in order.
- Note "loss of set" errors.
- Note responses that are perseverations of earlier items.
- Observe whether the examinee learns from errors made during the practice items. Examinees may also appear to learn from errors made within one item (e.g., miss the first trial, but get the next two trials correct).
- Note whether a client responds by giving the numbers first and then the letters requested or whether the client produces the opposite pattern in responses.
- Anxiety, distractibility, and concentration problems may impact performance on this test. Observe any behaviors that may indicate such difficulties.
- Observe and note any strategies that an examinee may use during this task. For example, a participant may keep track of numbers on one hand and letters on another. Other strategies include rehearsal and "chunking." An examinee who closes his or her eyes while being administered the items (and, perhaps, while responding) is probably using a visualization strategy or attempting to increase attention and focus by blocking out visual distractions.
- Note whether there is a pattern in the errors (e.g., missing only the letters, but getting all of the numbers correct). This may indicate stimulus overload or an advantage for processing letters or numbers.
- Note errors suggestive of hearing difficulty, such as incorrectly repeating letters that only have phonemic similarity to the target stimuli (e.g., the letter T vs. D or V).

Spatial Span

Administration of this subtest requires the stimulus booklet for the instructions, the protocol sheet for the items, and the plastic, three-dimensional, blue block-board. In this subtest, the examiner touches a sequence of blocks in view of the examinee, who is asked to repeat the sequence in the exact order. This task has items that are administered forward for the first half and backward for the second. Items are delivered at a rate of one block per second. There is no sample for the Spatial Span Forward, but there is one for the reverse condition. If an examinee makes an error on this practice item, the examiner teaches the correct response and gives a second example, but does not teach the response. The discontinue rule for both Spatial Span Forward and Spatial Span Backward is to stop after scores of 0 on both trials within an item. Clinicians should be careful not to touch the blocks audibly, as this provides an auditory cue regarding the number of items in a span.

Behaviors to Observe
- Recording exact responses allows for error analyses that detect sequencing, omission errors, and loss of set, which have specific clinical relevance.
- Indicate on the protocol when the client appears to have lost the item, so that it is clear when the client is making a guess (which clinicians should encourage as guesses are not penalized).
- Note whether the client attempts to use a problem-solving strategy such as chunking. Some examinees use such a strategy at the beginning of the task, and others learn a strategy as they progress through the task.
- Note whether errors are due to transposing block sequences, omitting, or substituting blocks.
- Attention and anxiety can impact this test; therefore such difficulties should be noted, if relevant.
- Watch for rapid repetition of taps or repetition of the span before the examiner has completed the series. Such behavior may indicate impulsivity.
- Observe whether there is a pattern of failing the first trial and then responding correctly to the second trial. Such a response pattern may indicate learning or a "warm-up" effect.

Mental Control (Optional)

Administration of this subtest requires the stimulus booklet for the instructions for each item, a stopwatch, and the protocol sheet to record responses. Items consist of recitation of over-learned sequences and manipulation of such sequences in a new format that requires holding information in working memory. Examiners should note omissions with a slash mark and record the amount of time needed to complete each item.

Behaviors to Observe
- Look for late sequence problems such that counting to 20 or reciting the alphabet contain errors later in the string.
- Note restarting, as well as loss of set errors (e.g., reversing the order to increasing numbers for the 20–1 item or beginning to state the months in their usual order in the Months Backward item. For the last item, 6s/Days, the examinee might begin reciting the numbers by six without alternation between numbers and months).
- Note strategies such as counting on fingers or writing "in the air" (e.g., for counting by sixes).

Digit Span (Optional)

Administration of this subtest requires the stimulus booklet for the instructions for both Digit Span Forward and Digit Span Backward conditions, and the protocol sheet to record responses. Strings of numbers of increasing length are presented auditorily, and the examinee is asked to repeat them back verbatim. After the examinee scores 0 points on both trials of an item, the subtest is discontinued. However, even if Digit Span Forward is discontinued, Digit Span Backward must be administered.

Behaviors to Observe
- Take note of exact output so that omission and sequencing errors can be distinguished, as well as perseveration to previous items.
- Note strategies, such as writing on an imaginary piece of paper or closing his or her eyes for increased concentration.
- Note whether the client attempts to use a problem-solving strategy such as chunking. Some examinees use such a strategy from the be-

ginning; others learn a strategy as they progress through the task. Chunking can be noted in the protocol with use of periods to denote pauses in between groups (e.g., "543 . . . 679").

- Note whether errors are due to transposing, omitting, or replacing numbers.
- Attention, hearing impairment, and anxiety can impact this test, therefore, these difficulties should be noted where relevant.
- The examiner should watch for rapid repetition of digits or repetition of the digits before the examiner has completed the series. Such behavior may be indicative of impulsivity.
- The examiner should observe whether there is a pattern of failing the first trial and then responding correctly to the second trial. Such a response pattern may indicate learning or a "warm-up" effect.

Logical Memory II

Administration of this subtest requires the stimulus booklet for the instructions and the protocol sheet to record responses. The client's responses may also be audiotaped. This is the first of five subtests that comprise Stimulus Booklet 2, representing the recall conditions for previously administered subtests. This task requires the client to recall the two stories administered earlier in the session and give as much detail of the original stories as possible. Thereafter, the examiner administers a recognition condition, which asks specific questions about the first and second stories, and the client responds with *Yes* or *No*. If only parts of the WMS-III are administered, or if administration was particularly fast, the clinician should be sure that at least 25 min have passed after administering Logical Memory I and beginning this subtest. Again, it is important to note the time at which the examinee completes Logical Memory I, although there is no prompt to do so in the test materials. If the examiner fails to record the exact time at which the examinee completed Logical Memory I, then (a) he or she could obtain an estimate from the time at which testing was begun (because Logical Memory is either the first or second subtest administered), or (b) the examiner could estimate from the "actual" time recorded on Item 14 of the Information and Orientation subtest (if it was given).

Some clients may draw a complete blank during this subtest. The examiner should give a few moments to see whether the examinee can recall the stories after consideration, and if needed, provide the cue for the first story. "The story was about a woman who was robbed." The client is allowed no further help. For the second story the prompt is, "The story was about a weather bulletin." If the examinee appears to "freeze up" and become anxious, reassure him or her with statements that this portion is meant to be somewhat challenging, and that relaxing can help retrieval.

For the recognition section that immediately follows, the correct answer appears in green bold ink, and this should be circled if that response was given by the examinee. If the item is wrong, a slash is suggested.

If more than 25 to 35 min have elapsed in the test administration, the examiner must note in the report text the reason for this time lapse (e.g., the client proceeded extremely slowly through the protocol, required a break because of an emotional outburst, etc.). A prolonged lapse between Logical Memory I and II could negatively affect performance, and make the norms less valid.

Behaviors to Observe

- Pay attention to statements like "This is the kind of thing I can't do anymore," suggesting insight into the types of day-to-day memory problems the individual may be experiencing, which may be part of the referral reason.
- Note consistent responses of *Yes* or *No* (indications of guessing).
- The individual may indicate that he or she is guessing or become resistant to this procedure if he or she recalls very little or nothing about the stories (e.g., "How can I answer when I don't remember anything?"). In this situation, the examiner should encourage the client to guess, as sometimes these results may be more accurate than the examinee expects (e.g., the client may have a feeling or a very mild sense of familiarity about one item).

Faces II

Administration of this subtest requires the stimulus booklet for the instructions and the protocol sheet to record responses. The task is to examine a set of faces and identify whether each is one of the original set to be remembered.

Individuals who are not on the original list are different from the foils presented at immediate recall condition. The clinician exposes each face for as long as the examinee needs to produce a response. If only parts of the WMS-III are being administered, or if administration was particularly fast, clinicians should be sure that at least 25 min have passed between administration of Faces I and Faces II. It is important to note the time at which Faces I is completed, although there is no prompt to write it down in the test materials.

Behaviors to Observe

The same behaviors that were important to observe during Faces I are also important to observe during Faces II.

- Note responses such as "I remember her because she's so pretty," or "unusual looking."
- Comments on the cultural group or race of the faces can be revealing as well (e.g., "I know there was an African-American person in the group").
- Make note of items to which the client takes an excessive amount of time to respond. There may be an identifiable pattern of facial types that are more challenging to the client.
- Note any responses that suggest a strategy used for recognition, such as "I know that one was in the group because they look like someone I know."
- Statements about a client's ability to recognize faces from day to day can reveal the level of insight into potential face identification or recognition difficulties experienced in daily life.

Verbal Paired Associates II

Administration of this subtest requires the stimulus booklet for the instructions and the protocol sheet to record responses. The task requires the client to recall as many word pairs as possible. The examiner presents the first word of a pair and the client is asked to recall the word that goes with it. The recognition part of the task requires the client to identify which pairs of words were in the original group that he or she was asked to remember earlier. The examiner should time administration of this subtest so that at least 25 min have elapsed since the administration of Verbal Paired Associates I. Although there is no prompt to do so in the test materials, it is a good idea for examiners to note the time at which Verbal Paired Associates I was completed. For the recognition portion, the examiner can score items (0 or 1 point) on-line as he or she administers them.

Behaviors to Observe

- Individuals with serious memory disturbance can experience confusion about task demands. Slow delivery of instructions can circumvent the confusion. The examinee may say, "I can't recall what words went together at all," or, "I can't remember my strategy to link the words," which is suggestive of where the problem in recall occurs.
- Recording exact responses can provide clues about whether there is confusion between items and whether errors are semantically or literally related to the correct response. If the client raises the inflection at the end of the word, the examiner should indicate the client's uncertainty on the record form with a question mark.

Family Pictures II

Administration of this subtest requires the stimulus booklet for the instructions and the protocol sheet to record responses. This subtest requires the client to recall the characters in each of the four scenes of Family Pictures I, where they were, and what they were doing. Examiners should time administration of this subtest so that at least 25 min have elapsed since the administration of Family Pictures I. Although there is no prompt to do so in the test materials, it is a good idea for examiners to note the completion time after administering Family Pictures I.

Behaviors to Observe

- Note if the client has stronger recollection of specific characteristics or class of elements (e.g., the client recalls specific people better than their actions, recalls people and actions better than their locations, or recalls locations and actions of people accurately, but not the specific individuals involved).
- Note statements indicating that the client has "lost it," in the interim of the delay, or statements such as, "I'm not good at remembering visual things."

Word Lists II (Optional)

Administration of this subtest requires the stimulus booklet for the instructions and the protocol sheet to record responses. This task requires the client to recall the list of words that was read over repeated trials (and not the second distractor list given later in Word Lists I). Examiners should record responses verbatim so that errors can be analyzed with respect to source memory difficulties (if they came from other parts of the test, such as the word pairs, or the Verbal Paired Associates Recognition stimuli).

If the client begins to respond before the examiner has said the whole word, the examiner should slow the client down until he or she has heard the word completely. The recognition condition consists of single words that are read aloud directly from the protocol form, and the client is asked whether each word was on the original list. The examiner should time administration of this subtest so that at least 25 min have elapsed between administration of Word List I and Word List II. Although there is no prompt to do so in the test materials, it is a good idea for examiners to note the completion time after administering Word List I.

Behaviors to Observe
- Note repetitive *Yes* or *No* responses or other cues in the recognition format that sound as if the individual is not processing the items or is guessing.
- The examiner can note words that the client endorses with confidence as well as words for which the client seems less certain.

Visual Reproduction II (Optional)

Administration of this subtest requires the stimulus booklet for the instructions and prompts (if needed) and the protocol sheet to record responses. There are four conditions of this subtest: recall, recognition, copy, and discrimination and recognition. The recall condition asks the client to draw the designs from memory. The recognition condition displays single designs, and the examinee says *Yes* or *No* as to whether the designs were presented originally in Visual Reproduction I. The copy condition allows the examinee to draw the design with the target in view in order to rule out visual-motor problems in interpreting the drawing scores. The discrimination and recognition condition tests whether visual-perceptual difficulties can account for problems in drawing the designs from memory. The client looks at the target on top and finds the matching design in a multiple-choice format that includes six designs. If only parts of the WMS-III are administered, or if administration was particularly fast, examiners should be sure that at least 25 min have passed between the administration of Visual Reproduction I and Visual Reproduction II. Although there is no prompt to do so in the test materials, it is a good idea for examiners to note the completion time after administering Visual Reproduction I.

Behaviors to Observe

- Examiners should note confabulation errors (where parts of one drawing now appear on parts of another) and emphasis on details, inner elements, or the overall gestalt of the design. Errors of rotation may occur, and examiners should note problems in sizes and proportion (smaller, larger). Any of these errors may indicate visual-perceptual, visual-motor integration, or visual memory difficulties. Administration of all four components of Visual Reproduction II can assist in differentiating between etiologies for difficulties observed.
- Observe whether the client appears overwhelmed for items on which there are two designs. This may indicate that the client is unable to recall more than one design at a time or fails to use a strategy to recall them both.
- If the examinee indicates that he or she feels certain an item is correct or that he or she is guessing at an item, note this in the protocol.
- On the multiple-choice condition, it is possible for an examinee to endorse items that are very similar or not at all alike, and this provides clues about the individual's encoding of the visual designs. Observe whether the individual looks at all the possibilities before responding, or whether responses are impulsive and haphazard.
- The copy condition can assess problems in visual-motor skills, and the discrimination condition can examine visual-perceptual problems for overall test interpretation purposes.

CAUTION

Common Examiner Pitfalls

Subtest	Error
Information and Orientation	• Failing to give the last three items
Logical Memory I	• Failing to pace the item properly by providing natural inflections and pauses; failing to read loudly or clearly
Faces I and II	• Failing to turn the pages evenly every 2 s while simultaneously watching to be sure the client is looking at each item carefully
Verbal Paired Associates I and II	• Failing to read the items at a rate of one pair every 3 s; providing too much time for responses (only 5 s allowed)
Family Pictures I and II	• Failing to place the stimuli book in the middle of the client's visual field
	• Forgetting to introduce the theme of each scene while turning the pages and letting the client view them for 10 s each
	• Failing to query in the proper sequence for People, Location of each, followed by activities of each individual
	• Failing to query about whether there were any other characters in the scene before moving to the next item
Word Lists I and II	• Failing to read the items at a uniform pace, at one word per 1.5 seconds
Visual Reproduction I	• Failing to place the book in the middle of visual field
	• Failing to encourage the client to draw everything he or she remembers, especially if the individual is hesitant to put down aspects of which he or she is uncertain
Letter-Number Sequencing	• Failing to read the items in a uniform speed (the rule is to administer one item per second)
Spatial Span	• Failing to touch the blocks at a uniform pace (while no guidelines are provided, touching one block per second is a good rule of thumb)
	• Fumbling with item administration and picking up a pencil fast enough to begin recording

A *tip* is to use the non-dominant hand to administer the item and the dominant hand to record the response.

Another good *tip* is to lift your finger high enough off the spatial span board so as not to assist a strategy of visually drawing a design to connect the blocks. A further tip is to touch the blocks silently so that an auditory strategy is not provided.

- Exposing the numbers on the blocks (this could stimulate use of a numbered strategy that not all clients are provided)

Mental Control (Optional)

- Committing errors in recording because the client restarted or self-corrected midway through (in which case it is necessary to write a verbatim response on a new line)

Digit Span (Optional)

- Failing to read the items at a rate of one item per second

- Dropping voice inflection on the last item for both forward and backward conditions

🖎 TEST YOURSELF 🖎

1. **Whenever feasible, it is generally best to administer the WMS-III in one session.** True or False?

2. **Which of the following represents good test form when the examinees are clients with special needs?**

   (a) Flexible administration targeted toward obtaining only qualitative data, because clinical interpretation of a modified test administration is close to meaningless

   (b) Close adherence to the standardized administration, even when this means the client's capabilities are underestimated

   (c) Maintenance of as near-standard administration as possible, with departures stated in the report and interpretive statements about the results made accordingly

   (d) Selection of only subtests that the individual can successfully complete without modification of interpretative statements

3. **Which of the following does *not* characterize possible concepts for interpretation from the WMS-III on the basis of Index scores?**

   (a) Visual-versus-verbal memory, and the neurobiological underpinnings subserving these capabilities in the brain, domain-specific material

   (b) Immediate recall of pictorial information, delayed recall of pictorial information

   (c) Auditory delayed versus auditory recognition capabilities

   (d) Visual delayed versus visual recognition capabilities

4. **An immediate memory problem should be conceptually distinguished from memory loss, and is separable in the WMS-III.** True or False?

5. **Testing in a noisy environment with many things happening in the background is suggested because this is how memory works in the real world.** True or False?

6. **Which one of the following capabilities is not included, with respect to immediate memory capabilities, on the WMS-III?**

   (a) Multitasking between more than one immediate recall task at a time

   (b) Auditory-versus-visual immediate memory

   (c) Working memory

   (d) Visual span memory

7. **Rapport with a client is generally established at the beginning of the session and does not change throughout the test administration.** True or False?

8. **A retrieval deficit is discerned through comparison of**

   (a) Immediate and Delayed Indexes.

   (b) Verbal and Visual Delayed Indexes.

   (c) Auditory Delayed and Auditory Recognition Delayed Indexes.

   (d) Working Memory and General Memory Indexes.

9. **The instructions on the WMS-III are the most explicit of all the WMS versions, and, therefore, the test does not require familiarity before the first administration.** True or False?

10. **Which of the following statements is false?**

   (a) The WMS-III does not make a distinction between learning and memory processes.

   (b) The WMS-III includes the most theoretically and empirically derived indexes when compared to previous versions.

   (c) The WMS-III has a new Recognition Index that was not included in previous versions.

   (d) The entire WMS-III takes less than two hours to administer.

(continued)

11. **The WMS-III allows administration of a partial battery to suit specific clinical questions.** True or False?

12. **In most situations it is advantageous to administer both immediate and delayed parts of subtests.** True or False?

Answers: 1. True; 2. c; 3. d; 4. True; 5. False; 6. a; 7. False; 8. c; 9. False; 10. a; 11. True; 12. True

Three

HOW TO SCORE THE WMS-III

TYPES OF SCORES

The WMS-III provides three types of scores: raw scores, scaled scores, and Indexes. The raw score for each subtest administered is computed first. The raw score is the sum of points earned on a subtest. However, the raw score alone is meaningless, as it is not norm-referenced. To interpret an examinee's performance, the raw scores must be translated into standard scores (either scaled scores or Indexes). Rapid Reference 3.1 lists the metrics for various types of standard scores. The subtest scaled scores, Supplementary subtest scores, and the Auditory Process Composite subtest scores (see Table D.2 and D.3 in the *WMS-III Administration and Scoring Manual*) have a mean of 10 and a standard deviation of 3, ranging from 1 to 19. Some subtests have truncated floors and ceilings depending on the age group in consideration (e.g., for 45–54 year olds, the Verbal Paired Associates II Recall Total Score has a scaled score range of 4 to 13; see Table D.1 in the *Administration and Scoring Manual*, p. 135).

The Index scores are obtained by summing the scaled scores that comprise the specific Index; the *WMS-III Administration and Scoring Manual* (Table E.1) provides the conversion. The Indexes have a mean of 100 and a standard deviation of 15 (ranging from 45 to 155), with some Indexes having a slightly higher floor (e.g., the Auditory Immediate Index Floor is 47; see Table E.1 in the *WMS-III Administration and Scoring Manual*, p. 195).

Because the scores have been smoothed and normalized to fit a bell curve, most individuals earn scores on the WMS-III that are within 1 SD from the mean. Specifically, about two thirds of the examinees earn indexes between 85 and 115. The number of examinees whose scores are 2 SDs from the mean (from 70 to 130) is about 95%. A very small number of examinees obtain scores that are higher than 130 (about 2.2%) or lower than 70 (also about

≡*Rapid Reference 3.1*

Standard Score Metrics

Type of Standard Score	Mean	Standard Deviation	Range of Values
Scaled Score	10	3	1–19
Index	100	15	45–155

2.2%). For the subtest scaled scores, corresponding values are as follows: About 66% score between 7 and 13, and about 95% score between 4 and 16; the extreme 2.2% in each "tail" earn scaled scores of 1 to 3 (very low functioning) and 17 to 19 (very high functioning).

Changes in the Protocol Forms and Tables

The WMS-III protocol form and the conversion tables are more straightforward and less ambiguous than those in the previous version. For the WMS-III, the range of possible scores is indicated for each subtest on the protocol forms and is labeled clearly for easy transfer to the profile page. Additionally, on the specific subtests as well as the profile pages, items that are not included in scores are noted in gray and green, respectively, to reduce chances of examiner calculation errors and to clearly note which subtests are part of which index. The subtest and index norms tables themselves have been reorganized; they are clearly labeled, and the tables are lined to make reading and finding conversions easier. Use of color for many tables also differentiates different types of scores (e.g., raw score versus scaled score).

SCORING THE WMS-III: PRIMARY SUBTESTS

Raw Scores

The first step in the process of scoring is obtaining raw scores for each of the administered subtests. As customary, all that is necessary to calculate the subtests' raw scores is careful addition. The best way to maintain accuracy is to calculate each score twice. Light green shading in the subtest pages easily identifies subtest scores used to calculate Primary Index scores. Examiners should transfer the raw scores for each subtest to the Score Conversion Page. The subtests are ordered according to the administration sequence. For the Auditory Recognition Delayed Total Score Calculation, sum the Logical Memory II Recognition Total Score and the Verbal Paired Associates II Recognition Total Score. A separate box below the main table on the Score Conversion Page is provided for this calculation. Transfer the sum to the raw score box for Auditory Recognition Delayed Total Score.

Scaled Scores

To determine the examinee's scaled scores, examiners need (a) the individual's chronological age, (b) his or her subtest raw scores from the record form, and (c) Table D.1 of the *WMS-III Administration and Scoring Manual* (Wechsler, 1997). *Note:* When calculating chronological age be careful not to round the dates; consider the client's exact age with respect to years, months, and days. An examinee whose age is 79 years, 11 months, and 29 days does not have that age rounded to 80 years, 0 months; the look-up table for this individual is the page for the 75–79 year range and *not* the page for the 80–84 year range. Rapid Reference 3.2 lists the steps to convert raw scores into scaled scores.

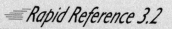

Rapid Reference 3.2

How to Convert Raw Scores to Scaled Scores

1. Transfer the total raw scores for each subtest from the inside of the protocol sheet to the appropriate spot on the score conversion page.

2. For each subtest, find the scaled score equivalent to the obtained raw score. These scores may be found by looking in Table D.1 of the *WMS-III Administration and Scoring Manual* on the page that lists the examinee's age.

3. Record each subtest's scaled score under all of the possible columns on the record form (i.e., the columns for each of the eight indexes).

4. *Optional step:* If you wish to compare scores with the reference group, scores may be obtained from Table D.2 of the *WMS-III Administration and Scoring Manual* and are recorded on the right-hand column of the score conversion page.

Examiners should look up the raw scores for each subtest on the page that contains the examinee's exact chronological age and enter the scores across the line in the white boxes under "Age-Adjusted Scaled Scores."

Note that the WMS-R did not use derived subtests scaled scores; rather, raw scores of the contributing subtests were summed and that sum was converted into age-adjusted Index scores. The WMS-R also used interpolated normative scores for three age groups (18–19, 25–34, and 45–54). This interpolation had a questionable effect on the norms, as memory performance over time may not be linear. The WMS-III compares each individual's scores with those of an equivalent age group to derive age-corrected subtests scaled scores, which are then summed to construct the Index scores. However, the *WMS-III Administration and Scoring Manual* still allows examiners to compare an adolescent's or adult's scores with those of the 20- to 34-year-old reference group, which may be useful if comparing old scores from a WMS-R.

Converting Scaled Scores to Index Scores

Once the scaled scores are entered across all white boxes in the row on the Score Conversion Page, examiners calculate the Indexes. Scaled scores entered in more than one white box in a row are included in more than one index (e.g., Logical Memory I Recall Total Score is part of both the Auditory Immediate Index and the Immediate Memory Index). The following steps help to ensure proper calculation of the Index scores:

1. Calculate the sum of the appropriate subtests' scaled scores by columns for the Auditory Immediate, Visual Immediate, Immediate Memory, Auditory Delayed, Visual Delayed, Auditory Recognition Delayed, General Memory, and Working Memory Indexes. The white boxes in that column denote the scaled scores to use for each column (e.g., the Auditory Immediate Index is composed of the sum of subtests in its column: Logical Memory I Recall Total Score and Verbal Paired Associates I Recall Total Score). In the gray box of the Sum of Scaled Scores row record the sums of the scaled scores for each Index at the bottom of each column.

2. To transfer these sums from the Sums of Scaled scores line on the Profile page of the record form to the Primary Indexes section of

the Profile page, follow the colored, dotted-line arrows across the page.

3. To find the Index score for each sum of scaled scores, locate the individual index table in Appendix E.1 of the *WMS-III Administration and Scoring Manual*. In the table, locate the sum of scaled scores for that Index in the first column and record the Index score found in the second column on that line. These tables are not differentiated by age because the age conversions have already been done. Record the Index score for each sum of scaled scores in the Index Scores line. Record the percentile rank in the next line of the table in the Percentiles box for that index. Finally, decide the desired confidence level (90% or 95%). Record the chosen confidence level in the Confidence Intervals box. Record the range for each index.

4. Plot the respective Indexes under Index scores heading for a visual display of the client's Index strengths and weaknesses.

Supplementary Scores

The same general rules previously described apply to the Auditory Process Subtest Scores and the Supplementary Scores on the Supplementary Score Conversion Profile page. These scores on the subtest pages are *not* in light green boxes. They are clearly labeled to match the headings in the tables. Again, examiners should transfer the raw scores to the appropriate lines (ordered by administration) and convert the raw scores to scaled scores using Tables D.2 for the Auditory Process Composite and D.3 for the Supplemental Subtest Scores in the *WMS-III Administration and Scoring Manual*. Sum the scores in the white boxes in each column and enter this sum on the Sums of Scaled Scores line for the Single-Trial Learning, Learning Slope, and Retention columns. Transfer the sum to the Composite Scores box by following the arrows. A separate box is provided to obtain the Retrieval Total Score. Enter the age-adjusted scaled scores calculated on the Score Conversion page into the formula and place the result (rounded to the nearest whole number) under the Retrieval Column. As with the scaled scores, plotting the Composite Scores gives a visual rendering of the individual's strengths and weaknesses.

For the Supplemental Subtest Total Scores age-adjusted scaled scores can be recorded for most subtests (in white boxes), but only percentile ranks can be calculated for Information and Orientation and for Visual-Reproduction Discrimination Total Score (recorded in the light green boxes).

Subtests Requiring Judgment

Logical Memory I and II

Scoring individual story units is easier than in previous versions of the *WMS* because the criteria are provided directly on the scoring page. However, scoring the thematic unit is slightly more difficult and requires judgment. The idea underlying the scoring of thematic units is to obtain an indicator of whether the examinee encoded the gist of the story even if he or she did not encode the exact wording. For both story unit and thematic unit, Appendix A of the *WMS-III Administration and Scoring Manual* assists the examiner in deciding between 0 and 1 point.

Family Pictures I and II

This subtest has three categories to score: character, location, and activity. Character refers to the specific identity of the individual in the scene. Location refers to the specific quadrant of the picture in which that individual is depicted, and activity refers to the actions of the specific character included in the scene. The scoring for character and location is straightforward and is scored as 0 or 1; the examinee must correctly name the character and correctly select the location (1–4). For the examinee to obtain full credit for the activity category, his or her response must include both the *object* being acted upon and the *action* itself. Activity is scored as 0, 1, or 2 (a separate point for action and object) and is the most complex score for this subtest, but Appendix B of the *WMS-III Administration and Scoring Manual* provides clarification of acceptable actions and objects. If the client's response is not found in the examples, the examiner should consider the principle or concept that holds the exemplars together and make a judgment whether the verbalization fulfills the principle.

Visual Reproduction

This is the most complex subtest with respect to scoring on the test, with multiple scoring criteria for each design. The examiner must be vigilant about the scoring principles for each item, because there are if-then statements for some items. For example, on Design C, there is a notation between Item 4 and 5 that states, "If there are fewer than or more than four medium-sized squares or rectangles, criterion 5–9 should be scored zero (0)" (*WMS-III Administration and Scoring Manual,* p. 105). An examiner who is rushing through the scoring process and fails to note this point may give too many points for a production.

Subtest-by-Subtest Scoring Keys

Some subtests require 0- and 1-point scoring and others award more than 1 point per item. Overall, the majority of the WMS-III subtests require binary scoring, but there are also subtle nuances of which the examiner should be aware (see the Don't Forget Box on this page).

DON'T FORGET

Subtest-by-Subtest Scoring Keys

Subtest	Individual Item Score Ranges	Scoring Pointers
Information and Orientation	0 or 1	Score during testing.
Logical Memory I and II	0–1 for both story unit and thematic unit	Write out output verbatim, score later.
Faces I and II	0–1	Score during testing by circling correct responses; make a slash mark through incorrect responses and assign a numeric score for each item during testing.
Verbal Paired Associates I and II	0–1 for each pair recalled	Write down output if wrong, score during testing.
Family Pictures I and II	0–1 for character & location; 1–2 for activity	Score character and location during testing by circling correct responses, slashing incorrect. Write down activity, and, unless the response is fully correct or incorrect (2, 0 points), come back and score activity later.

(continued)

Subtest	Individual Item Score Ranges	Scoring Pointers
Word Lists I and II	I point per word	Write down sequence of word production by numbering the items. Enter highest number in the box below columns and score during testing.
Visual Reproduction I and II: Recall	0–2 for each item	Score after test session.
Visual Reproduction I: Recognition	0–1	Score while testing.
Visual Reproduction I: Copy	0–2 for each item	Score after test session.
Visual Reproduction I: Discrimination	0–1	Score while testing.
Letter-Number Sequencing	0–3 (I pt/trial)	Write down output verbatim and score during testing.
Spatial Span	0–2 (I pt/trial)	Write down output verbatim and score during testing.
Mental Control (Optional)	0–5	Write down output verbatim and score during testing. Recall that each item gets a number of error score (accuracy) and potential bonus points.
Digit Span (Optional)	0–2 (I pt/trial)	Write down output verbatim and score during testing.

Computer Scoring Procedures

A computerized WMS-III "Scoring Assistant" for IBM and Macintosh computers is available from The Psychological Corporation (1997). The Scoring Assistant for the Wechsler Scales for Adults (SAWS-A) creates a summary of results from the WMS-III profile, including the following tables:

- Raw scores for each task (including a breakdown of subtests such as Digits Forward Total Score, Digits Backward Total Score; Story A Recall Units, Story A Thematic Units; and Scores for each design in the Visual Reproduction at Immediate, Delayed, and Direct Copy Condition)

- Summary of the WMS-III Primary Subtest scores (raw scores, age scaled scores and reference scaled scores)
- Summary of the Primary Index scores, including sums of the scaled scores, Index scores, confidence intervals, percentiles and qualitative descriptions
- Summary of the Supplemental Subtest scores including raw scores, Age and Reference scaled scores and Age and Reference percentiles
- Primary Index Differences and whether they are significant, as well as cumulative percentages of the normative group that received scores greater than or equal to the amount of difference
- Ability-Memory Differences (Using the WAIS-III IQ) for both predicted memory method and simple difference method

The program also generates graphs with confidence intervals for the following:

Primary Subtest scaled scores

Primary Index scores

Auditory Composite scores using percentile scores

The benefit of using a computerized scoring program is that it significantly reduces both scoring time and examiner error, as it eliminates the need to look up scores in multiple tables. It simply requires the examiner to calculate raw scores and enter them into the computer. These raw scores then convert automatically into the appropriate scaled scores, Indexes, and graphs using the examinee's calculated chronological age.

Research on Scoring Errors

Sullivan (2000) examined the common errors five trainee psychologists made when they were scoring the WMS-R. The test designers conceptualized scoring the protocols by having stages that parallel errors on Wechsler's intelligence scales (Conner & Woodall, 1983). Two of these stages of scoring are relevant to the WMS-III, as basic aspects of scoring have not changed, with the exception of weighted-scores that are part of the WMS-R scoring procedures but not the WMS-III. One stage includes assigning scores for each item, summing them to produce a subtest total, and transcribing them from pages within the record to the profile page (in the case of the WMS-R, the cover). This stage is susceptible to errors in judgment (e.g., incorrect application of scoring criteria), mathematics (e.g., incorrect summation), transcription (e.g., incorrect transfer of results from one part of the protocol to another), and timing (e.g., failure to take into account time limits for task completion). The next stage involves converting scores to Indexes. This phase is susceptible to errors of summation and errors due to erroneous use of conversion tables. Sullivan (2000) observed the most common errors on Information/Orientation, Logical Memory I and II, and Visual Reproduction I and II, where the maximum discrepancy was between trainee-scored protocols and the "gold standard" determined by scores produced by three experienced psychologists. Errors were made on the Information/Orientation subtest because the year of testing on the record form was different from the year in which protocols were scored. Errors on Logical Memory and Visual Reproduction were most often due to errors of judgment. Subtest errors were compounded when Index scores were calculated, causing different level-of-performance indicators. While the Information and Orientation subtest includes clear 0 or 1 scoring on both the WMS-R and WMS-III, the Logical Memory and Visual Reproduction subtests on the WMS-R have been revised in the WMS-III to provide more explicit scoring criteria, reducing the need for subjective judgment on the part of the tester. Whether these revisions successfully reduce inter-examiner error is yet to be studied. Examiners are more likely to improve the accuracy of their scoring by learning to administer the WMS-III through a structured course and with supervised experience, or (if this is not available or feasible) by having a complete protocol re-scored by a more experienced clinician for comparison of discrepancies. Such a double-checking procedure is likely to reduce systematic errors made by an individual clinician who is just learning the WMS-III.

✎ TEST YOURSELF ✎

1. What is a subtest that contributed to the WMS-R Visual Immediate Index, but is now a supplemental subtest on the WMS-III?

2. Immediate and Delayed Memory Index includes scores derived from recognition paradigms for visual material, while for the auditory/verbal information, the delayed and recognition scores are divided into separate indexes. True or False?

3. Which of the following is *false* with respect to why raw scores must be converted into scaled scores?

(a) For interpretation, scaled scores can be compared to one another directly.

(b) Scaled scores are calculated relative to age norms, whereas raw scores are not.

(c) Scaled scores have the same means and standard deviations, while raw scores do not.

(d) Raw scores are comparable from subtest to subtest but not from composite to composite.

4. One of the new design features of the test protocol scoring sheets is that it is constructed so that entering raw scores onto the scaled score conversion is explicitly labeled with respect to which number goes where, and transferring scores is a matter of following dotting lines. True or False?

5. Which of the following is false?

(a) The WMS-III allows for comparison of scaled scores of Immediate and Delayed Recall for the same information.

(b) The WMS-III allows for comparison between Indexes, with tables provided in the *Manual* for discerning differences required for significance.

(c) The subtests that comprise the Primary Indexes differ from the Supplemental Subtests because material with Primary Indexes focuses on visual material and Supplemental Subtests focus on verbal material.

(d) The Word Lists subtest allows examination of a learning curve.

6. The General Memory Index reflects

(a) both immediate and delayed scaled scores.

(b) a combination of delayed scaled scores only.

(c) a combination of immediate visual and verbal memory scaled scores.

(d) a combination of auditory/verbal scaled scores only.

7. Indexes that include the term "Auditory" refer to auditorily processed verbal information. True or False?

Answers: 1. Visual Reproduction; 2. True; 3. d; 4. True; 5. c; 6. b; 7. True

Four

HOW TO INTERPRET THE WMS-III

One improvement to the latest version of the WMS is that it provides more objective scores than previous versions. However, this benefit can also create challenges when trying to make sense of the complexity of multiple scores. The goal of this chapter is to help examiners organize the 11 primary subtest scaled scores and eight primary Index scores, plus all supplemental scores that the WMS-III yields. This chapter first provides an analysis of each individual subtest, and then a framework for step-by-step interpretation of the different scores obtained when the complete WMS-III is administered (Indexes, scaled scores, and supplemental scores). Ultimately, the goal of this chapter is to help examiners integrate the WMS-III test scores with each other and with background variables, behavioral variables, and supplemental test data.

ANALYSIS OF EACH WMS-III SUBTEST

The WMS-III subtests are analyzed in three different categories, empirical, cognitive, and clinical. The empirical analysis considers subtest reliability; the cognitive analysis summarizes the cognitive abilities that each subtest is believed to measure; and the clinical analysis presents factors to consider about each subtest from a clinical perspective.

Empirical Analysis

When interpreting test results, examiners should consider the reliability of the WMS-III subtests, and interpret subtests that are less reliable (< .80) with caution. In chapter 1 (Rapid Reference 1.3) we present the reliabilities of each of the subtests. Five subtests have average split-half reliability coefficients under .80, warranting caution during interpretation:

Subtest	Average Split-Half r_{xx}
Auditory Recognition Delayed	.74
Faces I	.74
Faces II	.74
Spatial Span	.79
Logical Memory II	.79

All Primary WMS-III subtests have test-retest reliability coefficients under .80, but the three subtests with the lowest values (under .70) cause the most concern and require the most cautious interpretation:

Subtest	Average Test-Retest r_{12}
Faces II	.62
Family Pictures I	.66
Faces I	.67

Cognitive Analysis

In addition to the empirical data presented for each subtest (see Rapid Reference 1.3 for all subtest reliabilities), we analyze the abilities measured by each WMS-III subtest. The majority of the shared abilities listed are from the Cattell-Horn-Carroll *Gf-Gc* model (CHC) (Flanagan, McGrew, & Ortiz, 2000). This model integrates the theories of Carroll (1993), Cattell (1941, 1957), Horn and Cattell (1966, 1967), and Horn (1965, 1989). The many similarities among these theories led Flanagan and colleagues to simplify and integrate them into a single theory (Flanagan et al., 2000). Within the CHC model, there are many terms and abbreviations. In the next few pages, we provide a foundation to understand this terminology.

The CHC theory focuses on two levels of human ability: broad abilities (such as Fluid Intelligence and Crystallized Intelligence), and narrow abilities (such as working memory and memory span). Flanagan and colleagues (2000), give a detailed presentation of the broad and narrow abilities but in this chapter we present the subset of narrow and broad CHC abilities that are relevant to the WMS-III. According to Flanagan and colleagues, the WMS-

III assesses four broad abilities: Short-term Memory (*Gsm*), Visual Processing (*Gv*), Long-term Storage and Retrieval (*Glr*), and Crystallized Intelligence (*Gc*). Flanagan and colleagues conceptualize Short-term Memory as the "ability to apprehend and hold information in immediate awareness and then use it within a few seconds" (p. 31). They define Visual Processing as "the ability to generate, perceive, analyze, synthesize, store, retrieve, manipulate, transform, and think with visual patterns and stimuli" (p. 42). Long-term Storage and Retrieval is conceptualized as "the ability to store information in and fluently retrieve new or previously acquired information from long-term memory" (p. 43). Crystallized intelligence refers to "the breadth and depth of a person's acquired knowledge of a culture and the effective application of this knowledge" (p. 30). Table 4.1 lists the narrow CHC abilities that are measured by the WMS-III.

Besides those abilities captured by the CHC theory, we have included abilities apparently measured by the test, as suggested in the WMS-R/WMS-III literature. This list of abilities should not be thought of as exhaustive. An individual's performance on the WMS-III is usually related to a unique set of variables. Most often a client's skills or deficits will be apparent in two or more subtests, so we stress examination of those abilities that are shared by two or between them. Examiners should use these hypothesized abilities flexibly and adapt them as necessary to include individual clinical experience and theoretical beliefs. Unique abilities measured by individual subtests are denoted with an asterisk.

Clinical Considerations

There are two additional lists that follow the list of abilities measured by each subtest: influences affecting subtests and clinical considerations. The influences that we list are those variables that may impinge on the client's performance. The clinical considerations are suggestions to aid in interpreting each subtest. These clinical points come from data in the literature as well as our own clinical experience with the instrument. Like all of the hypotheses we suggest, the clinical considerations are just that—points to consider. Such hypotheses should be well-supported with other data, as the nature of interpreting clinical information is very complex.

Table 4.1 Narrow CHC Abilities Tapped by WMS-III

Broad Ability	Narrow Ability	Definition
Gsm	Memory Span (MS)	Ability to attend to and immediately recall temporally ordered elements in the correct order after a single presentation.
	Working Memory (MW)	Ability to temporarily store and perform a set of cognitive operations on information that requires divided attention and the management of the limited capacity of short-term memory.
Gv	Visual Memory (MV)	Ability to form and store a mental representation or image of a visual stimulus and then recognize or recall it later.
	Visualization (Vz)	Ability to mentally manipulate objects or visual patterns and to "see" how they would appear under altered conditions.
	Spatial Relations	Ability to rapidly perceive and manipulate relatively simple visual patterns or to maintain orientation with respect to objects in space.
Glr	Free Recall Memory	Ability to recall as many unrelated items as possible, in any order, after a large collection of items is presented.
	Meaningful Memory	Ability to recall a set of items where there is a meaningful relation between items or the items comprise a meaningful story or connected discourse.
	Associative Memory (MA)	Ability to recall one part of a previously learned but unrelated pair of items when the other part is presented (i.e., paired-associative learning).
Gc	Listening Ability	Ability to listen and comprehend oral communications.

Note: Gsm = Short-Term Memory; *Gv* = Visual Processing; *Glr* = Long-Term Storage and Retrieval; *Gc* = Crystallized Intelligence.

Source: Adapted from "The Wechsler Intelligence Scales and Gf-Gc theory," by D. P. Flanagan, K. S. McGrew, and S. O. Ortiz (2000) Boston, MA: Allyn & Bacon.

PRIMARY WMS-III SUBTESTS: AUDITORY PRESENTATION

Logical Memory I and II

Abilities Shared with Other Subtests
- Crystallized Intelligence (*Gc*) (CHC theory)
- Long-term Storage and Retrieval (*Glr*) (CHC theory)
- Meaningful memory (CHC theory)
- Recall of prose

Influences Affecting Subtest Scores
- Attention span
- Concentration
- Distractibility
- Educational Opportunities
- Hearing difficulties
- Language processing
- Verbal rehearsal
- Visual elaboration

Clinical Considerations
- Subtle hearing impairment may be hypothesized if the client recalls words that are slight variations of those that were told in the story (e.g., repeating "Hannah" rather than "Anna" or "tall" rather than "small")
- Attention/concentration difficulties may be apparent if the examinee's gaze seems to drift and difficulties recalling the story coincide with the changed gaze patterns.
- Examine the pattern of errors made in forgetting to provide insight into emotional issues related to memory difficulties. For example, clients who cannot accurately recall numerical values in the stories (such as the dollar amount, the number of children, the number of days, the amount of rain, or the temperature) may suggest anxiety about numbers. Such an individual may state that he or she has "a mental block" when it comes to numbers.
- Embellishing stories extensively may be an attempt to overcompensate for an inability to remember. Such embellishment may arise in a person who doesn't want to appear "stupid" or who is trying to hide

his or her deficits. Individuals with more serious psychiatric conditions or neurological diagnoses may also produce confabulation or extreme embellishment in stories.

- Recency or primacy effects may be present in a client's retelling of the stories. Some individuals may be able to hold the beginning part of the story in mind, but forget (or perhaps are unable to attend to) the end, while other people may remember only the ending of the story because it is what was most recently heard.

- Examiners should contrast errors on the Thematic score versus Total Recall score to address the hypothesis that the client is a simultaneous (versus sequential) processor. For example, if a client can remember the global gist of the story, but not the linear details of it, he or she may have stronger simultaneous or holistic processing abilities.

Verbal Paired Associates I and II

Abilities Shared with Other Subtests
- Associative memory
- Long-term Storage and Retrieval (*Glr*) (CHC theory)
- Learning novel world pairs

Influences Affecting Subtest Scores
- Hearing difficulties
- Visual elaboration
- Verbal rehearsal
- Self-organizational abilities

Clinical Considerations
- This task taps the ability to actively associate unrelated words. Some clients may use a visualization strategy, while others may try to memorize the pairs rotely.
- Motivation is especially important in this task. Observe level of apparent effort, as well as signs of fatigue or boredom, which could impact performance.
- Observe the client's reaction when his or her nonresponse is followed by your statement of the correct response. Some individuals

may become unduly frustrated or later state that they feel they are "stupid" or have a "bad memory." Others may react more positively once they understand the task demands.

Letter-Number Sequencing

Abilities Shared with Other Subtests
- Short-term Memory (*Gsm*) (CHC theory)
- Working memory
- Facility with over-learned sequences

Influences Affecting Subtest Scores
- Attention span
- Concentration
- Distractibility
- Verbal rehearsal
- Visual elaboration
- Verbal processing
- Motivation

Clinical Considerations
- Sequencing, poor short-term memory, inattention, distractibility, or anxiety may cause difficulties on Letter-Number Sequencing. Evidence of sequencing problems includes correctly remembering the numbers and letters, but in the wrong sequence. Short-term memory may be implicated if part of the sequence is correct but some of the numbers or letters are forgotten.
- Observe the examinee for signs of "stimulus overload," which can lead to frustration. Statements such as "That is too much to remember at once," or "How about just the numbers?" indicate that an examinee may be overwhelmed with the amount of auditory stimuli.
- Letter-Number Sequencing is more conceptually related to Digits Backward than Digits Forward. Both the backward span and Letter-Number Sequencing require the examinee to mentally manipulate or visualize the stimuli. (Some examinees who rely on visualization strategies will close their eyes during the administration of the items

or during their response.) If the examinee generated these strategies in to respond to Digits Backward, he or she may benefit from using those or similar strategies on Letter-Number Sequencing.

- As there are three trials for each item, clients have an opportunity to develop and test strategies. The clinician may question the examinee after the test is complete to gather information about any strategies that he or she may have generated to complete the task.
- Like Digit Span, the skills required for this test are impaired more by state (test) anxiety than by trait (chronic) anxiety.
- Whereas number sequences are automatic for most adolescents and adults, the precise alphabetic sequence has not been adequately "overlearned" for many individuals. Note whether some examinees consistently make errors on the letters but get all numbers right. Consider reading problems, such as illiteracy or dyslexia.

PRIMARY SUBTESTS: VISUAL PRESENTATION

Faces I and II

Abilities Shared with Other Subtests
- Visual Processing (*Gv*)
- Visual memory
- Long-term Memory (*Glr*)
- Meaningful memory
- Memory for facial stimuli

Influences Affecting Subtest Scores
- Attention/concentration
- Reflectivity/impulsivity
- Premorbid facial processing abilities
- Verbal elaboration

Clinical Considerations
- Record the examinee's verbalizations during the test to provide clues regarding how he or she is encoding information. Statements such as "I remember this person's hair, or this unusual nose," versus "This

person gives me a funny feeling, or seems they could be up to something," reveal different strategies for recall.
- Verbalizations such as "They all look alike" may indicate that the client is having difficulty distinguishing the essential features of the face.

Family Pictures I and II

Abilities Shared with Other Subtests
- Long-term Memory (*Glr*) (CHC theory)
- Associative memory
- Visual Processing (*Gv*) (CHC theory)
- Visual memory
- Spatial relations
- Memory for location & activity of people

Influences Affecting Subtest Scores
- Environmental stimulation
- Concentration
- Verbal rehearsal
- Visual-perceptual processing capabilities
- Attention to visual detail

Clinical Considerations
- Record verbalizations during the test to provide clues regarding how the examinee is encoding information.
- Analyze whether the individual is confusing the family members within gender class (father versus grandfather) or activities in specific spaces (mowing the lawn versus other lawn activities).

Spatial Span

Abilities Shared with Other Subtests
- Short-term Memory (*Gsm*) (CHC theory)
- Memory span
- Visual Processing (*Gv*) (CHC theory)
- Visual memory
- Rote visual recall

Influences Affecting Subtest Scores
- Attention span
- Concentration
- Distractibility
- Verbal rehearsal
- Visual elaboration
- Ability to get into novel learning set
- Impulsivity

Clinical Considerations
- Record responses to help to discern whether failure is due to poor sequential ability (right numbers in wrong order) or to poor rote memory (skipping blocks, but otherwise correctly repeating the series). Responses that bear little relationship to the actual stimuli may reveal problems with inattention, distractibility, or anxiety. Note behavior such as beginning a response before the item is fully administered.
- After the task, test the limits and question whether the examinee used any strategy, in order to help differentiate among poor strategy generation (e.g., chunking), low motivation, anxiety, distractibility, sequencing problems, and memory problems.
- Spatial Span Backward, which requires mental manipulation of the sequence of tapped blocks, is more impacted by poor working memory ability than is Digits Forward. Therefore, those who have better working memory ability may perform better on Digits Backward.
- Typically adults and adolescents produce forward spatial spans that are longer than backward spans. Longer backward than forward spatial spans occur relatively rarely within the normal population of adults and are, therefore, noteworthy. One explanation for a longer backward spatial span is that individuals may find it to be more challenging and worthy of sustaining effort, or individuals may have better skill at representational (high level) tasks than at automatic (overlearned) tasks (such as Spatial Span Forward).
- Less-than-ideal testing conditions may adversely affect performance on this subtest (visual distractions), and visual impairment may make a client vulnerable to failure.

- Examinees may demonstrate impulsivity by beginning to respond before the examiner has completed tapping the series of blocks or by repeating the block sequence very rapidly.
- Examinees may demonstrate learning ability by making errors on the first trial but passing the second trial. Examiners should look for this pattern in other subtests as well (Digit Span, Letter-Number Sequencing, Word Lists).

OPTIONAL SUBTESTS: AUDITORY PRESENTATION

Information and Orientation

Abilities Shared with Other Subtests
- This subtest measures unique abilities, most notably episodic memory of personal information such as name, age, and birthdate as well as information pertaining to the current state (date, time, city, etc.)

Influences Affecting Performance
- Disorientation
- Inattention
- Malingering
- Thought disorder

Clinical Considerations
- This is a good measure to provide a first examination of whether the patient is oriented to time, place, and test situation. The examiner can obtain initial information on level of effort or possible malingering.
- The findings on this subtest can determine the appropriateness of a memory test or the examinee's ability to be validly tested on the more demanding and complex facets of the WMS-III.

Word Lists I and II

Abilities Shared with Other Subtests
- Long-term Memory (*Glr*) (CHC theory)
- Free recall memory
- Associative memory

- Anxiety
- List learning

Influences Affecting Subtest Scores
- Attention span
- Concentration distractibility
- Hearing difficulties
- Verbal rehearsal
- Visual elaboration

Clinical Considerations
- The examiner should be alert to unusual performances, such as recall of different words across trials or a decreasing learning curve, which suggest problematic effort.

Mental Control

Abilities Shared with Other Subtests
- Short-term Memory (*Gsm*) (CHC theory)
- Working memory
- Ability to multitask

Influences Affecting Subtest Scores
- Attention span
- Concentration
- Distractibility
- Reflectivity/impulsivity
- Anxiety

Clinical Considerations
- Clients may exhibit stimulus overload when presented with too much information to store and hold in working memory. When clients are in such a state, they may have a "glazed" look in their eyes, may refuse to attempt the items, or may verbalize their frustration and feelings of being overwhelmed.
- Multitasking can be challenging for some individuals, and clients may demonstrate such difficulty by being able to recite the overlearned

portion of the lists (e.g., they can count by sixes and separately can recite the days of the week), but cannot do the two tasks together.

- Some clients may have a perfectionistic style that is reflected by a slow, methodical recitation of the lists. Such people are not likely to earn bonus points for speedy performance.
- Other clients may be more concerned with producing the information rapidly (e.g., they are extremely motivated by the stopwatch), but the information that they present is not very accurate. Such clients often comment on the stopwatch or ask how quickly they completed an item.

Digit Span

Abilities Shared with Other Subtests
- Short-term Memory (*Gsm*) (CHC theory)
- Memory span
- Working memory
- Immediate rote recall

Influences Affecting Subtest Scores
- Attention span
- Concentration
- Distractibility
- Hearing difficulties
- Organization
- Verbal rehearsal
- Visual elaboration
- Anxiety

Clinical Considerations
- Record responses to help to discern whether failure is due to poor sequential ability (right numbers in wrong order) or to poor rote memory (forgetting digits, but otherwise correctly repeating the series). Clients may demonstrate problems with inattention, distractibility, or anxiety in responses that bear little relationship to the actual stimuli.

- After the task, test the limits and question whether the examinee used any strategy in order to help differentiate among poor strategy generation (e.g., chunking), low motivation, anxiety, distractibility, sequencing problems, and memory problems.
- Digits Backward, which requires mental manipulation or visualization of the numbers, is more impacted by number ability than is Digits Forward. Therefore, clients who have better number ability may perform better on Digits Backward.
- The median forward span stays constant from ages 16–54, with a length of 7 digits; after age 54, the length of the forward span remains consistently at 6 digits. A similar trend is noted in the backward span, with a median backward span of 5 for 16–54 year olds, and a median backward span of 4 for almost all individuals older than 54. For more detailed information on forward and backward spans see Table F.5 in the *WMS-III Administration and Scoring Manual* (Wechsler, 1997).
- Typically, adults and adolescents produce forward spans that are 2 digits longer than backward spans. Longer backward than forward spans occur relatively rarely within the normal population of adults (less than 4% of the time, averaging across all ages) and are, therefore, noteworthy (Wechsler, 1997, Table F.6). One explanation for a longer backward span is that individuals may find it more challenging and worthy of sustaining effort, or individuals may have better skill at representational (high level) tasks than at automatic (overlearned) tasks (such as Digits Forward).
- Less-than-ideal testing conditions may adversely affect performance on this subtest (visual or auditory distractions), and hearing impairment may make a client vulnerable to failure.
- Repeating digits seems to be more impaired by state anxiety (or test anxiety) than by chronic (trait) anxiety.
- Clients may demonstrate impulsivity by beginning to respond before the examiner has completed the series of digits or by repeating the digits very rapidly.
- Clients may demonstrate learning ability by making errors on the first trial but being able to pass the second trial. Look for this pattern in other subtests (Letter-Number Sequencing, Word Lists).

OPTIONAL WMS-III SUBTESTS: VISUAL PRESENTATION

Visual Reproduction I and II

Abilities Shared with Other Subtests
- Free recall memory
- Long-term Memory (*Glr*) (for Visual Reproduction II)
- Visual memory
- Visual Processing (*Gv*) (CHC theory)
- Visualization (for Visual Reproduction II)
- Visual-motor reproduction

Influences Affecting Subtest Scores
- Concentration (for Visual Reproduction II)
- Environmental stimulation
- Planning
- Reflectivity/impulsivity (for Visual Reproduction II)
- Verbal elaboration
- Vision difficulties
- Visual acuity
- Visual-motor coordination
- Visual-perceptual abilities
- Visual-spatial abilities

Clinical Considerations
- Note frequent checking back to the covered stimulus book while drawing, which could indicate that the client is trying to visualize the object that had been shown previously. Requests that the stimuli be shown again indicate the individual's difficulty encoding the design.
- Difficulties in replicating the drawings in proportion, using only one side of page, and problematic pencil grasp or tremor may reveal neurological problems.
- Rapid, careless drawings may indicate lack of effort or motivation.
- During the discrimination portion of Visual Reproduction II, the client may become overwhelmed by all of the visual stimuli. He or she may indicate such stimulus overload by comments such as "There are too many to tell." The client may also indicate overload by covering up some of the six foils with his or her hands to reduce visual distraction.

STEP-BY-STEP PROCEDURES FOR INTERPRETING THE ENTIRE WMS-III PROFILE

This section details seven steps for interpreting complete WMS-III profiles.

Step 1.	Examine the immediate-versus-delayed memory within the auditory and visual modalities.
Step 2.	Examine memory within the separate auditory-versus-visual modalities.
Step 3.	Examine the most global scores: Immediate Memory and General Memory.
Step 4.	Analyze the Working Memory Index where it is compared to Immediate and Delayed Memory.
Steps 5 and 6.	Determine strengths and weaknesses in the subtest profile.
Step 7.	Interpret the numerous supplemental scores.

Throughout the steps, we stress how to determine the interpretability and practical meaningfulness of the Indexes. The empirical framework we present is a "cookbook" approach, so examiners must know when to deviate from the steps and use clinical information to reject empirical rules in favor of alternative interpretations of the data. To best understand each individual's profile, examiners should always try to use knowledge of theory and clinical sense, paired with their conceptual understanding of the WMS-III.

We have developed a *WMS-III Interpretation Worksheet* (see Appendix B) that helps outline the steps that we discuss in this section. We also illustrate how to walk through the steps in the WMS-III Interpretation Worksheet by using the data from Natalie L.'s profile (see Table 4.2). Ms. L. is a 47-year-old woman with concerns about recent memory-related deficits related to a head injury acquired three months ago during a car accident. The last chapter of this book presents Ms. L.'s profile and another client's profile as illustrative case reports to demonstrate how the empirical framework translates into understanding actual clinical cases.

Step 1: Compare and Interpret Immediate and Delayed Memory within each Modality

In Step 1 we explore the temporal nature of memory to closely examine short-term and long-term memory. To make in-depth temporal comparisons, it is

Table 4.2 Wechsler Memory Scale–Third Edition (WMS-III) Score Summary for Natalie L.

Primary Indexes	Index Score	Percentile Rank	Confidence Interval (95%)
Auditory Immediate	89	23	83–97
Visual Immediate	112	79	100–120
Immediate Memory	100	50	92–108
Auditory Delayed	77	6	71–89
Visual Delayed	112	79	100–120
Auditory Recognition Delayed	75	5	70–93
General Memory	87	19	80–96
Working Memory	88	21	80–99

Primary Subtests	Age-Scaled Score	Percentile Rank
Logical Memory I Total Recall	8	25
Faces I Recognition Total	11	63
Verbal Paired Associates I Recall Total	8	25
Family Pictures I Recall Total	13	84
Letter-Number Sequencing Total	7	16
Spatial Span Total	9	37
Logical Memory II Recall Total	4	2
Faces II Recognition Total	10	50
Verbal Paired Associates II Recall Total	8	25
Family Pictures II Recall Total	14	91
Auditory Recognition Delayed Total	5	5

necessary to compare scores within each modality (i.e., immediate-versus-delayed memory within the auditory modality and immediate-versus-delayed memory within the visual modality). Thus, we begin by comparing performance on the Auditory Immediate and the Auditory Delayed Indexes. Table F.1 in the *WMS-III Administration and Scoring Manual* (Wechsler, 1997, p. 205) gives values for statistical significance between the Primary Index scores at the .05 and .15 levels. The .15 level is too liberal for most testing purposes (15% contains too much built-in error). We present difference values at the .01 and .05 levels, using the averages of all ages. Rapid Reference 4.1 and the WMS-III

≡Rapid Reference 4.1

Example of Natalie L.'s Auditory Immediate versus Auditory Delayed, Visual Immediate versus Visual Delayed, and Auditory Delayed and Auditory Recognition Delayed Index Comparisons from Step 1

Step 1: Compare and Interpret Immediate and Delayed Memory within each Modality.

Auditory Immediate Index	Auditory Delayed Index	Difference	Is there a significant difference? Significant ($p < .01$)	Significant ($p < .05$)	Not Significant
89	77	12	18 or more	13–17	(0–12)

Visual Immediate Index	Visual Delayed Index	Difference	Is there a significant difference? Significant ($p < .01$)	Significant ($p < .05$)	Not Significant
112	112	0	23 or more	17–22	(0–16)

Auditory Delayed Index	Auditory Recognition Delayed Index	Difference	Is there a significant difference? Significant ($p < .01$)	Significant ($p < .05$)	Not Significant
77	75	2	24 or more	18–23	(0–17)

Interpretation Worksheet detail the process of determining significance and include the values needed for significance. A significant discrepancy between these two indexes is 13 points (at the .05 level) and 18 points (at the .01 level). Next, compare the Visual Immediate Index and Visual Delayed Index. For this comparison, a significant discrepancy is 17 points at $p < .05$ and 23 points at $p < .01$. Rapid Reference 4.1 and Appendix B provide examples of how to examine these discrepancies.

The .05 level of confidence is appropriate to interpret discrepancy scores for most testing purposes. Because difference scores can be more unreliable than other types of scores, examiners should choose at least a 95% level of confidence. Because we want to generate useful hypotheses in the profile, a 99% confidence level is too conservative to allow flexible interpretation. However, clinicians should decide the level of confidence they are willing to accept.

Significantly lower performance on delayed memory indexes relative to immediate memory performance may indicate deficits in a person's ability to retain previously learned material. A delayed memory deficit suggests mesial temporal dysfunction, and this should be highlighted in a protocol where it exists. However, a more uncommon occurrence of lower immediate memory relative to delayed memory (or scores that are similarly depressed) may indicate initial poor learning, but not rapid forgetting.

Examiners can make another type of within-modality comparison from the delayed memory indexes within the auditory modality. One of the indexes, Auditory Delayed, measures a client's delayed memory recall, whereas another, Auditory Recognition Delayed, measures a client's ability to recognize the information presented. The size of the Auditory Delayed versus Auditory Recognition Delayed discrepancy needed for significance is 18 points at the .05 level and 24 points at the .01 level.

A discrepancy between a relatively high Auditory Recognition Delayed score when compared to Auditory Delayed suggests a retrieval deficit. This pattern could represent evidence for frontal-executive dysfunction or for subcortical dysfunction.

An additional interpretive consideration from the findings of Step 1 is the effect of a significant Auditory Delayed-Auditory Recognition Delayed discrepancy on the General (Delayed) Memory Index. As the "Decision Tree before Step 3" in the *WMS-III Interpretation Worksheet* (Appendix B) shows, if a significant Auditory Delayed versus Auditory Recognition Delayed discrep-

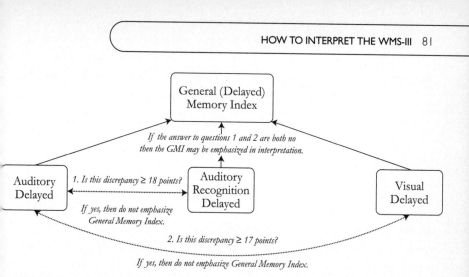

Figure 4.1 **Pictorial Representation of the Auditory Delayed versus Auditory Recognition Delayed Comparison**

ancy exists, then the General (Delayed) Memory Index should probably not be emphasized in interpretation. Figure 4.1 provides a pictorial representation of this point, and Step 3 gives more rationale for why examiners should or should not emphasize the Immediate Memory and General Memory Indexes.

The comparisons made in Step 1, as well as subsequent steps, focus on differences that are statistically significant. However, *statistical significance* tells us nothing about how *frequently* a discrepancy of a given magnitude occurs in the normal population. In interpreting a discrepancy, it is also important to understand how common or rare it is. Therefore, in this and subsequent steps, we address the size of a discrepancy needed to be considered abnormal, as well as significant. In the case of the three comparisons made in Step 1, the values needed for abnormality are actually *smaller* than the values needed for significance at the .01 level. For example, an 18-point discrepancy is necessary for significance at the .01 level for the Auditory Immediate versus Auditory Delayed comparison, but only 11 points are necessary for the discrepancy to be considered abnormal. Similarly, in the Visual Immediate versus Visual Delayed comparison, 23 points are needed for significance ($p < .01$), but 13 points are needed for abnormality; in the Auditory Delayed versus Auditory Recognition Delayed comparison, 24 points are needed for significance ($p < .01$) but only 9 points are needed for abnormality. These instances where the values needed for abnormality are smaller than those needed for significance are more uncommon than the opposite pattern and may be due, in part, to the relatively low reliability of the Indexes, but it can also indicate that statistically significant discrepancies are fairly uncommon in the normal population.

Step 2: Compare and Interpret Memory between Auditory and Visual Modalities

In Step 1 we examine the temporal nature of memory, comparing differences between short-term and long-term memory. In Step 2 we examine the nature of the stimuli that are to be remembered. Specifically, this step determines whether a client's auditory memory is differentially impaired compared to his or her visual memory. To complete the analysis, examine the auditory versus visual modalities separately in the immediate memory conditions and the delayed memory conditions.

Within immediate memory, calculate the size of the auditory-versus-visual discrepancy. An Auditory Immediate-Visual Immediate discrepancy of 15 points is needed for significance at the .05 level, and a discrepancy of 19 points is needed for significance at the .01 level. Within delayed memory, also calculate the size of the auditory-versus-visual discrepancy. An Auditory Delayed-Visual Delayed discrepancy of 16 points is needed for significance at the .05 level, and a discrepancy of 22 points is needed for significance at the .01 level (see Rapid Reference 4.2 and Appendix B).

Regardless of what level of confidence examiners choose to accept, a lack of significant findings in the size of the discrepancy needs to be interpreted as a discrepancy that is due to chance. Accordingly, we conclude that the abilities in the two modalities are not differentially impaired.

As in Step 1, the size of the discrepancies needed for abnormality should be examined in addition to the magnitude needed for significance. However, unlike the comparisons in Step 1, the values needed for abnormality in the Step 2 comparisons are larger than those needed for statistical significance. The values are as follows:

—Auditory Immediate versus Visual Immediate: 25 points needed for abnormality.
—Auditory Delayed versus Visual Delayed: 24 points needed for abnormality.

Thus, when interpreting these discrepancies, in addition to considering whether the indexes are significantly discrepant from one another, consider

≡Rapid Reference 4.2

Example of Natalie L.'s Auditory Immediate vs. Visual Immediate and Auditory Delayed vs. Visual Delayed Comparisons

Step 2: Compare and Interpret Memory between Auditory and Visual Modalities.

Auditory Immediate Index	Visual Immediate Index	Difference	Is there a significant difference?		
			Significant (p < .01)	Significant (p < .05)	Not Significant
89	112	23	19 or more	15–18	0–14

Auditory Delayed Index	Visual Delayed Index	Difference	Is there a significant difference?		
			Significant (p < .01)	Significant (p < .05)	Not Significant
77	112	35	22 or more	16–21	0–15

how unusual or rare the discrepancies are. An abnormally large discrepancy (one that occurs in less than 15% of the population) may be more clinically meaningful than one that occurs commonly (or more frequently) in the normal population.

Differential performances can suggest lateralized differences in hemispheric function. Dramatic differences should prompt the examiner to discern potential differences between primary verbal and visual-spatial capabilities, as well as problems with auditory-visual versus attention alone.

An additional interpretive consideration from the findings of Step 2 is the effect of a significant Auditory Immediate-Visual Immediate discrepancy on the Immediate Memory Index and the effect of a significant Auditory Delayed-Visual Delayed discrepancy on the General (Delayed) Memory Index. As the "Decision Tree before Step 3" in the *WMS-III Interpretation Worksheet* (Appendix B) shows, if a significant Auditory Immediate versus Visual Immediate discrepancy exists, then the Immediate Memory Index should probably not be emphasized in interpretation (see Figure 4.2). Likewise, if a significant

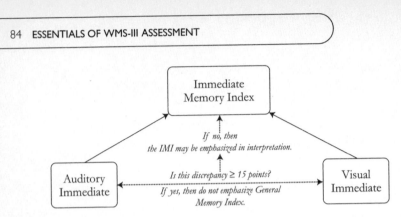

Figure 4.2 Pictorial Representation of the Auditory Immediate versus Visual Immediate Comparison

Auditory Delayed versus Visual Delayed discrepancy exists, then the General (Delayed) Memory Index should probably not be emphasized in interpretation. Step 3 provides more rationale for why examiners should or should not emphasize the Immediate Memory and General Memory Indexes.

Step 3: A. Compare Immediate Memory Index to General (Delayed) Memory Index; B. Compare Auditory Immediate and Visual Immediate Indexes to General (Delayed) Memory Index; C. Compare Auditory Delayed, Visual Delayed, and Auditory Recognition Delayed Indexes to Immediate Memory Index

The Immediate Memory Index is the most global measure of immediate memory available on the WMS-III and is composed of two other Primary Indexes: Auditory Immediate and Visual Immediate (see Figure 4.3). Likewise, the General Memory Index is the most global measure of delayed memory available on the WMS-III, and is composed of three other Primary Indexes: Auditory Delayed, Auditory Recognition Delayed, and Visual Delayed (see Figure 4.4). Both the Immediate Memory and General Memory Indexes have strong reliabilities (both .91), and are, therefore, good indexes to contrast in our profile interpretation.

However, because other indexes comprise the Immediate and General Memory Indexes, before continuing with Step 3, it is important to consider whether contrasting these two indexes will provide meaningful information. Thus, as the "Decision Tree before Step 3" illustrates (see Interpretive Worksheet and Figure 4.5), examiners must decide which part of Step 3 (part A, B,

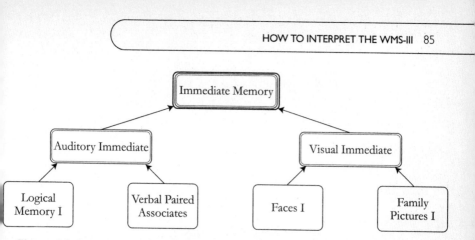

Figure 4.3 Subtests and Indexes Measuring Immediate Memory

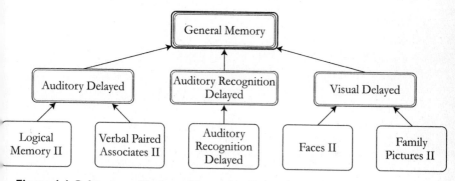

Figure 4.4 Subtests and Indexes Measuring Delayed Memory

or C) provides the most useful interpretive information. If significant differences were found in Step 1 between Auditory Immediate and Visual Immediate Indexes, then the Immediate Memory Index really represents nothing more than the average of very discrepant abilities, and probably should not be emphasized in interpretation. Likewise, if significant discrepancies were found between the Auditory Delayed and Visual Delayed Indexes in Step 1 or the Auditory Delayed and Auditory Recognition Delayed Indexes in Step 2, then the General (Delayed) Memory Index is not very meaningful, and therefore should not be emphasized in the interpretation. Following this logic, if neither the Immediate Memory or General (Delayed) Memory Indexes are meaningful because of discrepancies uncovered in Steps 1 or 2, then the comparison between them, which we make here in Step 3, is also not meaningful. In such a situation, clinicians may choose to skip Step 3 and move onto the next step

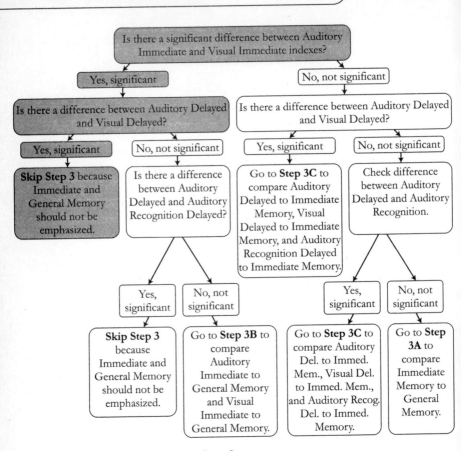

Figure 4.5 Decision Tree before Step 3

to see if they may find more clinically meaningful information. However, if one or both of the Indexes can be meaningfully interpreted, then there are discrepancies that can be meaningfully calculated and interpreted. In Natalie L.'s case, the "Decision Tree Before Step 3" reveals that her Immediate Memory and General (Delayed) Memory Indexes should not be emphasized because there are significant discrepancies between both the Auditory and Visual Immediate Indexes and the Auditory and Visual Delayed Indexes. Therefore, in her case, it is not necessary to complete the remaining comparisons in Step 3; ultimately her Immediate Memory and General Memory Indexes are not emphasized in interpretation.

As shown in Figure 4.6, if the two Indexes that compose the Immediate

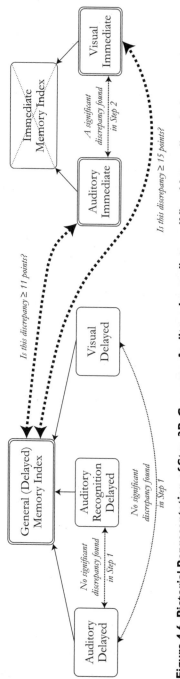

Figure 4.6 Pictorial Representation of Step 3B: Compare Auditory Immediate and Visual Immediate Indexes to General (Delayed) Memory Index (if Step 2 determined that the Immediate Memory Index should not be emphasized)

Memory Index (Auditory Immediate and Visual Immediate) are significantly different from one another, but the General (Delayed) Memory Index is meaningful, then it is wiser to compare the General Memory Index to the separate Auditory Immediate and Visual Immediate Indexes (Step 3B), rather than comparing the General Memory Index to Immediate Memory Index. Similarly, as shown in Figure 4.7, if any of the three General (Delayed) Memory Indexes are discrepant from one another (Auditory Delayed, Auditory Recognition Delayed, and Visual Delayed), but the Immediate Memory Index is meaningful, then it is wiser to compare separately the Auditory Delayed, Auditory Recognition Delayed, and Visual Delayed Indexes to the Immediate Memory Index (Step 3C). Rapid Reference 4.3 and the WMS-III Interpretation Worksheet present the size of the discrepancies needed for each of these comparisons. However, as Figure 4.8 shows, if both the Immediate Memory and General Memory Indexes are meaningfully interpretable then clinicians can interpret the discrepancy between them.

The size of discrepancy between the two indexes, Immediate Memory and General Memory, provides information about the temporal nature of memory. Namely, it reveals if memory deficits are more severe in the short-term or long-term. First, calculate the size of the Immediate Memory versus General (Delayed) Memory discrepancy and then determine whether the value is large enough to be statistically significant. The overall values for the Immediate Memory versus the General Memory Index discrepancy are 12 points at the .05 level and 16 points at the .01 level (Rapid Reference 4.4 summarizes these values). The magnitude of the value needed to be considered abnormally large or unusual is smaller than the value needed for statistical significance; only an 11-point Immediate versus General Memory discrepancy is needed for abnormality. Thus, all statistically significant differences in this comparison also occur in less than 15% of the normal population.

If the Immediate Memory and General Memory Indexes do not differ significantly, then you must consider the short-term and long-term memory to be equally strong (or weak). If the discrepancy is not large enough to reach significance, you must assume that it exists due to chance. Thus, refrain from making bold statements about the difference between a client's immediate versus delayed memory, if the data on which you are basing your statement is an 11-point discrepancy or smaller. On the other hand, if the discrepancy is large enough to be considered statistically significant, then you should make an in-

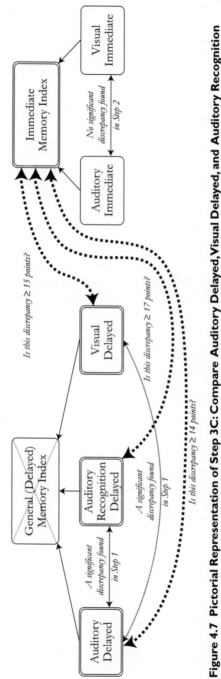

Figure 4.7 Pictorial Representation of Step 3C: Compare Auditory Delayed, Visual Delayed, and Auditory Recognition Delayed Indexes to Immediate Memory Index (if Step 1 determined that the General (Delayed) Memory Index should not be emphasized)

Excerpt from *WMS-III Interpretation Worksheet* showing General Memory vs. Auditory Immediate and Visual Immediate Comparisons and Immediate Memory vs. Auditory Immediate, Visual Immediate, and Auditory Recognition Comparisons

Step 3B: Compare Auditory Immediate and Visual Immediate Indexes to General (Delayed) Memory Index.

Auditory Immediate Index	General Memory Index	Difference	Is there a significant difference?		
			Significant ($p < .01$)	Significant ($p < .05$)	Not Significant
			15 or more	11–14	0–10

Visual Immediate Index	General Memory Index	Difference	Is there a significant difference?		
			Significant ($p < .01$)	Significant ($p < .05$)	Not Significant
			20 or more	15–19	0–14

Step 3C: Compare Auditory Delayed, Visual Delayed, and Auditory Recognition Delayed Indexes to Immediate Memory Index.

Auditory Delayed	Immediate Memory Index	Difference	Is there a significant difference?		
			Significant ($p < .01$)	Significant ($p < .05$)	Not Significant
			18 or more	14–17	0–13

Visual Delayed	Immediate Memory Index	Difference	Is there a significant difference?		
			Significant ($p < .01$)	Significant ($p < .05$)	Not Significant
			20 or more	15–19	0–14

Auditory Recognition Delayed	Immediate Memory Index	Difference	Is there a significant difference?		
			Significant ($p < .01$)	Significant ($p < .05$)	Not Significant
			22 or more	17–21	0–16

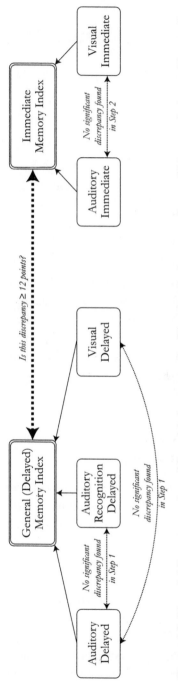

Figure 4.8 Pictorial Representation of Step 3A: Interpret the Discrepancy between General Memory Index and Immediate Memory Index (if they were both found to be meaningful in Steps 1 and 2)

Rapid Reference 4.4

**Excerpt from *WMS-III Interpretation Worksheet* showing
Immediate Memory vs. General (Delayed) Memory Comparisons**

**Step 3A: Compare Immediate Memory Index to General (Delayed)
Memory Index.**

Immediate Memory Index	General Memory Index	Difference	Is there a significant difference?		
			Significant ($p < .01$)	Significant ($p < .05$)	Not Significant
			16 or more	12–15	0–11

terpretation based on the client's differential performance on the two indexes. For example, a client whose General (Delayed) Memory Index is significantly higher than Immediate Memory Index may have better long-term than short-term memory due to encoding difficulties. Such a pattern is rare and could suggest malingering. The reverse pattern, a significantly higher Immediate Memory Index than General (Delayed) Memory Index, suggests bilateral or unilateral mesial temporal dysfunction.

Step 4: Compare and Interpret Working Memory with Immediate and General (Delayed) Memory

Working memory is an active part of how we process information, and, like immediate memory, refers to the temporary storage of information. Researchers view immediate or short-term memory as a passive form of memory, whereas working memory is an active form. The WMS-III Working Memory Index is composed of one auditory subtest (Letter-Number Sequencing) and one visual subtest (Spatial Span). Thus, for interpretation, it is useful to compare the Working Memory Index to (a) the Immediate Memory Index, (b) the Auditory Immediate Index, (c) the Visual Immediate Index, and (d) the General (Delayed) Memory Index.

The size of the Working Memory versus Immediate Memory discrepancy needed to achieve significance is 14 points (at the .05 level) and 19 points (at the .01 level). For the Working Memory versus General (Delayed) Memory comparison, a 14-point discrepancy is needed for significance at the .05 level, and an 18-point discrepancy is needed at the .01 level. Across the separate modalities, the size of the discrepancy needed for the Working Memory versus Auditory Immediate Indexes is 13 points (at the .05 level) and 18 points (at the .01 level). For the Working Memory versus Visual Immediate comparison, a 17-point discrepancy is needed for significance at the .05 level and a 22-point discrepancy is needed for significance at the .01 level.

The results of the four comparisons may reveal several things. One possibility is that a low Working Memory Index in conjunction with relatively low Immediate Memory or Delayed Memory Indexes signifies that a client's attentional abilities are affecting his or her ability to learn the material initially. It is also possible that a client may have a relatively poor Working Memory Index, a relatively strong Visual Immediate Index, and relatively weak Auditory Immediate Index. In such a case, a feasible interpretation may be that the client has impaired complex attentional abilities in the auditory modality but intact attentional abilities in the visual modality. Cross-checking the subtest scaled scores on Letter-Number Sequencing and Spatial Span can help confirm such a hypothesis.

Step 5: Interpret Significant Strengths and Weaknesses of the WMS-III Subtest Profile

Steps 1 to 4 examine the global scores, but in Step 5 we begin to look at an individual's unique WMS-III subtest profile. Although examining the profile at this level of detail is controversial (Flanagan, McGrew, & Ortiz, 2000), we feel it is a justifiable means by which to gather more clinical information and to develop additional hypotheses about a client's memory functioning. Kaufman (1994) and Flanagan, McGrew, and Ortiz (2000) review some of the controversy surrounding the empirical method of calculating strengths and weaknesses based on an examinee's own mean score. We recognize that the WMS-III individual subtests are not as reliable as the Index scores, and we, therefore, urge caution when making bold assumptions about subtest fluctuations within the profile. However, the approach we advocate for the Steps that pertain to ipsative analysis of subtest scaled scores is the same as our overall approach to interpretation: Clinicians must support hypotheses with multiple sources of data, and reject hypotheses that are not supported clinically, theo-retically, or with other data.

With that caution stated, Step 5 calls for an ipsative comparison of an indi-vidual's mean performance on all subtests with each subtest administered. An ipsative comparison examines how well a person is performing on each sub-test relative to his or her own average subtest score. Such a comparison is dif-ferent from a comparison with the normative group. For example, when a person earns a subtest scaled score of 11, he or she is performing in the Aver-age range compared to others that are his or her age in the normative group. However, the scaled score of 11 may be considered extremely high (and a rel-ative strength) if the client's overall mean subtest scaled score is 6.

Examiners can calculate the overall subtest scaled score mean in one of two ways: (1) Average the scaled scores from all of the WMS-III subtests administered, or (2) average all of the auditory subtests and then separately average all of the visual subtests (see Rapid Reference 4.5). How do you decide which of the two ways to calculate the mean or means? First, determine whether ab-normally large differences exist between the Auditory Immediate Index and Visual Immediate Index or between the Auditory Delayed and Visual Delayed Indexes. These two difference scores were calculated during Step 2. A dis-crepancy of 25 points is considered abnormally large for the Auditory-Visual Immediate Index comparison, and a discrepancy of 24 points is considered abnormally large for the Auditory-Visual Delayed condition. If neither the Au-ditory-Visual Immediate Index discrepancy or the Auditory-Visual Delayed Index discrepancy is abnormally large, then use the mean of all WMS-III sub-tests for the calculations in Step 5. However, if abnormally large Auditory-Visual Index discrepancies exist in either the Immediate or Delayed con-ditions, calculate separate means for the auditory and visual subtests. Once you calculate that mean (or these means), round the mean(s) to the nearest whole number. Rounding simplifies the next calculations and reduces the chance of making errors (but does not compromise statistical examination).

Once you record the mean scaled score, round it, and then calculate the dif-ferences between each of the subtest scaled scores and the mean. The subtests that have higher scores than the overall mean will have positive valences and those that have lower scores will have negative valences. When recording the difference scores, be sure to record the valence with a plus (+) or minus (−) sign (see Rapid Reference 4.6 and WMS-III Interpretation Worksheet).

≡Rapid Reference 4.5

Example of Calculating Natalie L.'s Subtests Mean in Step 5

A. Determine which mean you should use to calculate strengths and weaknesses:

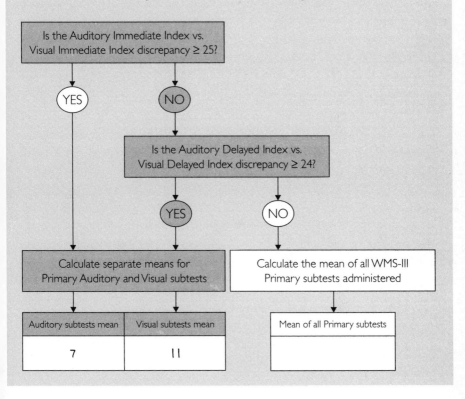

Step 5 of the WMS-III Interpretive worksheet summarizes the size of the differences needed (see Rapid Reference 4.6 and Appendix B). Table 4.3 presents exact values (for the overall sample and three broad age groups) for determining the significance of each discrepancy between individual scaled scores and the mean of the 11 Primary Subtests. Tables 4.4 and 4.5 present analogous exact values using the means of the Auditory subtests and the Visual subtests separately. Although you may use the exact values specific to particular age groups (Tables 4.3–4.5), the rounded values across all ages are

≡ Rapid Reference 4.6

Example of Recording Difference between WMS-III Subtests and Scaled Score Mean

| | Scaled Score | Rounded Mean | Scaled Score vs. Mean Difference | Size of Difference Needed for Significance | | | Strength or Weakness (S or W) | Percentile Rank (See Table 4.6) |
				Overall	Auditory/ Visual			
Auditory Subtests								
Logical Memory I	8	7	1	±3	±3			25
Verbal Paired Associates I	8	7	1	±2	±2			25
Letter-Number Sequencing	7	7	0	±4	±3			16
Logical Memory II	4	7	–3	±4	±3		W	2
Verbal Paired Associates II	8	7	1	±3	±3			25
Auditory Recognition Delayed	5	7	–2	±4	±4			5
Visual Subtests								
Faces I	11	11	0	±4	±4			63
Family Pictures I	13	11	+2	±4	±4			84
Spatial Span	9	11	–2	±4	±4			37
Faces II	10	11	–1	±4	±4			50
Family Pictures II	14	11	+3	±3	±3		S	91

Table 4.3 Differences between Individual Subtest Scaled Scores and Mean Scaled Score for 11 Primary WMS-III Subtests at .01 and .05 Levels of Confidence for Three Broad Age Groups and the Total Sample

WMS-III Primary Subtests	Ages 16–29		Ages 30–64		Ages 65–89		All Ages	
	.01	.05	.01	.05	.01	.05	.01	.05
Logical Memory I	3.64	3.13	3.45	2.97	3.53	3.04	3.48	2.97
Faces I	4.58	3.94	4.64	4.00	5.35	4.60	4.78	4.09
Verbal Paired Associates I	3.01	2.59	2.55	2.20	2.62	2.26	2.69	2.30
Family Pictures I	4.47	3.85	4.03	3.47	4.39	3.78	4.24	3.62
Letter-Number Sequencing	4.35	3.75	4.25	3.66	4.04	3.48	4.15	3.55
Spatial Span	4.12	3.55	4.28	3.69	4.82	4.15	4.35	3.72
Logical Memory II	4.90	4.22	4.42	3.81	4.23	3.64	4.44	3.80
Faces II	4.66	4.01	4.55	3.92	5.32	4.58	4.78	4.09
Verbal Paired Associates II	4.23	3.64	3.81	3.28	4.08	3.51	3.98	3.41
Family Pictures II	4.47	3.85	3.86	3.32	3.78	3.26	3.98	3.41
Auditory Recognition Delayed	5.00	4.31	5.10	4.39	4.61	3.97	4.81	4.12

Source: From Cole, J. C., Lopez, B. L., & McLeod, J. S. (2001) Comprehensive Tables for determination of strengths and weaknesses on the WMS-III. Manuscript submitted for publication.

sufficient to calculate strengths and weaknesses; they also minimize the risk of clerical error and reduce dependency on tables.

If the difference between a WMS-III subtest scaled score and the individual's mean is large enough to be statistically significant, consider it a strength (if above the mean) or weakness (if below the mean). On the WMS-III Interpretation Worksheet, strengths and weaknesses are denoted by the letters *S* and *W*, respectively. However, if the scaled scores do not deviate *significantly* from the appropriate mean, then consider them to be chance fluctuations. Do not interpret nonsignificant differences as strengths or weaknesses, per se, but use such differences to support hypotheses (see Step 6).

The WMS-III Interpretation Worksheet also has a column to record the

Table 4.4 Differences between Individual Subtest Scaled Scores and Mean Scaled Scores for 6 WMS-III Auditory Memory Subtests at .01 and .05 Levels of Confidence for Three Broad Age Groups and the Total Sample

Age Group	Logical Memory I		Verbal Paired Associates I		Letter-Number Sequencing		Logical Memory II		Verbal Paired Associates II		Auditory Recognition Delayed	
	.05	.01	.05	.01	.05	.01	.05	.01	.05	.01	.05	.01
16–29	2.76	3.29	2.36	2.80	3.24	3.85	3.61	4.29	3.16	3.75	3.67	4.37
30–64	2.62	3.12	2.04	2.43	3.15	3.74	3.27	3.88	2.86	3.40	3.73	4.43
65–89	2.64	3.13	2.04	2.42	2.98	3.54	3.10	3.69	3.00	3.57	3.36	4.00
All Ages	2.67	3.18	2.16	2.56	3.13	3.72	3.33	3.95	3.01	3.58	3.58	4.26

Source: From Cole, J. C., Lopez, B. L., & McLeod, J. S. (2001). Comprehensive Tables for determination of strengths and weaknesses on the WMS-III. Manuscript submitted for publication.

Table 4.5 Differences between Individual Subtest Scaled Scores and Mean Scaled Scores for 5 Visual Primary WMS-III Subtests at .01 and .05 Levels of Confidence for Three Broad Age Groups and the Total Sample

Age Group	Faces I .05	Faces I .01	Family Pictures I .05	Family Pictures I .01	Spatial Span .05	Spatial Span .01	Faces II .05	Faces II .01	Family Pictures II .05	Family Pictures II .01
16–29	3.27	3.92	3.21	3.85	3.01	3.60	3.32	3.98	3.21	3.84
30–64	3.29	3.94	2.93	3.51	3.08	3.68	3.24	3.88	2.83	3.39
65–89	3.79	4.54	3.22	3.86	3.48	4.17	3.78	4.53	2.88	3.45
All Ages	3.93	4.56	3.54	4.11	3.63	4.22	3.93	4.56	3.35	3.89

Source: From Cole, J. C., Lopez, B. L., & McLeod, J. S. (2001). Comprehensive Tables for determination of strengths and weaknesses on the WMS-III. Manuscript submitted for publication.

percentile rank equivalent of each of the subtest scaled scores (see Rapid Reference 4.6 and Appendix B). Although these percentile ranks are not used in psychometric comparisons, when used in a written report, a metric such as percentile rank is extremely effective for communicating to professionals and laypersons alike. The scaled score's mean of 10 and standard deviation of 3 are unfamiliar to most people (except, perhaps, other psychologists), but most will understand the commonly used percentile rank. The WMS-III *Manual* does not provide percentile ranks for the scaled score values, therefore we list them in Table 4.6.

Step 6: Generate Hypotheses about the Fluctuations in the WMS-III Profile

In this step examiners not only analyze the scores obtained from the WMS-III profile, but also integrate data from observed behaviors, background information, and supplemental testing in order to confirm or disconfirm hypotheses. For some clients the Immediate Memory versus General (Delayed) Memory dichotomy or the Immediate versus Delayed dichotomies do not provide an adequate explanation of the WMS-III profile. A multitude of

Table 4.6 National Percentile Ranks Corresponding to Scaled Scores

Percentile Rank	Scaled Score	Percentile Rank	Scaled Score
99.9	19	37	9
99.6	18	25	8
99	17	16	7
98	16	9	6
95	15	5	5
91	14	2	4
84	13	1	3
75	12	0.5	2
63	11	0.1	1
50	10		

strengths and weaknesses that need to be explained by alternative hypotheses may appear in a client's memory profile. Steps 1 through 5 provide a framework that navigates clinicians through the global scores down to the empirical determination of relative strengths and weaknesses in the subtest profile. Step 6 creates meaning from the strengths and weaknesses.

To begin creating hypotheses derived from the WMS-III profile, examiners should investigate the subtest scaled scores that deviate significantly from the examinee's own mean performance. The goal is to uncover hypotheses regarding abilities shared by two or more subtests or concerning influences that may have affected the test scores. Information should be consistent across the entire profile, and whenever feasible, should be supported by clinical observations, background information, and supplementary cognitive or achievement measures. Examiners should only use a subtest-specific hypothesis when the detective work to find global strengths or weaknesses is futile. At times there may not be any significant fluctuations within the subtest profile itself. In such a case, if questions still remain after the index scores are thoroughly examined, then it may be necessary to administer supplementary subtests that measure abilities not adequately tapped by the WMS-III.

INTRODUCTION TO WMS-III SUBTEST INTERPRETIVE TABLES

Researchers hypothesize that each WMS-III subtest measures numerous abilities. We have organized these abilities in list format in Rapid Reference 4.7. This list of shared abilities facilitates the detective process. The information in the shared abilities table summarizes the material that was included in the subtest-by-subtest analysis at the beginning of this chapter. Many of the hypotheses contained within the list are from Flanagan, McGrew, and Ortiz (2000). The list organizes the shared abilities alphabetically and then follows with a list of influences that may affect performance on the subtests.

The shared abilities named in Rapid Reference 4.7 are not exhaustive; rather, the information is intended to illustrate and provide a good guideline for clinicians. It should be referenced as a framework that is open to expansion. Examiners should incorporate their expertise and the individuality of each person tested into the detective work involved in profile analysis.

Guidelines for Using Information in the Shared Abilities Table

By glancing at Rapid Reference 4.7, examiners can see that there is a great deal of information with which to contend. The following section provides a sequential guide to generate hypotheses. There are five guidelines, which, if followed, help identify potential strengths and weaknesses evident from the WMS-III profile. We use Natalie L.'s subtest profile as an example of this process.

Guideline 1: Choose one of the strengths (S) *or weaknesses* (W) *determined in Step 5.* Write down all shared abilities (and influences affecting performance) that involve this subtest (see Rapid Reference 4.7).

This section goes through each of these guidelines using Ms. L.'s first relative weakness revealed in Step 5: Logical Memory II. Figure 4.9 shows part of the Shared Abilities Worksheet, specifically for Logical Memory II.

Guideline 2: Consider each ability, one-by-one, to determine how the examinee performed on the other subtest or subtests that also measure the identified abilities. In Step 5, examiners determined the relative strengths and weaknesses in the subtest profile by considering whether the score deviated significantly from the pertinent

Rapid Reference 4.7

WMS-III Subtests' Shared Abilities Table

| | Immediate Subtests | | | | | | | | | | Delayed Subtests | | | | | | |
| | Primary Subtests | | | | | | Optional Subtests | | | | Primary Subtests | | | | | Optional | |
Ability	LMI	FaI	VPAI	FPI	LNS	SpSp	WLI	VRI	MC	DS	LMII	FaII	VPAII	FPII	ARD	WLII	VRII
Associative memory			VPAI	FPI									VPAII	FPII		WLII	
Crystallized Intelligence (Gc)	LMI										LMII						
Free Recall Memory							WLI	VRI								WLII	VRII
Long-term Storage & Retrieval (Glr)	LMI	FaI	VPAI	FPI			WLI				LMII	FaII	VPAII	FPII		WLII	VRII
Meaningful Memory	LMI	FaI									LMII	FaII					
Memory Span						SpSp				DS							
Short-term Memory (Gsm)					LNS	SpSp			MC	DS							
Spatial Relations				FPI										FPII			
Visual Memory		FaI	VPAI	FPI		SpSp		VRI				FaII		FPII			VRII
Visual Processing (Gv)		FaI	VPAI	FPI		SpSp		VRI				FaII		FPII			VRII

	LMI	Fal	VPAI	FPI	LNS	SpSp	WLI	VRI	MC	DS	LMII	Fall	VPAII	FPII	WLII	VRII
Visualization																VRII
Working Memory																

Influences

	LMI	Fal	VPAI	FPI	LNS	SpSp	WLI	VRI	MC	DS	LMII	Fall	VPAII	FPII	WLII	VRII
Attention Span	LMI			FPI	LNS	SpSp	WLI		MC	DS	LMII				WLII	
Concentration	LMI	Fal		FPI	LNS	SpSp	WLI		MC	DS	LMII	Fall		FPII	WLII	VRII
Distractibility	LMI				LNS	SpSp	WLI		MC	DS	LMII				WLII	
Educational Opportunities	LMI										LMII					
Environmental Stimulation				FPI				VRI						FPII	WLII	VRII
Hearing Difficulties	LMI		VPAI				WLI			DS	LMII		VPAII		WLII	
Language Stimulation	LMI										LMII					
Organization Planning										DS						
Reflectivity/Impulsivity		Fal						VRI	MC			Fall				VRII
Verbal Rehearsal	LMI		VPAI	FPI	LNS	SpSp	WLI			DS	LMII		VPAII	FPII	WLII	
Visual Acuity								VRI								
Visual Elaboration	LMI	Fal	VPAI		LNS	SpSp	WLI	VRI		DS	LMII	Fall	VPAII		WLII	VRII
Visual-motor Coordination								VRI								VRII

Note: LMI = Logical Memory I; Fal = Faces I; VPAI = Verbal Paired Associates I; FPI = Family Pictures I; LNS = Letter-Number Sequencing; SpSp = Spatial Span; WLI = Word Lists I; VRI = Visual Reproduction I; MC = Mental Control; DS = Digit Span; LMII = Logical Memory II; Fall = Faces II; VPAII = Verbal Paired Associates II; FPII = Family Pictures II; WLII = Word Lists II; VRII = Visual Reproduction II; ARD = Auditory Recognition Delayed.

	Immediate Primary Subtests						Delayed Primary Subtests				
	LMI	FaI	VPAI	FPI	LNS	SpSp	LMII	FaII	VPAII	FPII	ARD
Ability											
Crystallized Intelligence (*Gc*)	+						−				
Long-Term Storage and Retrieval (*Glr*)	+	0	+	+			−	−	+	+	
Meaningful Memory	+	0					−	−			
Influences											
Attention span	+				0	−	−				
Concentration	+	0		+	0	−	−	−		+	
Distractibility	+				0	−					
Educational opportunities	+						−				
Hearing difficulties	+		+				−		+		
Language stimulation	+						−				
Verbal rehearsal	+		+	+	0	−	−			+	+
Visual elaboration	+	0	+		0	−	−	−		+	

Figure 4.9 Partial WMS-III Subtests' Shared Abilities Table for Natalie L.'s Weakness in Logical Memory II

mean subtest score. In the process of deciding which abilities explain the strength, the examiner must apply less stringent criteria. Thus, consider whether a person scores above, below, or equal to his or her own mean score on all pertinent subtests for an ability. Record this information on the list of shared abilities by writing one of the following symbols next to each subtest:

- "−" (indicating that performance is below the individual's mean subtest scaled score)
- "+" (indicating that performance is above the individual's mean subtest scaled score)
- "0" (indicating that performance is exactly at the individual's mean subtest scaled score).

Continuing with the example of Ms. L.'s relative weakness in Logical Memory II, Figure 4.9 also demonstrates how to fill in the empty squares with "+, −, or 0." For example, the first row lists Crystallized Intelligence as a hypothesized weak ability. The first subtest listed that possibly measures this ability is Logical Memory I (note the square in this column), and because Ms. L.'s Logical Memory I scaled score is 1 point above her Auditory subtests mean scaled score (see Rapid Reference 4.6), a "+" is placed in the box. Another subtest listed with Logical Memory I is Logical Memory II. These boxes are filled with the appropriate minus signs, as Ms. L.'s subtest score is below her mean scaled score. The next ability, Long-term Storage and Retrieval, lists eight subtests that may measure this ability. The examiner fills in the appropriate pluses, minuses, or zeros according to the difference between each of Ms. L.'s subtest scores and her mean scaled score (see Figure 4.9 for an example of a completed table).

Guideline 3: Consider each ability, one-by-one, to determine whether the ability should be considered a strong or weak one.   In general, shared strengths are those in which a person scores above his or her own mean score on all pertinent subtests, with at least one discrepancy reaching statistical significance. However, the Don't Forget Box on this page describes exceptions to this global rule for shared abilities. These rules should be considered rules of thumb, rather than rigid principles. There are instances when there is an overabundance of other clinical information from behavioral observations, background information, and supplementary testing data that supports a shared ability as a strength or

DON'T FORGET

Rules for Accepting and Rejecting Potential Hypotheses

Number of Subtests Constituting a Shared Ability	Rule for Interpreting Ability as a Strength (at least one subtest is a significant strength)	Rule for Interpreting Ability as a Weakness (at least one subtest is a significant weakness)
2	**All** subtests must be *above* the mean.	**All** subtests must be *below* the mean.
3 or 4	**At least 2 or 3** subtests must be *above* the mean, and **only one** subtest may be *equal to* the mean.	**At least 2 or 3** subtests must be *below* the mean, and **only one** subtest may be *equal to* the mean.
5 or more	**At least 4** subtests must be *above* the mean, and **only one** subtest may be *equal to* the mean or *less than* the mean.	**At least 4 subtests** must be *below* the mean, and **only one** subtest may be *equal to* the mean or *greater than* the mean.

Note: From *Essentials of WAIS-III Assessment* (p. 157), by A. S. Kaufman and E. O. Lichtenberger. New York: Wiley. Copyright © 1999 John Wiley & Sons. Reproduced with Permission.

weakness, even if these general guidelines are not met. In such instances of multiple sources of information, the rules listed here do not preclude clinicians from interpreting the strength or weakness.

Once the rules of thumb have been applied, circle strengths and weaknesses on the list of shared abilities. In Ms. L.'s example of Logical Memory II (shown in Figure 4.9), we examine each hypothesized ability to determine which ones may be considered strengths or weaknesses. Crystallized Intelligence is considered to underlie two subtests (Logical Memory I & Logical Memory II). By examining the pluses, minuses, and zeros that are filled in, we see that one subtest has a minus (indicating a score below the mean) and one has a plus (indicating a score above the mean). The rules for accepting and rejecting potential hypotheses tell us that for an ability to be considered a weakness when there are two or more subtests, both subtests must be below the mean. Thus, the examiner should not consider Crystallized Intelligence a weak ability, as there is not enough evidence in the WMS-III scores to support it.

The next ability to examine with Ms. L.'s profile is Long Term Storage and Retrieval, an ability measured by eight subtests. On five of the subtests, Ms. L. earned scores that are above her own mean, on two she earned scores that are below her mean, and on one other she scored at her mean. Because more than one test was above the mean, Long Term Storage and Retrieval cannot be considered as a hypothesized weak ability. The next ability, Meaningful Memory, follows the same pattern as Long Term Storage and Retrieval and cannot be considered a weak ability. In fact, none of the shared abilities listed with Logical Memory II have enough support with other subtests to be considered a hypothesized weak ability.

Guideline 4: Repeat Guidelines 1, 2, and 3 for every other significant strength that has not been accounted for. Next, follow analogous procedures for all significant strengths. Ms. L.'s relative strength in the WMS-III profile is Family Pictures II (see Figure 4.10 and Rapid Reference 4.6). After filling in the pluses, minuses, and zeros in the Shared Ability Worksheet for Family Pictures II, some hypothesized abilities appear to be possible explanations for Ms. L.'s strength in Family Pictures II: Associative Memory, Spatial Relations, and Environmental Stimulation. Before including any of these abilities in Ms. L.'s report, it is necessary to consider whether the behavioral observations, background information, and supplemental test data also support these hypotheses. Chapter 7 of this book presents the complete case report written about Ms. L.'s WMS-III

	Immediate Primary Subtests						Delayed Primary Subtests				
	LMI	FaI	VPAI	FPI	LNS	SpSp	LMII	FaII	VPAII	FPII	ARD
Ability											
Associative Memory			+	+					+	+	
Long-Term Storage and Retrieval (*Glr*)	+	0	+	+			−	+	+	+	
Spatial Relations				+						+	
Visual Memory		0		+		−		+		+	
Visual Processing (*Gv*)		0		+		−		+		+	
Influences											
Concentration	+	0		+	0	−	−	+		+	
Environmental stimulation				+						+	
Verbal rehearsal	+		+	+	0	−	−			+	+

Figure 4.10 Partial WMS-III Subtests' Shared Abilities Table for Natalie L.'s Strength in Family Pictures II

profile, which shows how all of the various strengths and weaknesses are integrated.

Guideline 5: If the client was administered Optional subtests, determine whether these offer further support for the hypothesized strong or weak abilities.   In addition to the 11 Primary subtests listed in the Shared Abilities Table (Rapid Reference 4.7), there are six Optional subtests that are also related to some of these abilities. If data on any of these Optional subtests are available, clinicians should incorporate the data in the process of hypothesis development. After using Guidelines 1 through 4 of Step 6 to determine if a particular ability is a relative strength or weakness, the examiner may use Optional subtests to provide further validation (or refutation) of this hypothesis. Thus, clinicians should examine each ability determined in the first four guidelines to be either relative strengths or weaknesses. For example, in Ms. L.'s case, Associative Memory was a hypothesized strong ability (see Figure 4.10). In addition to the four Primary subtests that measure this ability, two Optional subtests measure it as well: Word Lists I and Word Lists II. To determine whether the optional subtests offer further support for the hypothesis of strong associative memory, compare the age-adjusted scaled scores of Word Lists I and Word Lists II to the relevant mean of the subtest scaled scores. In this case, we compare the mean scaled score of the auditory subtests (7) to the scaled score on Word Lists I (9) and Word Lists II (8). Ms. L. scored above her mean scaled score on both of these subtests. *How far above the mean is not important for these comparisons.* Therefore, if an Optional subtest scaled score is above the mean subtest scaled score, then there is support for a strength, and if an Optional subtest scaled score is below the mean subtest scaled score, then there is support for a weakness.

As shown in Figure 4.11, note support from the optional subtests by circling "yes" (Y) and a lack of support for the hypothesis by circling "no" (N). We employ a simple rule of thumb in deciding whether the Optional subtests support the strengths or weaknesses demonstrated in the Primary subtests: *50% or more of the Optional subtests must support the hypothesis.* For example, if the examiner administered five or six Optional subtests to find extra validation for a *weakness,* at least three of those subtests must be marked "yes" (Y), indicating that they were below the mean scaled score. In Ms. L.'s case the other hypothesis underlying her strength in Family Pictures II is Environmental Stimulation. In addition to the support of the two Primary subtests, clinicians should examine both Visual Reproduction I and Visual Reproduction II to validate the hypothesis. The scaled scores for both Visual Reproduction I and II are 12, which is 1 point above the mean scaled score of 11 for the visual subtests. Thus, mark both Visual Reproduction I and II with "yes" (Y) indicating that they too support the hypothesis (see Figure 4.11).

Guideline 6: If the process of examining shared abilities uncovers no hypothesized strengths or weaknesses, then interpret the unique abilities that are presumably measured by significantly high or low subtests.   The primary focus for explaining significant discrepancies in a profile should be on shared abilities that link several subtests, especially when these hypothesized strengths and weaknesses are supported by background information, behavioral observations, and supplementary testing. However, sometimes, after examining the potential shared abilities, no hypothesized strengths or weaknesses are apparent. The examiner should then consider subtest-specific interpretations. The unique abilities are noted in the subtest-by-subtest description of abilities listed earlier in this chapter (denoted with an asterisk). Before interpreting a unique ability of a subtest, clinicians should consider the reliability of the subtest (check Rapid Reference 1.3). Examiners should use caution when considering those subtests with reliability coefficients under .80 before interpreting a unique ability.

Step 7: Follow Up Hypotheses with Supplementary WMS-III Scores

Clinicians may need to examine the supplemental WMS-III scores for several reasons: (a) Uncertainty may remain about the question posed in the "reason

	Immediate Subtests										Delayed Subtests						
	Primary Subtests						Optional Subtests				Primary Subtests					Optional	
	LMI	FaI	VPAI	FPI	LNS	SpSp	WLI	VRI	MC	DS	LMII	FaII	VPAII	FPII	ARD	WLII	VRII
Ability																	
Associative Memory			+	+			Y/N						+	+		Y/N	
Influences																	
Environmental stimulation				+				Y/N						+			Y/N

Figure 4.11 Partial WMS-III Subtests' Shared Abilities Table for Natalie L.'s Strength in Family Pictures II Incorporating Optional Subtests

for referral," even after the WMS-III Indexes and subtests have been evaluated; (b) further questions may have arisen in the evaluation of the Indexes and subtests, such that further hypotheses need validation; and (c) interesting, and perhaps unexpected, additional information may arise through examination of the rich supplemental data. Thus, we encourage clinicians to take the time to examine these supplemental scores, either to examine hypotheses further or just to complete a more in-depth exploration of the WMS-III profile.

A first glance at the page of supplemental scores on the WMS-III record form may make the numerous values—27 to be exact—seem a bit daunting. Each clinician needs to take an approach that suits his or her reason for exploring the supplemental information. We suggest the following two approaches: (a) If specific questions or hypotheses have arisen from the referral question or from earlier profile discrepancies, target your investigation with the particular supplemental scores most relevant to the hypotheses at hand, and (b) even if no specific hypotheses need further investigation, clinicians should scan briefly all of the supplemental scores to see if any of them are unusually high or low compared to the client's other scores. For our first suggested approach, we provide some guidance in Rapid Reference 4.8, which helps link various hypotheses with particular supplemental scores. For the second approach, which entails scanning all supplemental scores, we suggest beginning with those scores that are at least 1 SD above or below the normative mean of 10 or at least 1 SD above or below the client's own subtest mean. Review the data in Table 4.7 to determine the significance of the differences between each individual subtest and the mean of all supplemental subtests.

INTERPRETING THE FOUR COMPONENTS OF THE AUDITORY PROCESS COMPOSITES

Before interpreting the Auditory Process Composites, examiners need to convert the obtained percentile ranks to a metric that is more normally distributed. A table in the *WMS-III Interpretation Worksheet* (Appendix B) facilitates that conversion. The percentile ranks for each of the Composites (Single-Trial Learning, Learning Slope, Retention, and Retrieval) can be converted to standard scores (mean = 100; SD = 15) by looking at the appropriate column in the table listed under Step 7 of the *WMS-III Interpretation Worksheet*.

≡ Rapid Reference 4.8

Hypotheses and WMS-III Supplemental Subtests for Follow-Up

Visual-perceptual problems confounding performance on visual memory tasks	⇔	• Visual Reproduction II Discrimination
Visual-motor problems confounding performance on visual memory tasks	⇔	• Visual Reproduction II Copy
Visual Memory Problems	⇔	• Visual reproduction II Recall • Visual Reproduction II % Retention • Family Pictures II % Reproduction • Spatial Span Forward • Spatial Span Backward
Semantic memory problems with single trial exposures	⇔	• Logical Memory I Thematic Total • Logical Memory II Thematic Total
Problems learning over time (slope)	⇔	• Word Lists I Learning Slope
Working memory deficits	⇔	• Mental Control • Digit Span Backward • Spatial Span Backward
Deficits in the ventral vs. dorsal stream	⇔	• Family Pictures I (# of characters correct vs. # of location correct)
Malingering	⇔	• Information & Orientation • Recognition doesn't improve in comparison to recall (e.g., negative Retrieval Total Score) • Less than 50% correct on forced choice items • Lower score on Logical Memory I Thematic Score than Logical Memory I Total Recall Score
Episodic memory deficits	⇔	• Information and Orientation

Table 4.7 Differences between Individual Supplemental Subtest Scaled Scores and Mean Scaled Scores for 13 Supplementary WMS-III Subtests at .01 and .05 Levels of Confidence

WMS-III Supplementary Subtests	Ages 16–54		Ages 55–89		All Ages	
	.01	.05	.01	.05	.01	.05
Logical Memory I (Thematic)	4.7	4.0	4.4	3.8	4.6	3.9
Word Lists I (Recall)	4.6	3.9	4.0	3.5	4.3	3.7
Visual Reproduction I (Recall)	5.0	4.2	3.9	3.3	4.4	3.8
Spatial Span (Forward)	5.0	4.2	4.7	4.0	4.8	4.1
Spatial Span (Backward)	5.0	4.2	5.1	4.3	5.0	4.3
Mental Control	3.7	3.2	3.3	2.8	3.5	3.0
Digit Span	3.5	3.0	3.9	3.3	3.7	3.1
Logical Memory II (Thematic)	4.4	3.8	4.3	3.7	4.4	3.8
Word Lists II (Recall)	4.3	3.7	4.2	3.6	4.3	3.7
Word Lists II (Recognition)	5.3	4.3	4.2	3.6	4.6	3.9
Visual Reproduction II (Recall)	5.1	4.4	4.0	3.5	4.6	3.9
Visual Reproduction II (Recognition)	5.5	4.7	4.0	3.5	4.2	4.1
Visual Reproduction II (Copy)	5.0	4.2	4.8	4.1	4.9	4.2

Source: From Cole, J. C., Lopez, B. L., & McLeod, J. S. (2001). Comprehensive Tables for determination of strengths and weaknesses on the WMS-III. Manuscript submitted for publication.

Single-Trial Learning versus Learning Slope

Clinicians can often glean valuable information by examining the Auditory Immediate Index in conjunction with comparisons between Single-Trial Learning versus Learning Slope (see pages 195 and 210 in *WAIS-III and WMS-III Technical Manual*). The Single-Trial Learning score is very highly correlated with the Auditory Immediate Index, as it is comprises the first trial of both Logical Memory I stories and Verbal Paired Associates I. Single-Trial Learning is a measure of recall ability after a single presentation of material. In contrast,

Learning Slope is a measure of the relative increase from the first trial to the last trial for Logical Memory I Story B and Verbal Paired Associates I. Learning Slope must always be interpreted in the context of Single-Trial Learning. A high Learning Slope score indicates that the client has good learning ability relative to his or her performance on the initial trials. However, a low score on Learning Slope indicates that the client has limited ability to learn from multiple trials. An important caveat is that if Single-Trial Learning is very high, there can be a ceiling effect on the Learning Slope. For example, if a client initially recalls 48 of the 50 units of the first two Logical Memory I stories, then he or she can only improve his or her Learning Slope score by 2 raw-score points. In contrast, a client who performs very poorly on the first recall total score of Logical Memory I has greater room for improvement on subsequent trials of the story. Because of the possible ceiling effect, the *WAIS-III and WMS-III Technical Manual* (The Psychological Corporation, 1997) recommends that you not interpret the comparison between the Single-Trial Learning Composite and the Learning Slope Composite when the Single-Trial Learning Composite is relatively high.

Retention Composite versus Auditory Delayed Index

After examining the Auditory Delayed Index, clinicians have an additional follow-up comparison using the Auditory Delayed Index with Retention Composite (see pages 196–197 and 211 in the *WAIS-III and WMS-III Technical Manual*). Unlike the WMS-III Primary Indexes, the Retention Composite measures an individual's efficiency in delayed free recall relative to his or her own immediate memory. The information gleaned from the Primary Indexes, on the other hand, represents the individual's performance at the delayed point relative to his or her peers, rather than to his or her own performance. The percent-retention scaled scores from the Logical Memory II subtest and the Verbal Paired Associates II subtest are combined to create the Retention Composite. To adequately interpret the Retention Composite, examiners must consider the client's initial acquisition. If initial acquisition is low, there is little room for the person to remember less within the delayed conditions. The Retention Composite should be compared to the Auditory Delayed Index to make intra-examinee and inter-examinee comparisons. If the Auditory Delayed Index is low but the Retention Composite score is high, then the examinee's delayed recall performance is low compared to that of the normative group (inter-examinee comparison). However, this same pattern of scores also yields an intra-examinee comparison, which indicates that the examinee could later recall the information at a similar level of performance that he or she learned during the immediate condition. Confirmation of weak learning but adequate retention is available from a poor Immediate Auditory Index. An additional retrieval weakness is suggested if the individual has a relatively good recognition score relative to the Auditory Delayed Index.

Retrieval versus Free Recall

Examiners should also evaluate the Auditory Delayed Index in conjunction with the Retrieval Composite (see page 197 in the *WAIS-III and WMS-III Technical Manual*). The Retrieval Composite indicates the degree to which cueing increases information retrieval beyond the amount of information available through free recall. Calculate the Retrieval Composite by subtracting the average of Logical Memory II and Paired Associates II recall scaled scores from the combined Logical Memory II and Verbal Paired Associates II recognition scaled score (a.k.a., Auditory Recognition Delayed scaled score). The formula used to calculate the Retrieval Composite intrinsically compares the Auditory Recognition Delayed scaled score with the free recall scores. Therefore, high Retrieval Composite scores suggest that the client may have a retrieval problem because he or she cannot access as much information through free recall as he or she can through recognition. Low scores on the Retrieval Composite suggest that recognition is poorer than recall. Such low scores are unusual and may be due to a ceiling effect or may be due to distractors (i.e., foils) that interfere with retrieval. Another possible explanation for low Retrieval Composite scores is that the client has guessed on numerous items and has guessed quite poorly. Usually, an astute clinician can observe behaviors during the testing that help discern whether the client is simply guessing.

In addition to examining the Retrieval Composite, clinicians can compare the Auditory Delayed Index and Auditory Recognition Delayed Index to obtain information about delayed recall versus delayed recognition. If the client's immediate memory is intact (within the normal range on the Auditory Immediate Index), then significantly lower performance in both delayed recall and recognition suggests that the client was not able to retain previously learned information (over at least 25–35 min). For most people, retrieval is less demanding through recognition than through recall, so a low Auditory Delayed Index relative to the Auditory Recognition Delayed Index suggests some type of retrieval weakness or deficit.

INTEGRATING WMS-III DATA WITH WAIS-III

Because the WMS-III was co-normed with the WAIS-III, interpretation of intelligence quotient (IQ) memory discrepancies is much more accurate and sophisticated on the WMS-III than on previous versions. The IQ-memory comparisons are valuable because the underlying components of general intellectual ability are thought to be conceptually related to memory and learning (The Psychological Corporation, 1997). An examinee's IQs can serve as estimates of his or her probable level of memory ability because of the high correlations between IQ and memory. There are some cases in which general cognitive functioning (e.g., Full Scale IQ) declines at the same time as memory functions, such as in dementia. However, in instances such as focal brain injury, overall intellectual functioning may remain relatively stable, but the examinee shows focal memory impairment. Thus, when interpreting IQ-memory discrepancies, remember that the difference only reflects memory functioning relative to current intellectual functioning. In some cases it may be more informative to consider an individual's level of estimated or known premorbid intellectual functioning in comparison to his or her memory functioning.

The *WAIS-III and WMS-III Technical Manual* presents two methods for comparing WAIS-III and WMS-III scores: the predicted-difference method and the simple-difference method. Although many clinicians prefer the simple-difference method because of its implicitly simple nature, the predicted-difference method is statistically more sound because it takes into account the reliabilities and correlations between the measures as well as correcting for regression to the mean. In comparing the two tests, The Psychological Corporation (1997) recommends using the Full Scale IQ (FSIQ) as the estimate of intellectual ability unless there is a 10-point or greater discrepancy between the Verbal (V-IQ) and Performance (P-IQ) IQs. In such a case, the examiner should use the higher of the two IQ scores. However, recent analyses conducted by Ryan and Kreiner (in press) suggest that when there is marked scatter (i.e., 10 points or more on the FSIQ or 7 points or more on the VIQ or PIQ), then the PIQ is less accurate for predicting some of the WMS-III indexes. They suggest in such cases of significant WAIS-III scatter, WMS-III predictions may be made confidently only with the Full Scale or Verbal IQs. The Psychological Corporation (1997) also suggests that the General (Delayed) Memory Index is also the "best estimate of an examinee's memory functioning" (p. 213). However if there are significant differences between the visual and auditory components of the General Memory Index, it may be more appropriate to examine the modality-specific indexes.

Simple WAIS-III versus WMS-III Difference Method

Although it is not the preferred method of comparison, the simple-difference method is worthy of elaboration because of its frequent use. The calculations involved are straightforward; a WMS-III Primary Index is subtracted from the WAIS-III IQ (e.g., FSIQ minus General Memory Index). The discrepancy value is then examined to determine whether it is statistically significant at the .01 or .05 level. Tables C.1, C.2, and C.3 of the *WAIS-III and WMS-III Technical Manual* provide the values necessary for significance. Finally, the size of the discrepancy is examined to determine whether it is unusually large (i.e., does it occur frequently in the normal population). Tables C.4, C.5, and C.6 of the *WAIS-III and WMS-III Technical Manual* provide the values necessary to determine abnormality in the normal population. For example, a statistically significant FSIQ minus General Memory Index discrepancy is 9.9 points, but an unusually large discrepancy (≤ 15% of the population) is 13 points.

Predicted WAIS-III versus WMS-III Difference Method

This prediction formula is based on a regression equation rather than the simple difference between scores. However, as with the simple-difference method, clinicians should not only examine the significance of the discrepancy, but also the rarity of the difference. Tables B.1, B.2, and B.3 of the *WAIS-III and WMS-III Technical Manual* provide the predicted WMS-III scores based on the WAIS-III IQs, and Tables B.4, B.5, and B.6 provide the differences between the predicted and obtained scores that are required for significance.

Thus, the predicted-difference method requires an additional step beyond those taken in the simple-difference method:

1. Determine the predicted WMS-III score based on the WAIS-III IQ.
2. Subtract the obtained WMS-III score from the predicted WMS-III.
3. Determine whether the obtained-predicted WMS-III scores are *significantly* discrepant (Tables B.4, B.5, and B.6)
4. Determine whether the obtained-predicted WMS-III scores *unusually* discrepant (Tables B.7, B.8, and B.9). In interpreting a WAIS-III versus WMS-III discrepancy, bear in mind that the absence of a significant discrepancy is consistent with global neurocognitive impairment, in which memory is just one of many cognitive abilities that have declined. On the other hand, a significant and unusual IQ-memory discrepancy may indicate a more focal memory impairment in the context of the overall general cognitive abilities.

🐟 TEST YOURSELF 🐟

1. **To glean the most valuable information from the WMS-III, examine**
   (a) only the delayed memory scores.
   (b) only the immediate memory scores.
   (c) only the contrast between auditory and visual scores.
   (d) all facets of the test reviewed in the 7 steps of interpretation.

2. **Significantly lower performance on Delayed Memory Indexes relative to Immediate Memory indicates that the person never encoded the information in the first place.** True or False?

3. **If the discrepancy between the Auditory Immediate and Visual Immediate Indexes is large enough to be considered significant, then**
   (a) neither Index is able to be interpreted meaningfully.
   (b) the Immediate Memory Index is not able to be interpreted meaningfully.
   (c) the Delayed Memory Index is not able to be interpreted meaningfully.
   (d) only the Auditory Recognition Delayed Index can be interpreted.

(continued)

4. **Differential performance on auditory-versus-visual indexes can suggest**

   (a) working memory deficits.

   (b) lateralized differences in hemispheric functioning.

   (c) recognition memory deficits.

   (d) malingering.

5. **Significantly lower performance on Delayed Memory Indexes relative to Immediate Memory Indexes may indicate deficits in a person's ability to retain previously learned information.** True or False?

6. **Contrasting the Immediate and General (Delayed) Memory Indexes always provides meaningful information, even if there is significant variability between the Visual Immediate and Auditory Immediate Indexes or significant variability between the Visual Delayed and Auditory Delayed Indexes.** True or False?

7. **Working memory is conceptually similar to**

   (a) immediate memory.

   (b) delayed memory.

   (c) recognition memory.

   (d) processing speed.

8. **The best method for interpreting WMS-III subtests is to examine one subtest at a time and decide what each unique ability is that a single subtest alone measures.** True or False?

9. **The Learning Slope must always be interpreted in the context of**

   (a) Visual Delayed Index.

   (b) Visual Reproduction II.

   (c) Single-Trial Learning.

   (d) Retention.

10. **The significant discrepancy between the WAIS-III versus the WMS-III is consistent with global neurocognitive impairment.** True or False?

Answers: 1. d; 2. False; 3. b; 4. b; 5. True; 6. False; 7. a; 8. False; 9. c; 10. False

Five

STRENGTHS AND WEAKNESSES OF THE WMS-III

OVERVIEW OF ADVANTAGES AND DISADVANTAGES OF THE WMS-III

We have compiled the strengths and weaknesses of the WMS-III from our own clinical experience with the instrument as well as from published reviews (Flanagan et al., 2000; Franzen & Iverson, 2000; Mitrushina et al., 1999; Spreen & Strauss, 1998); they are summarized in Rapid References 5.1 through 5.5.

The psychometric qualities of the WMS-III are included among its major strengths. The split-half reliability coefficients are strong for all Indexes scales, and the validity of the instrument is well-documented through numerous studies. The WMS-III normative sample is excellent and well-stratified. The clinical usefulness and interpretability of the test are aided by the structure of the WMS-III and the fact that it was co-normed with the WAIS-III. The weaknesses found on the WMS-III are noted, but none are what we would consider *major*.

PERTINENT AREAS THAT ARE NOT MEASURED BY THE WMS-III

As we have noted, the WMS-III is one of the most comprehensive instruments for measuring memory. However, there are still areas of memory that the test assesses only partially or not at all, such as olfactory memory, kinesthetic memory, musical memory, procedural memory. Most of these types of memory are not of primary importance in a global memory assessment, and as such, there are not any or are very few tests available to tap these domains.

Bearing in mind the strengths and weaknesses of the WMS-III, as well as the few areas that are not measured well by the test, clinicians can make wise decisions about when it is necessary to supplement the WMS-III with other instruments, or perhaps use other instruments altogether.

≡Rapid Reference 5.1

Strengths and Weaknesses of WMS-III Test Development

Strengths

- The WMS-III extended the age range of the standardization sample from 74 to 89.

- Unlike the WMS-R, none of the WMS-III normative scores were interpolated.

- WMS-R Figural Memory and Visual Paired Associates were deleted from the WMS-III because of poor empirical evidence that they measured the constructs of visual memory.

- Recognition measures were added to the WMS-III, and an entire index is devoted to auditory recognition.

Weaknesses

- Retaining the name "General Memory Index" from the WMS-R is confusing as it contains completely different information (it used to be Immediate Memory and now is Delayed Memory). A more intuitive name for this Index could have been something like Global Delayed Memory.

- The new Family Pictures subtest is supposed to be the visual analog to the Logical Memory subtest; however, the family scenes that are pictured in the stimulus cards can be easily verbally encoded.

- The following subtests have inadequate floors: Family Pictures II (ages 85:0 to 89:11), Logical Memory II (ages 80:0 to 84:11), Verbal Paired Associates I (ages 65:0 to 89:11), Verbal Paired Associates II (ages 25:0 to 89:11), Visual Reproduction II (ages 65:0 to 89:11), and Word Lists II (ages 18:0 to 89:11) (Flanagan, McGrew, & Ortiz, 2000).

- The following subtests have inadequate ceilings: Family Pictures I (ages 16:0 to 34:11), Family Pictures II (ages 16:0 to 34:11), Verbal Paired Associates I (ages 16:0 to 44:11), Verbal Paired Associates II (ages 16:0 to 84:11), Visual Reproduction I (ages 16:0 to 34:11), and Word Lists II (ages 16:0 to 64:11) (Flanagan, McGrew, & Ortiz, 2000).

- There are no composite scores in the visual domain that are analogous to the Auditory Process Composites (J. Redfield, personal communication, January 8, 2001).

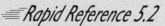

Rapid Reference 5.2

Strengths and Weaknesses of WMS-III Administration and Scoring

Strengths	Weaknesses
• The modernized format of the *Manual* and record form facilitate administration and scoring.	• The *Manual* does not present standardized administration guidelines regarding the speed of reading Logical Memory stories (Mitrushina et al., 1999).
• Scoring procedures for verbatim or near-verbatim recall of the Logical Memory stories have been tightened; the Manual offers numerous examples to improve interrater reliability (Mitrushina et al., 1999).	• The *Manual* also does not have a standardized procedure for the use of intonation, pauses, or inflections when presenting the Logical Memory stories.
• Scoring procedures for those who can recall the basic themes of the Logical Memory stories have been added.	• The test would have benefited from having an audiotaped administration of Logical Memory, thus offering more consistent presentation across examiners.
• Lines and arrows on the Score Summary page of the record form facilitate transferring scores from one column to another.	• The *Manual* gives an underestimation for the length of administration of the entire WMS-III. It indicates 45–55 minutes actual test time, but it is closer to 100 minutes.
	• To obtain a score on Logical Memory Recognition, it must be combined with Verbal Paired Associates recognition. This can be problematic because the two tasks measure quite different verbal material.
	• Although data on the difference between the backward and forward conditions of Digit Span can be obtained, there is no place to record these data on the record form (as there is on the WAIS-III).
	• The paper in the Visual Reproduction booklet is so thin that the drawn figures can "bleed" through the page currently being used (K. Blair, personal communication, December 5, 1998).
	• Examiners can only score Visual Reproduction reliably if they diligently use a ruler, protractor, and calculator. (F. Bardenhagen, personal communication, January 8, 2001).

Strengths and Weaknesses of WMS-III Reliability and Validity

Strengths

- Mean split-half reliability coefficients for the Indexes are strong for 7 of the 8 Indexes, ranging from .93 on Auditory Immediate to .82 on Visual Immediate.

- Of the 8 WMS-III Indexes, 5 have average stability coefficients at or above .80 (Auditory Immediate, Immediate Memory, Auditory Delayed, General Memory, and Working Memory). The Primary subtests with the highest stability coefficients are Verbal Paired Associates I and II and Logical Memory I and II.

- The *Manual* presents numerous studies supporting the validity of the WMS-III (e.g., samples of Alzheimer's disease, Huntington's disease, Parkinson's disease, traumatic brain injury, multiple sclerosis, temporal lobe epilepsy, alcoholism, schizophrenia, mental retardation, Attention-deficit Hyperactivity Disorder, and learning disabilities).

- Confirmatory factor analysis has supported the auditory-visual memory distinction in the WMS-III (Millis et al., 1999).

Weaknesses

- One of the WMS-III Indexes has a relatively low reliability coefficient: Auditory Delayed Recall (.74).

- The average stability coefficients for most WMS-III subtests are not strong. Three are in the .60s, four are in the low-.70s, four are in the mid- to high-.70s, and only one is above .80. Subtests with the lowest stability coefficients are Faces I and II and Family Pictures I.

- Of the 11 WMS-III subtests, 5 have average split-half reliability coefficients below .80: Faces I (.74), Spatial Span (.79), Logical Memory II (.79), Faces II (.74), and Auditory Recognition Delayed (.74).

- Logical Memory I and II appear to have a high degree of cultural loading, as well as a high degree of linguistic demands, which may result in bias against those for whom English is not their first language or who are from a nondominant culture.

- The intercorrelations between the subtests are too high for a memory scale and the correlation with IQ is too high. Thus, the scale is contaminated with too much general reasoning and is not a pure enough measure of memory (C. R. Reynolds, personal communication, January 4, 2001).

- The Visual Memory Index may be quite flawed. The Faces subtest appears to have insufficient commonality with Family Pictures (Millis, Malina, Bowers, & Ricker 1999)

- Support for separate immediate and delayed memory constructs in a normal sample have been questioned in confirmatory factor-analytic studies that have found that the immediate and delayed subtests do not load neatly on their respective factors (Millis et al., 1999).

Rapid Reference 5.4

Strengths and Weaknesses of WMS-III Standardization

Strengths

- WMS-III was stratified according to age, gender, race/ethnicity, education level, and geographic region, closely matching Census data.
- WMS-III was co-normed with the WAIS-III, allowing practitioners to identify discrepancies in IQ and memory while correcting for regression effects using co-normed tests.

Weaknesses

- Because the standardization version of the WMS-III contained more subtests than the published version of the WMS-III, it is possible that the effects of fatigue on the normative sample were greater than they are on a typical client being administered the test. Some clinicians have questioned why scores on some WMS-III subtests appear normal when their clients show clear impairment on other measures of similar ability.

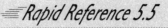

Rapid Reference 5.5

Strengths and Weaknesses of WMS-III Interpretation

Strengths

- The Manual offers helpful tables for interpreting Indexes (e.g., statistical significance and base rates for abnormality of differences).

- The thoroughness of the WMS-III allows for a finer-grained interpretation of multiple dimensions of memory: immediate vs. delayed, auditory vs. visual, and recall vs. recognition.

- Suggested interpretive comparisons for the Auditory Process Composites are useful.

- For comparisons between the WMS-III and WAIS-III, the Manual provides data on both the simple-difference method, as well as the predicted-difference method.

- The Mental Control and Information and Orientation subtests are much better normed and have many of the same items as other available mental status evaluations. Thus, they are valuable when screening for or documenting dementia (A. J. Phay, personal communication, January 22, 2001)

Weaknesses

- The WMS-III Manual does not provide guidance on possible interpretations when the entire battery is not given (which is a common practice among neuropsychologists).

- The three components of Family Pictures (content, location, and action) are not scored separately, which does not allow examiners to analyze the spatial rather than the figural aspects of visual memory.

- The stimuli for Family Pictures may be verbally encoded; thus, there may be an interaction between performance on this test and more verbally laden tests.

- The ability to verbally encode some of the nonverbal elements of the WMS-III inhibits the differentiation of right-left hemisphere distinctions and confounds the interpretation of the verbal-nonverbal distinction on the scales (C. R. Reynolds, personal communication, January 4, 2001)

- The significant ceiling effect on Verbal Paired Associates recognition renders it of little value for most clients except as a possible test for unsophisticated malingering (A. J. Phay, personal communication, January 22, 2001).

- There is little communality shared between Family Pictures and Faces. This lack of shared variance may present a problem when interpreting the Visual Memory Index score (Millis et al., 1999).

STRENGTHS AND WEAKNESSES OF THE WMS-III

🖎 TEST YOURSELF 🖎

1. **Which Index bears the same name on the WMS-R and WMS-III but has completely different content from one version to the next?**

    (a) Immediate Memory Index

    (b) Visual Delayed

    (c) Auditory Delayed

    (d) General Memory Index

2. **All WMS-III subtests have adequate ceilings and floors.** True or False?

3. **Which visual subtest can be visually encoded easily?**

    (a) Family Pictures

    (b) Faces

    (c) Spatial Span

    (d) Visual Reproduction

4. **Two verbal subtests are combined to obtain the Auditory Recognition Delayed score. This combination can be problematic because these two subtests, _____ and _____, measure quite different verbal material.**

    (a) Logical Memory and Letter-Number Sequencing

    (b) Verbal Paired Associates and Letter-Number Sequencing

    (c) Letter-Number Sequencing and Word Lists

    (d) Logical Memory and Verbal Paired Associates

5. **Because of its high degree of cultural loading as well as strong linguistic demands, Logical Memory I and II may be biased against those for whom English is not their first language or for those who are not from the dominant culture.** True or False?

6. **One weakness of the WMS-III *Manual* is that it does not provide data on the validity of the test in clinical samples such as patients with Alzheimer's disease, traumatic brain injury, schizophrenia, and other samples.** True or False?

7. **Because the WMS-III was co-normed with the WAIS-III, clinicians can identify discrepancies in IQ and memory while correcting for**

    (a) gender bias.

    (b) regression effects.

    (c) examiner scoring errors.

    (d) lack of client's motivation.

Answers: 1. d; 2. False; 3. a; 4. d; 5. True; 6. False; 7. b

Six

CLINICAL APPLICATIONS OF THE WMS-III

The WMS-III may prove to be more useful in differential diagnoses of many types of brain injury or diseases than previous test versions because the third version is theoretically designed to measure distinct facets of memory performances. This chapter is divided into three sections: The first section describes the use of the Wechsler Memory Scales in cases of brain damage, focusing on traumatic brain injury and temporal lobe epilepsy, the second section highlights abbreviated batteries for special populations, and the third section focuses on the effects of normal aging on memory and use of the WMS-III. Our focus is on the clinical presentation of commonly observed types of brain injury, dementia, psychiatric illnesses, and malingering; we shed light on *expected* patterns of findings on the WMS-III, given what is known about each disease state or disorder based on research on previous versions of the test, as well as WMS-III research when it exists. Future studies will determine whether the expected patterns we present are empirically founded on the WMS-III. Until then, this chapter serves as a guide that focuses on what is known about memory in various conditions, and the expected memory results on the WMS-III for each condition; in some cases, research on the WMS-III with small clinical samples is available and is discussed in the context of these expectancies. Although this chapter is devoted to memory, we have included, where relevant, information about other cognitive domains. For the interested reader, a more detailed treatment of the neuropsychological profiles associated with many disorders presented here is provided in *Clinical Syndromes in Adult Neuropsychology: The Practitioner's Handbook* (White, 1993), a book that is organized to illuminate the various cognitive domains that are affected in each disorder, over and above expected memory profiles.

RELATIONSHIP OF WECHSLER MEMORY SCALES TO BRAIN INJURY

WMS-III Findings on Patients with Brain Dysfunction

Hawkins (1998) examined data for several clinical samples that were tested during the standardization of the WAIS-III and WMS-III to determine if any indicators of brain dysfunction could be derived from graphic representations of the data. The clinical groups, which are described in detail in the *WAIS-III and WMS-III Technical Manual* (The Psychological Corporation, 1997), include patients with traumatic brain injury (TBI; $N = 22$), Alzheimer's disease ($N = 35$), Huntington's disease ($N = 15$), Parkinson's disease ($N = 10$), chronic alcohol abuse ($N = 28$), Korsakoff's syndrome ($N = 10$), and schizophrenia ($N = 42$), in addition to 25 patients with Multiple Sclerosis (MS). The data that were analyzed include the WMS-III Indexes for all samples and the WAIS-III IQs and Indexes for all but the MS sample. Hawkins graphed the data from each of the samples; means and standard deviations (SDs) on all variables appear in the *Manual* (The Psychological Corporation, 1997).

Hawkins (1998) found that the WAIS-III Processing Speed Index (PSI) is highly sensitive to brain dysfunction. For all seven clinical populations, the PSI was the low point in the WAIS-III profile (on average, nearly 1 SD below the high point on each profile). The Verbal Comprehension Index (VCI) was the high point for most of the population's profiles, except for TBI and Korsakoff's. The PSI was especially sensitive in Huntington's Disease and TBI. The average VCI-PSI discrepancy in Huntington's was 29 points, and the VCI-PSI discrepancy in TBI was 16 points.

Discrepancies between WMS-III Memory Indexes and WAIS-III IQs were weak indicators of brain dysfunction. In comparison to the FSIQ for all clinical samples, the WMS-III Indexes were significantly lower; the mean FSIQ-Immediate Memory Index difference, for example, was nearly 13 points. However, the FSIQ-Immediate Memory difference in 4 of the 7 clinical groups was less than 8 points, and 25% of the standardization sample had difference of 10 points or more. Thus, the IQ-Immediate Memory Index discrepancy is of limited utility as a clinical screening tool for brain dysfunction.

Hawkins also found that the WMS-III is sensitive to new learning deficiencies associated with Alzheimer's and Korsakoff's diseases. However, the Immediate and General (Delayed) Memory Indexes do not differ significantly in most clinical conditions. For the eight groups that Hawkins (1998) studied, the Immediate Memory Index and the General (Delayed) Memory Index were virtually identical, and the means correlated .98. Thus, the measures of delayed recall on the WMS-III do not appear to detect more than what was already detected by the measures of immediate recall. This finding contradicts earlier research on the WMS-R, but Hawkins (1998) suggests that the WMS-III Immediate Memory Index may be better able to capture deficits that typically become more apparent after delay.

Similar to previous research on the WMS and WMS-R, Hawkins' (1998) research found that the learning and retention of visuo-spatial information is more vulnerable than auditory retention to the effects of organic conditions. WMS-III Immediate Visual Memory was lower than Immediate Auditory Memory for 7 of the 8 clinical samples, and Visual Delayed was lower than Auditory Delayed in 6 of the 8 samples. Alzheimer's and Korsakoff's samples were exceptions, but all memory scores for these samples were uniformly low.

Hawkins (1998) also examined the difference between the WAIS-III VCI and the WMS-III Immediate Memory Index to determine the value of this discrepancy for identifying possible brain dysfunction. He found that, although there were generally large discrepancies between the VCI and Immediate Visual Memory Index in the seven principal clinical samples (mean difference was 17.6), the base rate in the standardization sample was presumed to be high for discrepancies of this size (Actual base rate data were not available for this comparison, so he estimated based on Verbal IQ-Immediate Visual Memory base rates of 17–18% for discrepancies of similar magnitude). His conclusion was that, despite the possible lack of sensitivity of this discrepancy evident in the comparison to base rates, the VCI-Immediate Visual Memory discrepancy warrants further investigation as a "red flag" for brain compromise.

WMS-R Findings in Patients with Closed Head Injury

Reid and Kelly (1993) studied differences of individuals with closed head injury and non-brain-injured individuals. They administered the WMS-R to 20 inpatients admitted to an acute head trauma rehabilitation unit (1 to 3 months post-injury) and to 20 neurologically normal participants who were matched according to education and age. As predicted, the patients with head injury performed worse than the control group on all WMS-R Indexes. Delayed memory performance was especially vulnerable in the head-injured group, as they scored an average of 30 index points lower than controls on measures of delayed recall. Patients with head injury also performed significantly worse than controls on measures of forgetting rates. Logical Memory and Visual Reproduction provided the largest discrepancies between the groups. Specifically, on Logical Memory, patients with head injury retained an average of 50% of the information, while controls retained 85%, and patients with head injury retained 60% of the information on the Visual Reproduction subtests, while controls retained 90%; Reid and Kelly concluded that the WMS-R provides a valid assessment of memory impairments in patients with closed head injury.

Similar findings on the ability of these memory tasks to discriminate between brain-injured and non-brain-injured patients were reported with Russell's revision of the WMS (Sherer, Nixon, Anderson, & Adams, 1992). However, Sherer and colleagues attempted to determine the *differential* effects of IQ and brain damage on the sensitivity of the WMS (Russell's revision). They analyzed the data for 64 individuals with brain injury and 64 age- and IQ-matched individuals without brain injury by dividing the samples into three groups based on IQ (FSIQs of 80–89, 90–99, and 100–109). Overall, the WMS Memory Quotient did significantly correlate with WAIS-R FSIQ ($r = .50$). Results showed that some subtests were only affected by IQ level and not by brain-damage status: Logical Memory I and Visual Reproduction I. However, Logical Memory II and Visual Reproduction II were affected by brain damage status even when both subject groups were equated on IQ. Several measures—including Information, Orientation Logical Memory percent recall, Visual Memory percent recall, and Associative Learning (as well as Hard Pairs, a subset of Associative Learning)—were affected by brain-damage status but not IQ level. Sherer and colleagues concluded that Logical Memory percent recall, Visual Memory percent recall, and the subset of Associative Learning (Hard Pairs) are the most useful WMS measures for assessing memory dysfunctions in patients with brain injury.

In addition to the studies examining the ability of the WMS or WMS-R to discriminate between individuals with and without brain injuries is a study that examined the test's ability to discriminate between TBI and dementia. Brooker (1997) examined 12 patients with mild TBI who were education-matched with 11 patients with mild dementia. There was a broad age range for the all-male samples, from 20 to 68 ($M = 47$) for the mild TBI group and from 27 to 75 (M

= 46) for the mild dementia group. Performances on the WMS-R subtests were obtained for all participants. The mild TBI participants had significantly higher scores on Verbal Paired Associates I and II, Visual Reproduction I and II, and Visual Paired Associates, in comparison to the mild dementia group. The groups were highly similar in their scores on Digit Span, Visual Span, Logical Memory I and II, and Figural Memory. The Attention/Concentration raw scores of the mild TBI and mild dementia groups did not differ significantly from that of a normal control group, indicating the lack of sensitivity of this measure to concentration problems that were subjectively reported by patients with brain injury.

Semantic Processing on WMS-R in Patients with Closed Head Injury

Haut, Petros, and Frank (1991) used the WMS-R Logical Memory subtest to discern whether there were differences between the semantic memories of 16 individuals with severe head injuries, 16 individuals with moderate injuries, and 16 individuals with normal neurological functioning. They hypothesized that varying levels of brain injury would affect participants' prose processing. As predicted, the authors found that overall recall of the stories declined as a function of the severity of the injury. However, they also found that the importance of the ideas contained within the stories influenced the recall of prose in patients with moderate and severe head injuries, as well as controls. Thus, all three groups were equally capable of distinguishing important from less important information in their recall. The authors concluded that semantic processing is intact in individuals with moderate and severe closed head injury, although the amount of information that is recalled declines with the severity of the patient's injury.

Another group of researchers also investigated the importance of informational units in the Logical Memory subtest for patients with head injury; Vakil, Arbell, Gozlan, Hoofien, and Blachstein (1992) analyzed the performance of 40 patients with closed head injury and 40 control participants on the WMS Logical Memory subtest. Results showed three main effects: (a) The control group (mean age = 25, mean education = 14) performed significantly better than the head-injured group (mean age = 30, mean education = 11), even with age and education covaried; (b) immediate recall was better than delayed recall; and, (c) important ideas were recalled better than less important details. In both groups, the rate of forgetting less important ideas over time was steeper than the rate of forgetting more important ideas. In the head-injured group, the ability both to retrieve the most important information from the stories and to retrieve it at a later time was more vulnerable than the ability to immediately recall such information.

WMS Patterns in Patients with Right versus Left Brain Injury

Vakil and colleagues (1992) administered one WMS subtest (Verbal Paired Associate Learning) and two other tasks (Gollin Incomplete Figure Test and Stylus Maze) to a sample of 20 patients with right-hemisphere damage, 20 patients with left-hemisphere damage, and 20 controls with no brain damage. Control patients outperformed both brain-damaged groups on all tasks, and right-hemisphere patients showed an advantage over left-hemisphere patients by demonstrating a steeper learning curve on the Verbal Paired Associate Learning task and in the amount learned on the task. As expected, the patients with right-hemisphere damage were more impaired on the spatial learning task (Stylus Maze), but the learning rate was not significantly different between the groups on this measure. However, the visual task that could be verbally coded (Gollin) did not distinguish between the two brain-damaged groups. Vakil and colleagues (1992) concluded that the total amount learned was a more sensitive index of learning ability than learning rate because it was able to distinguish between the patient groups and controls, as well as between the two patient groups.

Chlopan, Hagen, and Russell (1990) conducted further analysis of patients with right-versus-left brain injury. Their sample comprised five groups: 10 patients with left anterior lesions, 13 patients with right anterior lesions, 24 patients with left posterior lesions, 23 patients with right posterior lesions, and 47 non-injured controls. No significant differences were found between groups for age, education, or etiology of lesion. Chlopan and colleagues administered three memory tasks: WMS Logical Memory, WMS Figural Memory, and WAIS Digit Span. They predicted that patients with left posterior lesions would be most impaired on Logical Memory, and their prediction was fully supported in both the immediate and delayed conditions. Participants in the left posterior lesion group scored 6 to 9.5 points lower on the immediate recall of Logical Memory than the other groups, and scored 7 to 9.5 points lower than the other groups on the delayed recall portion of the test. For the Figural Memory subtest, all four of the brain-lesion groups scored significantly worse than the controls in the immediate and delayed conditions. In addition, the right posterior group was significantly more impaired than the right anterior group on the delayed recall of Figural Memory. On Digit Span (Digits Forward), the left posterior group was significantly impaired in relation to both the normal comparison and right anterior lesion groups. In contrast, for Digits Backward, the performances of both posterior groups were significantly impaired in relation to the controls, and no significant differences were found among the four lesion groups. Interestingly, on the overall Digit Span score, the right anterior lesion group scored higher than controls, suggesting that right anterior lesions do not impair Digit Span performance. Chlopan and colleagues conclude that impaired performance on the WMS Logical Memory task assists in localizing cortical lesions to the left posterior quadrant. In contrast, impairment on WMS Figural Memory is by itself of little use in localizing cortical lesions. When paired with Logical Memory, the difference between Logical Memory and Figural Memory may help to lateralize posterior cortical lesions. The pattern of scores on the WMS tasks did not help to identify anterior cortical lesions.

Attention and Concentration in Patients with Traumatic Brain Injury

Cicerone (1997) administered four neuropsychological measures of attention to a sample of 57 patients with mild TBI (mean age = 34.6, mean education = 14.8). Cicerone administered one measure from the WMS-R (Digit Span), in addition to Trails A and B, Paced Auditory Serial Addition Test, and the Continuous Performance Test of Attention. Cicerone found significant variability among the measures, observing impaired performance most often on the Paced Auditory Serial Addition Test and the Continuous Performance Test of Attention. The WMS-R Digit Span subtest was the least sensitive measure to mild TBI. Gass, Russell, and Hamilton (1990) also found that Digit Span, as well as Logical Memory (Immediate and Delayed) and Visual Reproduction (Immediate and Delayed), did not significantly differentiate between participants with subjective complaints of attentional and concentration difficulties from those without.

WMS Memory Quotient versus Full Scale IQ

Heilbronner, Buck, and Adams (1990) investigated the relationship of IQ to the memory quotient of the WMS in patients with and without brain damage. They administered either the WAIS or WAIS-R concurrently with the WMS to a sample of 177 patients (mean age = 37 years; mean education = 12 years). Findings indicate that neither WAIS-R FSIQ versus WMS Memory Quotient discrepancy or WAIS FSIQ versus WMS Memory Quotient discrepancy successfully discriminated between patients with and without brain damage. The WMS Memory Quotient itself was a better discriminator overall than discrepancy scores, but the total discrimination error rate for the Memory Quotient was also quite high (42% of the participants without brain damage and 35% of the participants with brain damage were misclassified). Thus, the authors do not recommend using the WMS Memory Quotient as a single index to screen for brain damage.

In a recent study of estimated premorbid WAIS-R IQ scores and WMS-R Indexes in participants with closed head injury, Tremont, Hoffman, Scott, Adams, and Nadolne (1997) compared the performance of those with mild versus moderate-to-severe injuries. Tremont and colleagues' sample was composed of 41 patients with mild head injury (mean age = 34, mean education = 13) and 41 with moderate-to-severe head injuries (mean age = 32, mean education = 13). The premorbid IQs were estimated by the Oklahoma Premorbid Intelligence Estimation, which has been shown to correlate .87 with obtained WAIS-R FS-IQs. Tremont and colleagues' results show that the two groups were not significantly different on IQs or WMS-R Indexes, except for WMS-R Visual Memory and WMS-R Delayed Recall, which were both lower for the group with moderate-to-severe head injuries. Results also show that the comparison between estimated premorbid IQs and WMS-R scores differentiated the groups. The most sensitive comparison in their study was between the estimated premorbid IQ and the WMS-R Delayed Recall Index, which was consistent with the notion that delayed memory functioning is the most sensitive in patients with brain injury. The authors conclude that their study demonstrates the usefulness of comparing estimated premorbid IQs with WMS-R Indexes to evaluate both the presence and degree of memory dysfunction.

Expected Performance on WMS-III for Patients with Brain Injury

Examination of the studies on the WMS and WMS-R and the one study on the WMS-III suggest that some patterns of performance may be expected on the WMS-III for patients with brain injury. We detail the findings of several pertinent studies on this topic in the beginning of this chapter, so here we highlight the application the data to clinical work. As the data on the WMS-III itself are quite limited, what is directly suggested from Hawkins' (1998) results requires validation with future studies. With that caveat in mind, Hawkins' data reveal that the discrepancies between WMS-III Indexes and WAIS-III IQs are weak indicators of brain dysfunction (similar findings were reported for the WMS-R). However, the WAIS-III Verbal Comprehension Index versus the WMS-III Immediate Memory Index discrepancy may potentially indicate brain dysfunction. Contrary to what has been reported on the WMS-R, measures of delayed recall of the WMS-III may not be more sensitive to brain dysfunction than Immediate Indexes. Yet, learning and retention of visual-spatial information is more vulnerable to brain dysfunction than auditory information. Thus, the WMS-III Visual Memory Indexes (Immediate and Delayed) may be lower than Auditory Memory Indexes (Immediate and Delayed) for patients with brain dysfunction.

In comparison to normally functioning individuals, patients with brain injury can be expected to have generally depressed scores on all WMS-III Indexes (Hawkins, 1998; Reid & Kelly, 1993). Unlike what Hawkins reported on the WMS-III, researchers have shown that WMS-R delayed memory performance is especially vulnerable to brain injury (Reid & Kelly, 1993). Therefore, it is unclear whether the Delayed < Immediate pattern will persist in subsequent WMS-III studies of patients with brain injury. It can be expected that forgetting rates on Logical Memory and Visual Reproduction will be lower than normal for patients with brain injury (Reid & Kelly, 1993; Sherer et al., 1992). In addition, Verbal Paired Associates may be sensitive to brain damage (Sherer et al., 1992). Within the Logical Memory subtest, patients with brain injury can be expected to recall more important story units than less important information (Haut et al., 1991; Vakil et al., 1992). Verbal Paired Associates and Visual Reproduction are useful subtests for differentiating patients with brain injury from those with dementia, and patients with dementia are likely to score lower than those with brain injury (Brooker, 1997).

For patients with lateralized lesions or dysfunction, individuals with affected left hemispheres are likely to have more depressed scores on auditory tasks such as Verbal Paired Associates (Vakil, Hoofien, & Blachstein, 1992), and Logical Memory (Chlopan et al., 1990). However, patients with right-hemisphere damage may not show as pronounced an affect in visual memory tasks (Chlopan et al., 1990; Vakil, Hoofien, & Blachstein, 1992). The small data on attention and concentration suggest that the WMS-R (and presumably the

≋Rapid Reference 6.1

Expected Findings for Patients with Brain Injury

- There is a discrepancy between WAIS-III *Verbal Comprehension Index* and the WMS-III *Immediate Memory Index.*
- Learning and retention of visual-spatial information is more vulnerable than auditory information to brain dysfunction.
    - Patients have lower WMS-III *Visual Memory Indexes* (Immediate and Delayed) than *Auditory Memory Indexes* (Immediate and Delayed).
- Patients have generally depressed scores on all *WMS-III Indexes.*
- Patients show higher-than-normal forgetting rates on *Logical Memory* and *Visual Reproduction.*
- When differentiating patients with brain injury from those with dementia, patients with brain injury have higher *Verbal Paired Associates* and *Visual Reproduction* scores than patients with dementia.
- Patients with lateralized lesions or dysfunction show
    - more depressed scores on auditory tasks such as *Verbal Paired Associates* and *Logical Memory* (for individuals with affected left hemispheres).
    - not as pronounced an affect in *visual memory tasks* (for patients with right-hemisphere damage).
- Measures of *delayed recall* on the WMS-III are *not* more sensitive to brain dysfunction than *immediate Indexes* (contrary to WMS-R findings).
- *Attention/concentration impairment* may *not* be gleaned from WMS-III due to lack of the instrument's sensitivity.

Note: Clinical judgment and other measures must be considered in addition to the aforementioned patterns of performance when making differential diagnoses.

WMS-III) may not be a sensitive measure of impairment in this domain (Cicerone, 1997; Gass et al., 1990). (See Rapid Reference 6.1 for expected findings for patients with head injury.)

Temporal Lobe Epilepsy and WMS-III and Earlier Versions of the Test

Epilepsy is a common disorder occurring in approximately 5 out of 1,000 people, or 2% of the population (McIntosh, 1992). One method of treatment for the intractable seizures of epilepsy is to resect the epileptogenic foci during surgery, although in many cases, treatment with anticonvulsant medications adequately reduces the frequency of seizures. Hippocampal sclerosis was found in 60% of a sample of individuals with treatment-resistant epilepsy and was related to deficits in recall, regardless of hemisphere (McMillan, Powell, Janota, & Polkey, 1987). Pre- and postoperative studies on the effects on neuro-psychological functioning have been fairly well-documented in patients with epilepsy.

Memory and Temporal Lobe Epilepsy—General

Memory deficits in individuals with right-versus-left temporal lobe epilepsy or after right or left temporal lobectomy have been examined to determine whether there is a differential effect on visual-versus-auditory modalities. Some have reported affected verbal memory following dominant temporal lobe resections (Penfield & Mathieson, 1974) and visual-spatial compromise following right-hemisphere temporal resection (Augustine & Novelly, 1981). However, these relationships have not been consistently reported (Lee, Loring, & Thompson, 1989). Generally, the literature suggests that patients who have undergone left temporal lobectomy obtain lower scores on tasks with auditorally presented material than on tasks with visually presented material; and, less certainly, patients who have undergone right temporal lobectomy obtain the opposite pattern (The Psychological Corporation, 1997).

WMS-III Data

Hawkins (1998) examined the small samples of patients with temporal lobe epilepsy tested during the standardization of the WMS-III to see whether there was evidence for lateralizing WMS-III modality-specific deficits. This sample was composed of 15 patients with left lobectomies and 12 patients with right lobectomies (see The Psychological Corporation, 1997, Tables 4.40 and 4.42 for background information and WMS-III and WAIS-III test scores). Patients with right lobectomies performed at substantially lower levels on visual memory tests relative to their auditory performances, and patients with left lobectomies did substantially poorer on the auditory memory subtests relative to the visual. However, patients with both right and left lobectomies had low Visual Memory Indexes. Specifically, patients with left lobectomies had mean Auditory Immediate and Delayed Indexes of 78 and 75, respectively, in contrast to mean Visual Immediate and Delayed Indexes of 87 and 85. Conversely, patients with right lobectomies had mean Auditory Immediate and Delayed

Indexes of 95 and 94, versus mean Visual Immediate and Delayed Indexes of 84 and 84. The mean percentile ranks for the WMS-III Auditory Process Composites also indicate that the group with left temporal lobectomy scored lower than the group with right on the Single-Trial Learning, Learning Slope, and Retention composites. Poor retention scores suggest a worse storage deficit due to rapid forgetting over delays. Performance on the Retrieval Composite is relatively higher for the group with left lobectomy than the right, suggesting a retrieval deficit may underlie at least part of the memory problems. This pattern suggests that recognition aids retrieval more so for the group with left than right lobectomies.

These findings from the WMS-III *Manual* on right and left lobectomies are tentative, as the samples were not matched on premorbid functioning or any other demographic variable (Hawkins, 1998; The Psychological Corporation, 1997). Nonetheless, these data do suggest that a depressed auditory Index accompanied by a substantially less depressed visual Index indicates left hemisphere impairment. However, a depressed visual Index accompanied by a less depressed auditory Index may signal either diffuse/bilateral damage or specific right-hemisphere impairment. The evidence for the latter finding is that the mean difference between the Auditory and Visual Immediate Indexes was 11.5 for the patients with right hippocampectomies, which was similar to that of patients who abused alcohol (mean difference = 12.0) and patients with TBI (mean difference = 14.4).

WMS-R Data

Naugle, Chelune, Cheek, Lüders, and Awad (1993) examined discrepancies between visual and verbal modalities and immediate and delayed memory on the WMS-R with samples of patients with temporal lobe epilepsy. Specifically, 30 patients with left temporal lobectomy, 30 with right temporal lobectomy, and 60 control patients with epilepsy (nonsurgical) were administered the Logical Memory and Visual Reproduction subtests of the WMS-R. The subject groups were matched on age, gender, handedness, age at seizure onset, duration of epilepsy, and presurgical IQs. The right temporal group had a higher mean educational level. Examination of short-term memory (via the Verbal and Visual Memory Indexes) revealed no differences between the left and right temporal lobectomy groups prior to surgery. Postoperatively, the group with left-temporal lobectomies showed marked change in their pattern of performance, evidencing a Verbal-Visual Memory Index discrepancy of 13.5 points in favor of visual memory. This change in the left temporal lobectomy group was due primarily to a drop in verbal memory (Verbal memory change was –9 points and the visual memory change was +1 point). However, the right temporal lobectomy group showed little change, as the postsurgery mean discrepancy score was 2.8 points in favor of visual memory. This change was not associated with a drop in visual memory (changes in Verbal and Visual memory were both +0.4 points). In contrast, the nonsurgical controls displayed a small but significant discrepancy of 6.3 points in favor of verbal memory at retest, which represented a 4.6-point increase in the change score. The change in the control group's score appeared to be due mainly to an increase in verbal memory (7-point increase).

Naugle and colleagues (1993) also examined changes in short- versus long-term memory in the separate modalities, comparing scores on Logical Memory I and II scores and on Visual Reproduction I and II. The patients with left temporal lobectomy displayed a drop in their Logical Memory II-Visual Reproduction II difference scores from +1.2 prior to surgery to –11.9 after surgery, but the change in this difference score for the patients with right lobectomies changed from –3 points prior to surgery to +2.4 points after surgery. The change noted among the patients with left lobectomies was due to a significant decline in Logical Memory II and a significant increase in Visual Reproduction II following surgery. The patients with left lobectomies showed a smaller change in discrepancy score in the opposite direction following surgery, which was primarily due to a significant increase in Logical Memory II. Naugle and colleagues' findings were consistent with prior research showing that patients with left-temporal lobe epilepsy show significant drops in measures of verbal memory after surgery. In these data, the change in delayed memory discrepancy scores among the patients with left temporal lobectomies was also influenced by an increase in Visual Reproduction II scores. Overall, the findings from Naugle and colleagues' study show that upon retesting after surgery, the left temporal lobectomy was associated with a marked change in short-term and long-term memory discrepancy scores, primarily due to a drop in verbal memory. Right temporal lobectomy was not associated with a drop in visual memory, which suggests that the WMS-R reflects deficits in modality-specific memory following left, but not right, temporal lobectomy.

WMS (Russell) Data

The relationship of performance on Russell's adaptation of the WMS and quantitative MRI measures was examined in 19 preoperative patients with temporal lobe epilepsy (Lencz et al. 1992). Of the 19 patients, 10 had left temporal lobe epilepsy and 9 had right temporal lobe epilepsy. Findings show that the MRI raw measurements of the left hippocampus were significantly correlated with the percent retention Index of the WMS Logical Memory subtest for all patients. When examining the left and right groups separately, Lencz and colleagues found significant correlations between the Logical Memory percent retention and left hippocampal measures for only the left temporal lobe epilepsy patients. Neither the right hippocampal nor the right temporal lobe measures were correlated with scores on any of the verbal or nonverbal memory testing procedures. In conclusion, Lencz and colleagues stated that, although postsurgical pathological studies could have allowed for greater sensitivity and specificity within the hippocampus, their study with presurgical patients provided an opportunity to examine multiple areas of the brain in vivo.

WMS Data

Another study of hippocampal structures and neuropsychological test performance of individuals with temporal lobe epilepsy examined the relationship between verbal memory and hippocampal neuron loss. Sass and colleagues (1992) administered the WMS Logical Memory subtest (Immediate and Delayed), WAIS-R verbal subtests, and the Boston Naming Test to 28 patients with left temporal lobe epilepsy and 31 with right temporal lobe epilepsy prior to surgery. After the neuropsychological testing, all patients underwent anteromedial temporal lobectomy and radical hippocamectomy. The results of the neuropsychological testing revealed that patients with left temporal lobe epilepsy were significantly more impaired than those with right temporal lobe epilepsy on the WMS Logical Memory Subtest (immediate, delayed, and percent retention). The same pattern of impairment for the patients with left temporal lobe epilepsy, in contrast to the pattern for patients with right temporal lobe epilepsy, was also noted on the Boston Naming Test; however, the WAIS-R Verbal IQ did not significantly differentiate between the groups with right and left temporal lobe epilepsy. The neuronal loss in hippocampal subfield CA3 and the hilar area were significantly correlated with percent retention on Logical Memory for the left temporal lobe epilepsy patients only. However, neither the Boston Naming Test nor the Verbal IQ correlated significantly with neuron loss in any hippocampal subfield for either group. Sass and colleagues' (1992) interpretation of their findings was that left hippocampal neuron loss is correlated with aspects of memory, but not with language competency or general intellectual ability (even though the Logical Memory subtest was significantly correlated with the Boston Naming Test and the Verbal IQ, and all tests were sensitive to left temporal lobe epilepsy preoperatively).

Rausch and Babb (1993) further studied the relationship between hippocampal neuron loss and memory measures. Participants for this study included 25 patients who had temporal lobe epilepsy (12 left and 13 right); all patients underwent temporal lobe surgery. Rausch and Babb administered the following measures both before surgery and one year after surgery: WMS Verbal Paired Associates subtest; WMS Logical Memory subtest; WMS Visual Reproduction subtest; WAIS Full Scale, Verbal, and Performance IQs; and the Rey-Osterrieth Draw and Recall Test. Results show that degree of hippocampal neuron loss was significantly related to immediate and delayed performance on WMS Verbal Paired Associates in only the group with left temporal lobe epilepsy. Following surgery, the patients with right and left temporal lobe epilepsy had decreased scores on the word-pairs task, but patients with left temporal lobe epilepsy scored lower than those with right temporal lobe epilepsy. In contrast to the findings on Verbal Paired Associates, scores on WMS Logical Memory did not correlate significantly to degree of hippocampal neuron loss in either patient group. However, there was a significant negative effect of surgery on the immediate Logical Memory recall scores of patients with left, but not right, temporal lobe epilepsy. Thus, patients with left temporal lobe epilepsy had significantly lower postoperative Logical Memory (immediate condition) scores than those with right temporal lobe epilepsy. Similar results were found for the delayed recall condition of Logical Memory, with left temporal lobe epilepsy less than right pre- and postoperatively. No significant findings related to any of the visual measures. Results also showed that degree of hippocampal cell loss did not relate to IQ performance in patients with right or left temporal lobe epilepsy. However, patients with left temporal lobe epilepsy had significantly lower Verbal IQs than those with right temporal lobe epilepsy, both before and after surgery. Following surgery both groups improved their Performance IQs (the well-known practice effect for PIQ; see Kaufman & Lichtenberger, 1999), but only the patients with right temporal lobe epilepsy demonstrated improved Verbal IQs. Rausch and Babb (1993) concluded that their study provides evidence that the "left language-dominant hippocampus does not contribute uniformly to performance on different verbal memory tasks" (p. 815). Although the researchers found significant correlations between left hippocampal neuron loss and rote verbal learning and word-pairs learning, they did not find the same relation with logical prose, a more semantically complex task.

Expected Performance on WMS-III for Patients with Epilepsy

A specific pattern of memory performance is expected in individuals with various kinds of epilepsy (see Rapid Reference 6.2). Overall, intellectual capabil-

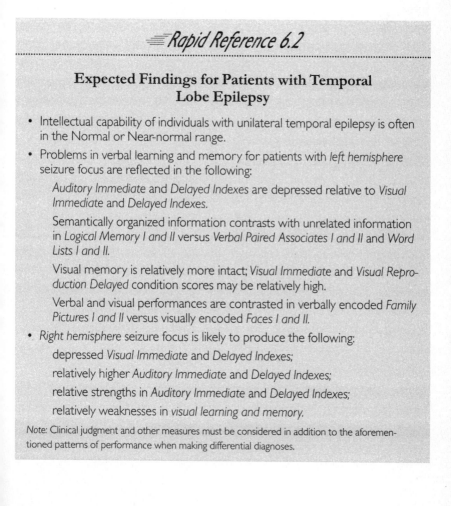

≡Rapid Reference 6.2

Expected Findings for Patients with Temporal Lobe Epilepsy

- Intellectual capability of individuals with unilateral temporal epilepsy is often in the Normal or Near-normal range.
- Problems in verbal learning and memory for patients with *left hemisphere* seizure focus are reflected in the following:

  Auditory Immediate and Delayed Indexes are depressed relative to Visual Immediate and Delayed Indexes.

  Semantically organized information contrasts with unrelated information in *Logical Memory I and II* versus *Verbal Paired Associates I and II* and *Word Lists I and II.*

  Visual memory is relatively more intact; *Visual Immediate* and *Visual Reproduction Delayed* condition scores may be relatively high.

  Verbal and visual performances are contrasted in verbally encoded *Family Pictures I and II* versus visually encoded *Faces I and II.*

- *Right hemisphere* seizure focus is likely to produce the following:

  depressed *Visual Immediate* and *Delayed Indexes;*

  relatively higher *Auditory Immediate* and *Delayed Indexes;*

  relative strengths in *Auditory Immediate* and *Delayed Indexes;*

  relative weaknesses in *visual learning and memory.*

Note: Clinical judgment and other measures must be considered in addition to the aforementioned patterns of performance when making differential diagnoses.

ity of individuals with unilateral temporal epilepsy is often in the normal or near-normal range, while memory performances are among the weakest in the protocol. Specifically, when assessing right or left temporal lobe epilepsy, a clinician may see a domain-specific pattern that is correlated with the side of seizure focus. A patient with a seizure focus in the dominant (presumably left) hemisphere is likely to exhibit problems in verbal learning and memory. This is usually reflected in depressed Auditory Immediate and Delayed Indexes relative to Visual Immediate and Delayed Indexes. Logical Memory I and II, Verbal Paired Associates I and II, and Word Lists I and II provide a contrast, over several trials, between semantically organized information and unrelated information. It is important to establish that visual memory, thought to be subserved primarily in the nondominant hemisphere, is relatively more intact. Visual Immediate and Visual Reproduction delayed condition scores may be relatively high. Administrating Faces I and II and Family Pictures I and II allows a contrast between verbal and visual performances. Clinicians who have used older versions of the WMS may want to use the Visual Reproduction I and II subtests as a replacement for Faces or Family Pictures. In contrast, the expected pattern for a patient with a seizure focus in the nondominant (presumably right) hemisphere would be the opposite of that for the patient with a dominant-hemisphere focus. Patients with right temporal lobe epilepsy usually demonstrate depressed Visual Immediate and Delayed Indexes and relatively higher Auditory Immediate and Delayed Indexes. Auditory Immediate and Delayed Indexes are likely to be relative strengths as well. Visual learning and memory are relatively weaker than verbal learning and memory, and test scores generally demonstrate this. Comparison of both verbal and visual memory encoding versus retrieval is an essential feature of the unilateral temporal lobe epilepsy, so that treatment recommendations can be made based on the individual's strengths and weaknesses in new learning. Bilateral or right hippocampal damage would be suggested by depressed auditory and visual indexes (see the previous section for support for these findings).

ABBREVIATED WMS-III BATTERIES FOR SPECIAL POPULATIONS

In this section, we address a neuropsychological approach to using the WMS-III. In the context of neuropsychological assessment, several testing variables may require selecting an abbreviated set of subtests to administer (see also Chapter 2 for a discussion of abbreviated batteries). Such variables frequently include the need to address a specific hypothesis of memory dysfunction and the need to balance time constraints with administering a comprehensive battery (including measures of language, visual-spatial and visual-motor functioning, judgment and problem solving, attention, and personality/emotional functioning), along with memory tests. To demonstrate a neuropsychological approach to interpreting a partial WMS-III battery, we present examples of common clinical referrals, along with suggestions to use select subtests for interpretation. These are not rigid rules of interpretation; the examiner should always use sound clinical judgment in considering specific factors pertaining to the case in question when determining which measures are best to administer and interpret. Note that translating data from groups that present mean data very rarely allows a direct one-to-one translation to individual data. While trends in these directions are expected, individual variation is likely to modify the findings.

General Interpretive Considerations

Often a comparison regarding an individual's capability to encode new information with what is retained after a delay is part of the referral issue. The Wechsler Memory Scales have allowed examination of forgetting rates over time for different material domains, and this feature is helpful in neuropsychological evaluations. For this reason, we strongly suggest administering both immediate and delayed portions (parts I and II) of tests that have two parts in order to maximize the utility of the WMS-III. An additional measure to administer routinely is the WAIS-III (to obtain an estimate of intellectual capabilities). Information about general cognitive functioning provides a context within which to interpret memory findings. While the relationship is imperfect, the higher the level of intelligence, the higher the expected level of memory performance. In particular, the WAIS-III subtests provide another means of comparing verbal and visual-spatial capabilities and also serve as a context to interpret differences between verbal and visually based memory problems. Other commonly included measures to supplement a partial or complete WMS-III battery are tests for frontal-executive function (e.g., the Wisconsin Card Sort or Trails A and B) and confrontational naming tasks (e.g., the Boston Naming Test or the Expressive Vocabulary Test).

Dementia

The hallmark of various dementing illnesses is a gradual loss of memory functioning accompanied by decline in one or more cognitive domains. Disease states that include dementia have different patterns of onset, types of memory dysfunction, courses of decline, and neurobiological bases. Memory decline generally represents a critical component of the disease process. Neuropsychological assessment and accurate diagnosis at the early stages are most important with respect to potential treatments and clinical care. In contrast, late stages of dementing diseases are characterized by severe dysfunction in several cognitive capabilities, which makes using neuropsychological data for differential diagnosis difficult. Therefore, in the late stages, interview data regarding onset and course of illness, particularly with detailed information on temporal order of observed deficits, are of increased importance to consider along with the neuropsychological data.

Alzheimer's Disease

Alzheimer's disease is the most common dementing illness. Approximately 11% of individuals over the age of 65 suffer from some form of dementia (Katzman, 1976, 1986; Mortimer, Schuman, & French, 1981) and of these cases, 50 to 70% may be attributed to Alzheimer's disease. Up to 50% of the population over the age of 85 may develop this disease (Evans et al., 1989). Alzheimer's disease includes a gradual course of cognitive decline that is most frequently heralded, in early stages, by a deficit in memory function and executive capabilities.

Summary of Neuropsychological Profile in Alzheimer's Disease

The robustness of neuropsychological markers for Alzheimer's disease is highlighted by a study that contrasts the sensitivity of neuropsychological, structural, and physiological measures of temporal-hippocampal system function (Zakzanis, 1998). The neuropsychological profile of early-stage Alzheimer's disease consists of problems in acquiring or retaining new information, which is disproportionate in its severity to problems in other cognitive domains (Masur, Sliwinski, Litpon, Blau, & Crystal, 1994; Storandt & Hill, 1989; Fuld, Masur, Blau, Crystal, & Aronson, 1990, Masur, Fuld, Blau, Crystal, & Aronson, 1990). The memory problem may be due more to impairment in *recall* than in *recognition.* Furthermore, the memory problems are nonspecific; that is, they are evident in both verbal and nonverbal domains (Stern, Richards, Sano, & Mayeux, 1993; Troster et al., 1993). Immediate simple attention is likely to be normal or close-to-normal at early stages of the disease. The patient is likely to demonstrate word-finding difficulties, in the form of semantic paraphasias and circumlocutory errors and may show these in free speech during testing. The patient may also demonstrate difficulties in executive system function. Problems on visuospatial tasks that are due to a conceptual problem rather than a primary visual-spatial deficit are frequently seen (Moss & Albert, 1992); specifically, the patient may show difficulties in drawing on command, but resolves these in copy conditions in early stages of the disease (Moss & Albert, 1992). Other studies reveal that Alzheimer's patients have greater visual-perceptual and visual-spatial deficits, which include problems in matching and copying designs on the Visual Reproduction subtest, than do patients with right frontal lobe lesions and normal controls (Haut, Weber, Wilhellm, Keefover, & Rankin, 1994). Patients with Alzheimer's disease also made more prior-figure intrusion errors than normal controls and more than patients with alcoholic Korsakoff's syndrome, Huntington's disease, and hippocampal damage (Jacobs, Troster, Butters, Salmon, & Cermak, 1990).

Inconsistencies in the Research on Alzheimer's Disease

While changes in memory function are among the presenting symptoms in Alzheimer's disease, there has been considerable debate about whether performance on immediate or delayed memory tasks provide the best discrimination between patients in the early stages of Alzheimer's disease and controls. Some studies have suggested that delayed recall is the best discriminatory measure available (Welsh, Butters, Hughes, Mohs, & Heyman, 1991, 1992), while others have found little or no evidence of abnormal delayed recall in individuals with Alzheimer's disease compared with uncompromised elderly individuals, particularly after controlling for the effects of immediate recall (Freed, Corkin, Growdon, & Nissen, 1989; Money, Kirk, & McNaughton, 1992; van der Hurk & Hodges, 1995). Chapman, White, and Storandt (1997) address the methodological problems in memory studies of Alzheimer's disease that could contribute to the varying outcomes. First, researchers have assessed memory abilities in a variety of ways, including both verbal stimuli (word lists or prose passages) and nonverbal stimuli (abstract designs). Second, procedures used for sample selection and dementia staging are inconsistent across studies, causing samples to vary widely with respect to severity. Third, researchers have used different statistical methods to evaluate memory retention over a delay interval (matching in immediate recall scores, savings or difference scores, and multiple regression). Robinson-Whelen and Storandt (1992) specifically point out that the inconsistency on rates of forgetting in patients with Alzheimer's disease are likely to be due, in part, to different methods of calculating savings. For example, Becker, Boller, Saxton, and McGonigle-Gibson (1987) used "immediate recall—delayed recall" as a measure of forgetting and concluded that the rate of forgetting was not significantly different for a group of patients with Alzheimer's disease than for normal controls. In contrast, Butters and colleagues (1988) used "delayed recall/immediate recall × 100" and concluded that patients with Alzheimer's disease forgot verbal information more rapidly than did the control group. Agreeing with Butters and colleagues (1988), Kopelman (1985) reported descriptive data on his samples (including mean immediate recall, delayed recall, and percentage-retained scores from WMS Logical Memory) and found that the control group retained 82%, while the group with dementia retained only 9% of their immediate recall after a 30-min delay. Fourth, a fundamental problem with change and ratio scores, such as percentages, is that they are correlated with, and dependent upon, initial scores (Robinson-Whelen & Storandt, 1992). Fifth, there is variability in the delay length over which retention is assessed, ranging from seconds to hours, and even days.

Expected Performance on WMS-III for Patients with Alzheimer's Disease
The most recent findings providing information on what to expect on the WMS-III for patients with Alzheimer's disease are from a sample of 36 individuals clinically diagnosed with probable Alzheimer's disease who were administered WMS-III and WAIS-III (The Psychological Corporation, 1997). The mean performances on the WMS-III memory indexes ranged from 60.4 for the General Memory Index to 80.4 for the Working Memory Index (WMI). With the exception of the WMI, mean scores on the Indexes were clearly impaired, with scores of 70 or below. Group performances on the memory indexes were much lower relative to the WAIS-III performances. The percentages of the sample scoring 70 or below on the Immediate Memory Index and General Memory Index were 71% and 89%; these contrast with the

percentages scoring below 70 on the WAIS-III scales: 9% (VIQ), 17% (PIQ), 9% (FSIQ). The WMS-III Auditory Process Composites showed that as a group, individuals with Alzheimer's disease demonstrated borderline-to-impaired recall performance after the first presentation of memory stimuli (Single-Trial Learning) and demonstrated little improvement with repeated exposure to the stimuli (Learning Slope). At delayed recall, they had marked difficulty recalling the limited information learned at the immediate condition, which was indicative of abnormal forgetting. Performance on the Recognition Index did not indicate that these individuals have greater access to previously learned information through recognition formats than spontaneous recall (The Psychological Corporation, 1997). These results suggest that impairment in both immediate and delayed recall conditions are notable within a clinical context.

The hallmark of mild-to-moderate-stage Alzheimer's Dementia is a near-normal immediate recall score, coupled with a significant drop in information retained over a delay. Clinicians can examine this issue with the Logical Memory subtest, by comparing Logical Memory I Recall Total Score and Logical Memory II Recall Total Score. Performances of more than 1 SD below normative expectations are often considered sufficient for impairment in day-to-day functioning. This comparison can be a good point for clinicians to begin their interpretation because the task has ecological validity for day-to-day activities (e.g., listening to a news story, being told of a meaningful event, being given new instructions to carry out a task). Examination of Logical Memory I First Recall Total Score (Supplementary Score) allows insight into performance for recalling semantic information in one trial, as the Logical Memory I Recall Total Score (Primary subtest) includes the score for the second administration of the second story.

Next the examiner should consider subtests that assess learning capabilities. Verbal list learning required in Verbal Paired Associates I and II and in Word Lists I and II allows the clinician to examine the efficiency for learning information over several trials, versus performance for semantic (Supplementary Score) information provided in one trial. Inadequate increase over trials in either list learning subtest would suggest a learning impairment and have repercussions for rehabilitation considerations. If a client does not profit from repeated exposure, then rehearsal alone is probably an ineffective way for that individual to learn important material. In such an outcome, the examiner may want to suggest more active techniques such as imagery, use of an acronym, and other methods. Even if only Verbal Paired Associates is administered, the Auditory Process Subtest Total Scores can be calculated and converted to auditory process composites, which allow comparison of Single-Trial Learning percentiles to Learning Slope, Retention, and Retrieval composites. Including Word Lists II allows the added advantage of detecting of potential proactive (interference of initial learning on later learning) or retroactive interference (interference of earlier administered items by later learning) in the process of new learning.

Furthermore, the client is likely to demonstrate memory impairments for both verbal and visual material (Moss & Albert, 1992; Moss, Albert, Butters, & Payne, 1986; Salmon, Granholm, McCullough, Butters, & Grant, 1989; Wilson, Bacon, Fox, & Kaszniak, 1983). If a discrepancy exists between the two, information can be gleaned about which modality allows the most information for better later retrieval. When time permits, the clinician should examine the pervasiveness of a memory deficit through administration of visual information as well. Clinicians who are accustomed to interpreting results of visual designs in previous versions of the WMS have the option of employing the supplementary Visual Reproduction I and II subtests to provide an analogous test of forgetting in the visual memory domain. Otherwise, Family Pictures I and II has ecological validity, in that scenic recall of meaningful information is also required in activities such as encoding newspaper photos or where a car is parked within a layout of a parking lot.

Frontal lobe dementia or subcortical dementias may be differentiated from Alzheimer's disease by a different pattern of memory difficulties, based on organizational problems in the retrieval component required by the WMS-III. These patterns are evident when comparing performances at delay conditions with the recognition formats. A poor performance at delay conditions of subtests, followed by a significantly better score on recognition paradigms (over and above what is expected for the norm), suggest a retrieval problem that could be part of a disease process and would prompt the clinician to consider frontal lobe or subcortical diagnoses (Troster et al., 1993). The examiner should compare General Memory and Auditory Recognition Delayed Total Score to find such a difference in memory performances. Digit Span Forward score should be normal or near-normal, although cognitive tracking required for Digits Backward and Letter-Number Sequencing may show decline. The patient may also experience orientation problems at early stages of Alzheimer's

Dementia (e.g., he or she may have trouble with the exact day of the week or month or may show some sporadic inconsistencies in retrieval of background information).

It is important to note, however, that a diagnosis of a memory impairment alone is not sufficient in making a diagnosis of dementia. An impairment in at least one other cognitive domain, such as language, visual-spatial processing, or problem solving and abstraction, is required for this diagnosis. Finally, when planning a test protocol for individuals with a dementing illness, the examiner should consider the stage at which the dementia is thought to have progressed. Individuals at early stages require more comprehensive testing across many cognitive domains in order to help with differential diagnoses and to characterize the individual's capabilities in detail. In moderate to late stages, individuals with a dementing illness will be more distractible, more prone to fatigue, more confused, and, therefore, less able to tolerate extended testing. Briefer batteries are more appropriate at these stages of the illness, as information regarding level of functioning can be clearly elucidated by administering fewer tests in each cognitive domain. (See Rapid Reference 6.3 for a summary of expected findings for patients with Alzheimer's disease.)

Parkinson's Disease

Parkinson's disease is a progressive neurodegenerative disorder of unknown etiology that is characterized by a severe loss of neurons in the substantia nigra. The illness is thought to affect 1 million individuals in North America, and the incidence and prevalence shows dramatic age-related increases (Civil, Whitehouse, Lanska, & Mayeux, 1993). The prevalence is approximately 150 to 200 cases per 100,000 people and increases after age 65 to nearly 1,100 per 100,000 (Kessler, 1972). Onset of signs and symptoms typically occur in the fifth and sixth decade of life, and are characterized by tremor, muscular rigidity, slowness of movement (bradykinesia), inability to initiate movement (akinesia), flexed posture, gait difficulties, abnormalities in speech, and problems with handwriting (White, Vasterling, Koroshetz, & Myers, 1992). The most characteristic motor abnormalities include chorea, ocular motor dysfunction, and disturbances of voluntary movement, particularly initiation of action (Folstein, 1989; Lanska & Whitehouse, 1989).

The characteristic pattern and progression of the cognitive deficits in

Rapid Reference 6.3

Expected Findings for Patients with Alzheimer's Disease

- Patients have impaired mean scores on the *WMS-III Indexes*, with scores of 70 or below, except on *Working Memory Index*.
- Patients show much lower performance on the *WMS-III Memory Indexes* relative to the *WAIS-III IQs*.
- On *Auditory Process Composites*, patients make little improvement with repeated exposure to the stimuli (*Learning Slope*) after the first presentation of memory stimuli (*Single-Trial Learning*).
- Patients have normal or near-normal performance on *Digit Span Forward*.
- Patients show decline in cognitive tracking required for *Digits Backward* and *Letter-Number Sequencing*.
- Patients show problems on *Orientation* questions at even early stages of the disease (i.e., in the exact day of the week or month, or some sporadic inconsistencies in retrieval of background information).
- Patients have near-normal or reduced *immediate recall* scores, coupled with a significant drop off of information over a delay on the *Logical Memory I Recall Total Score* and *Logical Memory II Recall*.
- Little recognition of information on the *Recognition Index* suggests rapid forgetting.
- Patients have reduced efficiency for learning information over several trials: They have *depressed Word Lists I and II* scores.
- Patients have memory impairments in both verbal and visual domains. The supplementary *Visual Reproduction I and II* subtests provide a test of forgetting in the visual memory domain.

Note: Clinical judgment and other measures must be considered in addition to the aforementioned patterns of performance when making differential diagnoses.

Parkinson's disease include generalized psychomotor slowing; impaired attention, cognitive tracking, flexibility, and executive functioning; deficits on visuospatial tasks; slow organization, slow learning of new information (particularly visuospatial), and difficulties in memory retrieval (White et al., 1992). At early stages, linguistic abilities (including reading and naming) and academic skills (such as spelling and long term memory—sometimes accompanied by effortful retrieval) are relatively intact. With disease progression, verbal fluency and reasoning skills become impaired. With further progression, the patient may have confusional episodes and develop widespread cognitive decline.

Other descriptors that are thought to be pathognomonic include micrographia (small writing), hypophonia (reduced volume of speech), dysarthria (slurred speech), and affective symptomology (White et al., 1992). Symptoms at the time of onset can be informative. Early in the disorder, patients may display unilateral motor symptoms suggestive of hemi-Parkinsonism. Other symptoms noted by referral sources or in the medical history can include confusion, hallucinations, dysphagia (difficulties swallowing), tremors, motor slowing, postural rigidity, masked facies, urinary incontinence, fatigue, and depression.

Parkinson's disease medications can affect test results, particularly on tasks of attention, arousal, executive functioning, and motor speed. Other medication side effects may include confusion and hallucinations; therefore, the clinician should note medications and dosages as well as any on-off phenomena, if observed (White et al., 1992). Most patients with Parkinson's disease experience some change in cognitive function early in the disorder and show a progressive deterioration in some functional capacities as the disease progresses (White et al., 1992). Mayeux and colleagues (1992) estimate that by 85 years of age, more than 65% of individuals with Parkinson's disease have dementia. Differences in the pattern of neuropsychological changes suggest ways in which the pathology underlying the dementias differs (Brown & Marsden, 1988; Cummings, 1986; Dubois, Boller, Pillon, & Agid, 1991; Mahler & Cummings, 1990; Whitehouse, 1986).

Summary of the Neuropsychological Profile for Parkinson's Disease

Studies have resulted in conflicting results with respect to verbal and visual memory in Parkinson's disease. Some investigators demonstrate both recall and recognition memory are impaired in Parkinson's disease (Gotham, Brown & Marsden, 1988; Halgin, Riklan, & Misiak, 1977; Helkala, Laulumaa, Soininen, & Riekkinen, 1989; Mortimer, Pirozzolo, Hansch, & Webster, 1982; Tweedy, Langer, & McDowell, 1982). Other investigators report that immediate recall or recognition are comparable to normal controls (Delis, Direnfeld, Alexander, & Kaplan, 1982; Sullivan, Sagar, Gabrieli, Corkin, & Growdon, 1989; Tweedy et al., 1982). Similarly, studies on visual memory report that participants with Parkinson's have slowed response times on tasks (Horn, 1974) and intact immediate recognition memory (Flowers, Pearce, & Pearce, 1984; Horn, 1974;

Sullivan & Sagar, 1988). One study found delayed recognition memory impaired relative to controls (Sullivan & Sagar, 1988), while another study found it intact (Flowers et al., 1994). White and colleagues (1992) concluded that the literature on Parkinson's Disease is limited by the heterogeneity of participants, including the potential confound of concurrent Alzheimer's disease in some studies that would not be detected by screening methods used in several studies. Their clinical experience suggests that even at very early stages, individuals with Parkinson's disease are slow in their ability to learn new material, particularly lists, paired associates, or visual material, and they are generally more efficient in learning and remembering verbal, versus spatial, information.

Expected Performance on the WMS-III for Patients with Parkinson's Disease

Verbal list learning and paired-associates performances are likely to demonstrate slow acquisition over trials, due to problems organizing unstructured material and retrieval difficulties. For material presented only once, immediate recall performances, particularly for visual material, may not be quite normal, but the drop-off between immediate and delayed recall should not be as severe as the drop-off observed in patients with Alzheimer's disease. In fact, there may be an increase in information provided at the delay condition, which is known as "inconsistent retrieval" in Parkinson's disease. Furthermore, recognition paradigms are likely to yield better scores than immediate recall, which would exceed the expected increase in normal individuals. Visuospatial memory scores may be depressed overall in comparison to verbal memory scores. Mental control performance is likely to be problematic and or slow. Tasks that require drawing may be completed in prolonged times and be labored due to problems with fine-motor control and tremor. Visuoperceptual tasks, without a motor component, may be problematic as well, due to a primary visuospatial deficit (White et al., 1992). (See Rapid Reference 6.4 for a summary of expected findings for patients with Parkinson's disease.)

Caveats Regarding Assessment of Dementia

While the described patterns constitute common expected outcomes on WMS-III testing, there is individual variation, such that Alzheimer's disease or Parkinson's disease should not necessarily be ruled out if the protocol does not

≡≡*Rapid Reference 6.4*

Expected Findings for Patients with Parkinson's Disease

- Patients show slow acquisition over trials, due to problems in organizing un-structured material; retrieval difficulties are evident in *verbal list learning* and *paired-associates* performances.
- Patients have sub-normal *immediate recall* performances, particularly for vi-sual material that is presented only once. However, the discrepancy be-tween immediate and delayed recall is not as severe as that observed in patients with Alzheimer's disease.
- Patients have stronger *recognition* than *immediate recall* (exceeding the ex-pected increase in normal individuals).
- Patients have depressed overall *visual-spatial* memory scores in comparison to *verbal memory* scores.
- Patients have problematic or slow performance on *mental control*.
- Patients have slow and labored performance on *drawing tasks* due to prob-lems with fine-motor control and tremor.
- Patients have difficulty on *visual-perceptual* tasks due to a primary visual-spatial deficit.

Note: Clinical judgment and other measures must be considered in addition to the aforemen-tioned patterns of performance when making differential diagnoses.

conform to the described memory profile. For example, it is not uncommon for individuals with Alzheimer's disease to obtain significantly better scores at recognition conditions in early stages of the disease. The examiner should con-sider performance in other cognitive domains outside of memory, including ex-ecutive function, language, visual-spatial processes, personality, and behavioral observation, as well as age of onset and course of progression, to allow for more accurate differential diagnoses. However, as is the case for memory, there are variations within other domains. A clinical approach that uses information from test patterns and observations made by the patient's medical team and close family members will be most successful at differential diagnoses.

Schizophrenia

Schizophrenia is a chronic psychiatric disorder characterized by positive symp-toms that include hallucinations, delusions, and thought disorders, and negative symptoms that include anhedonia, avolition, and flattening of affect (American Psychiatric Association, 1994; Andreasen & Carpenter, 1993). The lifetime prevalence is 0.5 to 1.0% (Andreasen & Carpenter, 1993). Peak age of onset for men is between 18 and 25 years, whereas women report a broader peak, ranging from about 26 to 45 years of age (Wyatt, Alexander, Egan, & Kirch, 1988). Limbic-diencephalic, prefrontal, and temporal lobe neocortical regions are the most common sites of structural and physiological dysfunction (Seidman, Cassens, Kremen, & Pepple, 1992).

Inconsistencies in the Research on Schizophrenia

The studies we review on schizophrenia and the Wechsler Memory Scales reveal variations in methodology that may be related to inconsistencies in the results on memory functioning noted across studies. Some of the variation between studies includes samples that are composed of participants of different severity, chronicity, and subtypes of schizophrenia. Some studies group all subtypes of schizophrenic individuals together but specify whether individuals are categorized as paranoid, catatonic, undifferentiated, or schizoaffective, while other studies do not specify the subcategories of their sample. Types of medication and duration of administration vary across samples, although the majority of studies specify the proportion of individuals who are on antipsychotic or anticholinergic medications, and some even indicate average doses. An important variable in these studies is the potential effect of medications, because the majority of patients with schizophrenia are treated with anticholinergics. While there is conflicting literature on specific effects, antipsychotics may improve memory function, while anticholinergic agents may impair cognitive ability (King, 1994; Stirling, Hellewell, & Hewitt, 1997). Level of cognitive impairment is also different across studies, with some selecting participants who are above or below a specified IQ level or Mini Mental Status Exam (MMSE) score in order to restrict samples to nondemented individuals. Recent studies have examined first-episode patients who have not yet been treated with medication, in an effort to characterize neuropsychological profiles early in the disease state and to address the potential medication-confound problem. There is demographic variation between and within studies with respect to selection of controls. Also, interpretation of memory data varies depending on whether specific aspects of memory are grouped together or parsed into components such as attention, immediate recall, delayed recall, and forgetting rate (savings), across a delay period. Hawkins, Hoffman and colleagues, (1997) suggest that interpreting verbal memory may be confounded with negative symptoms, because verbal test performances require socially assertive behavior. Debate also continues about whether memory deficits represent a selective impairment in the context of global cognitive impairment (Saykin, Gur, & Gur, 1991; Saykin et al., 1992) or are part of generalized dysfunction (Blanchard & Neale, 1994). Some researchers favor the view of a true amnestic impairment versus poorly organized initial absorption of information (Hawkins, Sullivan & Choi, 1997). In making this distinction, some researchers emphasize the frontal-executive dysfunction in this disease (Morice & Delahunty, 1996). Many emphasize that the true representation of cognitive deficits in schizophrenia include both memory and frontal-executive dysfunction, representing multiple, interconnected neurobehavioral deficiencies (Brewer, Edwards, Anderson, Robinson, & Pantelis, 1996; Hawkins et al., 1977; Nester et al., 1993).

Findings on WMS-III and Schizophrenia

Memory scores appear to be consistently affected in patients with schizophrenia. Several studies have examined the degree of this impairment in comparison with other clinical groups. Hawkins (1998) examined data presented in the technical manual of the WMS-III, comparing results produced by a group of schizophrenics ($N = 42$) to previous studies conducted using the WMS-R on individuals with schizophrenia. In his reformulation of published data from the *Manual,* he highlighted the better performances by patients with schizophrenia and traumatic brain injury compared to patients with Alzheimer's disease and Korsakoff's syndrome on both Immediate and General Memory indexes. Patients with schizophrenia were also able to learn verbally presented information over several trials at a rate comparable to that of TBI patients, where as learning slopes for patients with Alzheimer's disease and Korsakoff's syndrome were substantially impaired, in comparison. Furthermore, the study shows that General Memory Indexes are not substantially weaker than General Intellectual Indexes in patients with schizophrenia; on average, the Full Scale IQ-General Memory Index discrepancy for the schizophrenia group was 7.1 points. Reported average scores for specific WMS-III Indexes include an Auditory Immediate Index score of 83.3, Visual Immediate Index score of 82.3, Auditory Delayed Index score of 84.4, and Visual Delayed Index score of

79.3. Hawkins (1997) concludes that the memory difficulties in schizophrenia are consistent with the level of deficit reported in other domains, including speed of information processing, novel problem solving, and executive functioning, and therefore does not represent a selective impairment.

Several studies compared memory performances of individuals with schizophrenia versus performances of bipolar individuals on the WMS-III to contrast memory capabilities in two disease states that include psychotic symptoms. Results generally demonstrate milder clinical symptoms and cognitive impairments in bipolar participants. Hobart, Goldberg, Bartko, and Gold (1999) found significant differences between estimated FSIQs in favor of the bipolar group (schizophrenia mean = 69; bipolar mean = 76.3). Memory testing in both of the groups revealed higher scores for the bipolar group on Logical Memory I (schizophrenia mean = 4.6; bipolar mean = 6.7) and Visual Reproduction I (schizophrenia mean = 3.8; bipolar mean 6.0). No significant differences were observed between groups on Logical Memory II (schizophrenia mean = 3.8; bipolar mean = 6.4) and Visual Reproduction II (schizophrenia mean = 5.3; bipolar mean = 6.6).

Findings on WMS-R

Brewer and colleagues (1996) compared performances for select subtests of the WMS-R for patients with schizophrenia ($N = 26$) and controls ($N = 19$) who were matched on age and premorbid IQ. They found significant differences in favor of controls for Visual Reproduction I (schizophrenia mean = 28.5; control mean = 36.2) and Verbal Memory Index (schizophrenia mean = 77.7; control mean = 90.6).

Hawkins, Sullivan, and Choi (1997) reviewed the literature on the WMS-R and schizophrenia to address competing theories on the essential characteristics of memory dysfunction and their neurobiological bases. The two extremes of the discussion include the "general deficit state" hypothesis that patients with schizophrenia exhibit broad cognitive deficiencies, and the conclusion that memory deficiencies are especially pronounced. Hawkins, Sullivan, and Choi (1997) conclude that the literature supports an intermediary position. Patients with schizophrenia display broad cognitive deficiencies, but they experience especially pronounced difficulties in executive functioning, abstract reasoning, attention, concentration, and new learning. However, they do *not* demonstrate poor retention rates, which would reflect a failure to consolidate information for later retrieval (Sass et al., 1992). Hawkins, Sullivan, and Choi conclude that their study and others like it do not reveal abnormal savings scores; Delayed Recall indexes are *not* lower than IQ or immediate measures of recall. In sum, the WMS-R data presents little evidence of a primary amnestic disorder (Hawkins, Sullivan, & Choi, 1997).

Gold, Randolph, Carpenter, Goldberg, and Weinberger (1992) address performances of patients with schizophrenia relative to other clinical groups. The majority of their study patients ($N = 45$) obtained General Memory and Delayed Memory Indexes that *were* significantly different from their FSIQs on the WAIS-R. The degree of impairment in schizophrenia fell between 1 and 2 SDs on WMS-R Indexes. Average scores on the WMS-R Indexes, including general, verbal, visual, attention, and delay, were comparable. Full Scale IQ exceeded the General Memory Index by an average of 8.64 points, and the mean discrepancy between FSIQ and the Delayed Memory Index score was 5.13. Additionally, approximately one third of the participants had FSIQ versus General Memory Index and FSIQ versus Delayed Memory Index splits of 15 points or more. A difference of 15 or more points on FSIQ versus Delayed Memory Index is found in only 10% of normal participants (Bornstein, Chelune, & Prifitera, 1989). Next, Gold and colleagues (1992) found that verbal and visual memory indexes were nearly identical, suggesting equivalent levels of impairment across stimulus materials. Calculations of savings scores, which reflect retention of information from the immediate to the delayed conditions, revealed high percentages. For the Logical Memory and Visual Reproduction subtests, the mean score of patients with schizophrenia indicated a 74% savings on both, suggesting equivalent performances across modalities. In contrast, Hawkins, Sullivan, and Choi (1997) found that Visual Memory was substantially higher than the other WMS-R Indexes, which was due to the relative strength of visual new learning rather than a weakness in verbal learning. Gold and colleagues (1992) concluded that other nonmemory neuropsychological measures explained little of the variance in the IQ-memory comparisons, suggesting that memory dysfunction is a selective impairment, and not simply an indication of general cognitive deterioration in patients with schizophrenia. Additionally, attention and memory performances did not covary. The researchers also found that the discrepancies between IQ and Delayed and General Memory Indexes of patients with schizophrenia could not be attributed to anticholinergic medications.

Finally, several studies have documented a working memory deficit in schizophrenia (Dupre, Prieto, Davidson, & Davis, 1995; Keefe et al., 1992; Rossel and David, 1997), and some have suggested that a working memory deficit accounts for at least part of the frontal dysfunction observed (Gold et al., 1997). Brebion, Amador, Smith, and Gorman (1998) proposed that the slowed processing speed linked to cognitive disorders, including memory in aged populations, may also account for at least part of the observed difficulties in memory impairments in schizophrenia.

Expected Findings for Patients with Schizophrenia on the WMS-III

The *WAIS-III and WMS-III Technical Manual* (The Psychological Corporation, 1997) reported mean performances of 42 individuals with schizophrenia who were administered the WAIS-III and WMS-III (see Rapid Reference 6.5 for a summary of expected findings). Mildly lower scores on WMS-III General Memory Index compared to WAIS-III FSIQ are expected. On the WMS-III, Primary Indexes ranged from 79.1 (Immediate Memory Index) to 86.1 (Auditory Recognition Delayed Index). Participants scored in the Low-Average to Borderline ranges on every Primary Index. These results do not suggest trends with regard to auditory or visual modality-specific deficits. A pattern of reduced efficiency for acquiring new verbal information on repeated procedures

---

≡Rapid Reference 6.5

Expected Findings for Patients with Schizophrenia

- Patients have mildly lower WMS-III *General (Delayed) Memory Index* compared to *WAIS-III FSIQ.*
- *Primary Indexes* are in the Low Average to Average range.
- There is reduced efficiency for acquiring *new verbal information* on repeated procedures.
- Patients have a small advantage on the *Visual Immediate* and *Visual Delayed Indexes* over the *Verbal Immediate* and *Delayed* scores.
- Patients have lower *Working Memory Index* than *Delayed Index* scores.
- *Percent retention* scores for verbal and visual information are at or above approximately 75.

Note: Clinical judgment and other measures must be considered in addition to the aforementioned patterns of performance when making differential diagnoses.

is expected, but differences between immediate and delayed performances for verbal and visual material are not expected to be large; and percent retention scores should be at or above approximately 75 points. An advantage of the Visual Immediate and Delayed Indexes over the Verbal Immediate and Delayed scores may be observed (Hawkins, Sullivan, & Choi, 1997). Working Memory Index may be lower than Delayed Indexes. The premise that individuals with schizophrenia demonstrate impairments on tasks measuring attention, processing speed, and working memory was only mildly supported by mean scores on the WAIS-III: Verbal Comprehension Index (VCI) (93) > Working Memory Index (WMI) (85) and Perceptual Organization Index (POI) (90) > Processing Speed Index (PSI) (83) (The Psychological Corporation, 1997).

Substance Abuse

Alcohol and drug abuse are major problems in contemporary American society (Parsons, 1996). There has been a significant amount of research on the topic in the past few decades. In this section we focus on the memory and general cognitive effects of alcohol, amphetamine, cocaine, and marijuana abuse.

Methodological Issues

Many studies have demonstrated cognitive deficits in patients with chronic substance abuse (Pope & Yurgelun-Todd, 1996), but specific methodological issues affect the results of this line of research. First, studies often rely upon self-report data for length of time and frequency of substance use. This method of data collection is problematic, as many studies show that memory is affected as a result of substance abuse. Second, users often have a history of moving from one substance of choice to another, as well as combining substances, so that making distinctions between groups along length of time and frequency dimensions is difficult. Third, there is variability across studies with respect to operationalizing mild, moderate, and heavy usage, as well as periods of abstinence required before study. This variability, in turn, calls into question interpretation of cognitive deficits, as it is difficult to discern whether the findings result from withdrawal symptoms, residual effects of the drug in the system, and changes (damage) in the central nervous system. Fourth, choice of control groups vary: Some studies employ normal control groups, whose members have never had a history of abusing the substance studied; others use groups consisting of mild users, in order to partially account for lifestyle and background differences between groups. Fifth, another source of variability in studies includes the methods for studying cognitive changes. For example, many researchers examine effects on verbal and visual memory separately, while others do not (Pope & Yurgelun-Todd, 1996). Finally, criteria for inclusion differ between studies, although most try to rule out individuals with a history of head trauma, past psychiatric illness, and use of psychotropic medications.

Alcohol Abuse

Mann, Gunter, Stetter, and Ackermann's (1999) review of the literature reveals neuropsychological impairment across several countries. Studies conducted in the United States (Beatty, Hames, Blanco, Nixon, & Tivis, 1996; Nixon & Bowlby, 1996; Parsons, 1977; Tarter, 1980), Canada (Wilkinson, 1987), England (Acker, 1986), and Australia (Cala, Jones, Mastaglia, & Wiley, 1993) have demonstrated deficits in cognitive flexibility, problem solving, verbal and nonverbal abstraction, visual-motor coordination, learning, and memory, as well as specific intellectual functions. Specific findings on the WAIS (Wechsler, 1955) include depressed scores on Block Design, Digit Symbol, and Object Assembly, while other subtest scores appear relatively unaffected (Ellis & Oscar-Berman, 1989; Parsons & Farr, 1981). Many researchers agree that memory and learning difficulties endure beyond detoxification (Butters & Granholm, 1987; Ellis & Oscar-Berman, 1989), but the quality and severity of the impairment remain unclear. O'Mahony and Doherty (1996) address the inconsistent results across studies using the WMS. Early works indicated that alcohol abusers showed little, if any, deficit on the WMS (Parsons & Prigatano, 1977). Butters, Cermak, Montgomery, and Adinolfi (1977) found their alcoholic (non-Korsakoff's syndrome) sample did not differ from the control sample. Later studies varied with respect to demonstration of differences between alcoholic and nonalcoholic populations, as well as the obtained pattern of deficits. For example, Loberg (1980) found his sample of alcoholics to be superior to normal controls on the WMS. Nixon, Kujawski, Parsons, and Yohman (1987) and Shelton and Parsons (1987) reported deficits on both verbal and nonverbal subtests of the WMS. Hightower and Anderson (1986) showed verbal memory to be more deficient. O'Mahony and Doherty (1993) demonstrated deficits in both verbal and nonverbal memory on the WMS-R.

O'Mahony and Doherty (1996) attempted to clarify the typical alcoholic pattern on the WMS by studying two samples of detoxified, hospital-treated abusers who were administered a neuropsychological assessment. To address whether WAIS-R findings would conform to WAIS findings reported in the literature, they gave the WAIS to half the experimental group and the WAIS-R to the other. They administered the Logical Memory and Visual Reproduction subtests of the WMS, as well as Trails A and B. All test scores were age-scaled and transformed to yield a mean of 10 and an SD of 3. Their sample included 86 participants, the majority of whom were inpatients of a private general psychiatric hospital referred for assessment of suspected cognitive impairments associated with alcohol abuse. At the time of study, all inpatients were attending the hospital's alcohol treatment program. Exclusion criteria ruled out individuals with a primary diagnosis other than alcohol dependence; history of head injury; cerebrovascular accident or any other major medical disorder apart from liver disease; and abstinence duration of less than 3 weeks prior to the examination. No control group was used. Findings corroborate previous WAIS studies in that Block Design and Digit Symbol scores were below average on both versions of the intellectual assessment, and they were relatively lower than Vocabulary and Digit Span, which were at least average on both versions. Next, memory variables were significantly less than the normative 10 in every case including Logical Memory and Visual Reproduction Immediate and Delayed conditions. Both Trails tests also were significantly different from the normative value 10. While results are clear in this pure sample of participants, the authors caution that a selection effect was possible, as this group was referred for apparent clinical impairment, and therefore individuals were likely to suffer from mild to moderate cognitive impairment. However, these participants were also thought to represent the general population, as indexed by their Vocabulary subtest scores. The finding of deficit in both verbal and nonverbal memory functioning among these groups indicates that chronic (subcatastrophic) alcohol abuse *can* result in significant memory deficits that have adaptive significance.

Mann and colleagues (1999) studied a sample of German alcoholics to determine the effect of controlled abstinence on the *recovery* of cognitive test results. The alcohol dependent participants ($N = 49$) had been abstinent from alcohol for 18 to 30 days and took part in an inpatient treatment program that did not include cognitive rehabilitation. Patients had been alcohol dependent for an average of 11 years and the average daily alcohol consumption was about 18 standard drinks. They were compared to healthy males matched for age, education, and marital status ($N = 49$). Tests included the WMS and other tests used in German-speaking countries. These were administered at two time periods: at the beginning of the inpatient treatment (abstinence established 5 days before testing), and 5 weeks later. At the beginning of treatment, alcoholics scored significantly lower than matched controls on 5 out of 12 neuropsychological parameters including Trail Making B Time, Auditory Verbal Learning Test (AVLT) Immediate Recall, and tasks of verbal knowledge, nonverbal reasoning, and spatial imagination. The alcoholics showed impairment in verbal as well as nonverbal performance, which provides support for the "mild generalized dysfunction hypothesis" (Tivis, Beatty, Nixon, & Parson, 1995). They did not show any differences on the Benton Visual Retention test and Logical Memory test, which are related nonverbal and verbal memory functions. After several weeks of abstinence, differences between control individuals and patients were reduced to nonsignificant levels for all but the verbal short-term memory measure, the AVLT. Significant interaction effects confirmed that patients' neuropsychological performance increased significantly more than that of controls for verbal and nonverbal tests, as well as for complex cognitive tasks such as the Trail Making Test. No substantial correlations between duration and dependence of abuse and neuropsychological performance were established, suggesting that linear relationship between duration of alcohol dependence and neuropsychological performance may be too simplistic to describe the dose-response relation. The authors note that other studies have come to the same conclusion: An alcoholic's drinking history does not relate significantly to the speed or extent of recovery (Goldman, 1995). They conclude that specific drinking patterns, including repeated withdrawal, physical impairment induced by alcohol, and even personality characteristics should be considered as moderators when assessing dose-response patterns.

Amphetamine Abuse

McKetin and Mattick (1998) contrasted groups of participants who had high amphetamine dependence ($N = 11$) and low dependence ($N = 15$) to a normal control group on Indexes of the WMS-R. They found that severely dependent amphetamine users performed at approximately 0.5 SD below non–

drug using controls on the WMS-R Index of Verbal Memory, Attention/Concentration and Delayed Recall. Importantly, the magnitude of impairment in the highly dependent amphetamine users was less than what is considered clinical memory impairment (approximately 1 SD; Wechsler, 1987) and reflects a *mild* impairment that still falls within the range of normal functioning. The mildly dependent amphetamine users exhibited no evidence of impairment relative to non–drug using controls. An unexpected finding was that the low dependence group performed better than controls on the WMS-R Verbal Memory Index. This may have been due to the small sample size for the amphetamine users or due to other artifacts produced by a factor that was not measured. The authors note that they did not include variables such as use of tobacco and benzodiazepines, premorbid factors, fatigue, nutrition, and mood state, and also comment that cognitive impairment could be withdrawal-related. In addition, severely dependent users were more likely to inject amphetamine, which could make a different contribution to cognitive impairment, although researchers did not study this variable. They suggested a prospective study to better address whether cognitive impairment is related to amphetamine dependence, and to address the time course of such impairment (McKetin & Mattick, 1998).

Cocaine and Polydrug Abuse

Roselli and Ardila's (1996) review of the literature suggests that while acute behavioral effects of cocaine are relatively well known, the cognitive consequences of chronic cocaine abuse are less clearly defined. Washton and Gold (1984) report that 57% of their sample experienced memory problems. Manschreck and colleagues (1988) report persistent short-term memory disturbances. Press (1983) found worse, but nonsignificantly different, performance for cocaine abusers than normals on the Luria-Nebraska Neuropsychological Battery, with performance on a verbal memory subtest being most impaired in the cocaine abuser group. Mitteberg and Motta (1993) describe memory and learning difficulties in cocaine abusers. Ardila, Rosselli, & Strumwasser (1991) studied neuropsychological performances in 27 chronic freebase cocaine (crack) abusers. Performances were lower than expected for their age and educational levels as observed through significant impairment in short-term memory and attention. Neuropsychological test scores were correlated with lifetime amount of cocaine used, suggesting a direct relation between abuse and cognitive impairment. Bernal and colleagues (1994) administered a basic neuropsychological test battery to 64 adolescents who were divided into two groups, drug abusers and non–drug abusers. Psychoactive substances included marijuana, "basuco," solvent inhalation, gasoline inhalation, and alcohol. In general, performance was mildly, but nonsignificantly, lower in the user group than in the control group. Only some neuropsychological test scores correlated with the length of use and amount of psychoactive drug use. The authors conclude their review by noting that psychoactive substance abuse has been associated with conduct disorders and personality disorders. In antisocial personality disorders, there is a predisposition to develop psychoactive substance use. However, research that addresses developmental history, risk factors of brain dysfunction, and subjective phenomena found in drug users is scarce.

Rosselli and Ardila (1996) studied neuropsychological test performances of chronic cocaine-dependent and poly-drug abusers. They compared neuropsychological performances of cocaine-dependent participants ($N = 61$), poly-drug–dependent participants ($N = 59$), and normal controls ($N = 63$). Experimental participants were living under permanent supervision in rehabilitation centers, where drugs were unavailable. Most often, participants initially used marijuana, and then later began to use other psychoactive substances. None of the participants in the cocaine group had a history of alcohol dependence, but about one half of the experimental participants and one third of the controls used to drink alcohol at least once a week. About 80% of the participants in the dependent groups were smokers, which is approximately 10 times as many smokers than in the nondependent group. Parental age and level of education were not different among groups. Tests administered included the WMS, WAIS, Boston Naming Test, Trails, Wisconsin Card Sorting Test, Verbal Fluency, and Rey-Osterrieth Complex Figure (ROCF). There were no differences between the test profiles of the two user groups. Depressed scores were observed on some verbal memory subtests (Logical Memory-Immediate for both groups, and Delayed for the cocaine group only) and on nonverbal memory subtests (delayed reproduction of the ROCF, both groups). The WMS Memory Quotient correlated negatively with frequency and duration of use. The persistence and severity of these cognitive impairment abnormalities have been previously correlated with the amount of drug used (Cummings & Benson, 1992). Scores on the Wisconsin Card Sorting Test were approximately 1 SD below the normative scores, whereas scores on Trails, Verbal Fluency, copy of the ROCF, and naming subtests were within the normal range. Results supported the presence of a mild, but significant, persisting cognitive deficit associated with chronic cocaine and poly-drug abuse when compared with the normal control group. Persisting neuropsychological deficits in nonverbal abstraction, motor-perceptual integration, and memory have previously been described in substance-dependent patterns even after several drug-free months (Grant & Judd, 1976; Grant, Mohns, Miller, & Reitan, 1976; Mittenberg & Motta, 1993; Murray, Greene, & Adams, 1971).

Hypothesized reasons for a lack of difference between user groups were that some members of the poly-drug group had used cocaine, and while cocaine abusers had used cocaine as the primary drug, many had used other substances (Rosselli & Ardila, 1996). Isolating cognitive effects of different substances is therefore difficult. Age also appears to be an important variable when studying the effects of psychoactive substances on the brain (Bernal, Ardila, & Bateman, 1994). In their study, the experimental participants were young (mean age of all participants was 26, ranging between 15 and 48 years). Grant and Judd (1976) propose that chronic poly-drug abuse can produce a chronic dementia that may not reverse with abstinence. Dementia is more common among elderly alcoholics than it is among younger individuals who drink for a similar period of time (Cummings & Benson, 1992). Furthermore, dementia in alcoholics is more likely to occur after 10 to 15 years of continuous drinking than if the history was marked by periods of abstinences (Cummings & Benson, 1992). In Rosselli and Ardila's sample, the average length of cocaine abuse was limited and most users had frequent periods of abstinence.

Roselli and Ardilla's results were generally consistent with the neuropsychological profile usually found in chronic psychoactive substance abusers (Adams, Rennik, Schooff, & Keegan, 1975; Carlin, 1986; Carlin, Strauss, Grant, & Adams, 1978; Carlin & Trupin, 1977; Hartman, 1988; Mittenberg & Motta, 1993; Washton & Gold, 1984). Memory (followed by abstraction and attention) appeared most vulnerable to chronic cocaine use. Moreover, these results suggest that cocaine does not produce a pattern of neuropsychological deficits different from that of other psychoactive drugs. The researchers contrasted findings in the cocaine sample with those found previously for alcohol abusers. Attention, impaired abstraction, poor short-term memory (Cummings & Benson, 1992) and the absence of aphasic symptoms are similar between groups. In alcoholics, however, nonverbal performance is usually more affected than verbal skills and verbal fluency is usually unimpaired (Victor & Adams, 1985).

Marijuana Use

Pope and Yurgelun-Todd (1996) examined the residual effects of marijuana in Boston college students. This study contrasted performances of two samples of college undergraduates divided into heavy users ($N = 65$), who had smoked marijuana a median of 29 days of the past 30 days (range 22 to 30 days) and displayed cannabinoids in their urine, and light users ($N = 64$), who had smoked a median of one day in the last 30 days (range 0 to 9 days) and displayed no urinary cannabinoids. Participants received a battery of standard neuropsychological tests to assess general intellectual functioning (WAIS-R), abstraction ability (Wisconsin Card Sorting Test, WCST), sustained attention (Stroop), verbal fluency (Benton), and ability to learn and recall new verbal and visuospatial information [WMS, ROCF, and California Verbal Learning Test (CVLT)]. Analyses controlled for potential confounding variables in the two groups, including level of premorbid cognitive functioning and use of alcohol and other substances.

The findings suggest that heavy marijuana use is associated with reduced function of the attentional/executive system (as demonstrated through decreased mental flexibility and increased perseveration on the Wisconsin Card Sorting Task) and reduced learning (as observed on the CVLT). Interestingly, the ability to retain newly learned information after a temporal delay appeared intact in the heavy users, as exhibited by the absence of decay on the delayed recall conditions of the CVLT and ROCF. The authors suggest that while marijuana use may compromise some memory function, the principal effect is in the attentional/executive system, with recall memory functions remaining relatively unaffected. While multiple brain systems may be affected by marijuana use, the most pronounced effects appear to be in sustained attention, mediated by brain stem structures, and in the capacity to shift attention, associated with prefrontal cortices. Additionally, the findings were more prominent among men than women, despite there being no difference between male and female heavy users (in reported recent or lifetime marijuana consumption). The researchers suggest that men may ingest greater total dosages of cannabinoids during individual smoking episodes (Pope & Yurgelan-Todd, 1996).

Expected findings on the WMS-III for Patients with Substance Abuse

Studies of neuropsychological effects of alcohol abuse reveal dysfunction in verbal and visual memory, psychomotor speed, visual-spatial tasks with a timed component, and executive system and set-switching difficulties. For memory assessment, WMS-III Digit Span, Letter-Number Sequencing, Logical Memory I and II, Word Lists I and II, and Visual Reproduction I and II allow comparisons between learning and memory in both auditory and visual domains and immediate-versus-delayed performances (either or both can be affected in substance abuse). Problems in arousal, psychomotor speed, and visual-spatial functioning might be better detected through the WAIS-III than the WMS-III. Specifically, performances on Digit-Symbol Coding and Letter-Number Sequencing are likely to be below average. The visual-spatially loaded subtests of the Performance scale, such as Block Design and the supplementary Object Assembly, are likely to be lower than average as well. Arousal, psychomotor speed, and visual-spatial difficulties may also be present, but less evident, on the WMS-III (slight depression of Immediate and Delayed Visual Memory Indexes as well as the Auditory Delayed Index). Furthermore, careful behavioral observation may be revealing (e.g., time required for drawing figures, difficulties modulating attention, fatigue factors, need for breaks, etc.). Administering supplementary tests such as Visual Reproduction Copy and Discrimination Total Score can evaluate visual-spatial capabilities that may account for visual memory problems.

Cocaine and poly-drug use are likely to be associated with depressed scores on attention/concentration and short-term memory measures, including auditory, and perhaps to a lesser degree, visual memory deficits. Reduced performances are therefore expected on verbal memory measures, such as the Logical Memory and Associative Learning subtests; this poorer performance is expected to a lesser degree, for visual memory subtests such as the Faces II or Visual Reproduction II. General Memory performance is expected to decline as duration of use increases.

Individuals with substance abuse problems frequently use marijuana. Chronic marijuana use has been associated with reduced function of the attentional/executive system (as demonstrated through decreased mental flexibility and increased perseveration on tasks requiring hypothesis-testing and set maintenance and switching) and reduced learning, as observed on list learning tasks (e.g., CVLT), although retention of learned material is intact. Chronic

Rapid Reference 6.6

Expected Findings for Patients with Substance Abuse

Alcohol Abuse

- learning and memory deficits on *Logical Memory I and II* and *Visual Reproduction I and II*
- verbal learning problems on *Word Lists I and II* or *Verbal Paired Associates I and II*
- reduced *Working Memory* or *Processing Speed Indexes*

Amphetamine Abuse

- mildly reduced performances on *Verbal Memory* and *Attention/Concentration Indexes*
- difficulties in *delayed recall* conditions and *Working Memory Indexes*

Poly-substance Abuse

- difficulties in *attention*
- poor *short-term memory*
- difficulties in *verbal immediate, verbal delayed,* and *visual delayed* memory

Marijuana Abuse

- problems in *attention*
- relatively unaffected *recall memory* functions

Note: Clinical judgment and other measures must be considered in addition to the aforementioned patterns of performance when making differential diagnoses.

marijuana use may also negatively affect performance on learning and memory measures, such as Word List I and II and Verbal Paired Associates I and II, as well as supplemental measures of frontal-executive functioning outside of the WMS-III, such as the Wisconsin Card Sorting Test. (See Rapid Reference 6.6 for a summary of expected findings for patients with substance abuse.)

Malingering

Detection of malingering, or feigned illness for secondary gain, is an important consideration for clinicians, particularly for those who assess individuals involved in litigation after suffering a brain injury. Neuropsychologists are increasingly involved in areas of civil law where malingering is a possibility, including Worker's Compensation, disability/competency determination, and personal injury (McMahon & Satz, 1981). Bernard (1990) found little in his review of the literature addressing dissimulation on standardized tests commonly used by neuropsychologists. He emphasizes the importance of research in this area, particularly with respect to evaluation of memory functioning, as memory complaints are among the most common that neuropsychologists receive (Brandt, 1988). One survey found that the Wechsler Memory Scale was the most frequently used test, outranking the Halstead Reitan Neuropsychological Battery (Piotrowsky & Lubin, 1989). Despite the high rate of WMS usage, little information exists on feigned memory performances for the Wechsler Memory measures, as is the case for neuropsychological testing in general.

Methodological Issues

Iverson and Franzen (1996) present two general methodologies for studying malingering. The laboratory approach uses simulation designs to create scenarios that represent situations found in actual clinical practice. These include asking participants to simulate brain damage by performing on assessment procedures in a manner consistent with how they thought brain-damaged patients would perform (Benton & Spreen, 1961; Brandt, Rubinsky, & Lassen, 1985; Wiggins & Brandt, 1988). A variation of this methodology involves creating experimental malingering scenarios in which the examiner instructs the participant to simulate *malingering,* as opposed to *brain damage* (Bagby, Gillis, Toner, & Goldberg, 1991; Bernard, 1990; Hiscock & Hiscock, 1989; Iverson, Franzen, & McCracken, 1991). The second methodology employs actual malingerers or participants with inferred motivation to malinger, reporting findings from single cases (Binder, 1992, Pankratz, Binder, & Wilcox, 1987; Pankratz, Fausti, & Peed, 1975) and from group designs, which are limited by practical problems of locating and studying actual malingerers or identifying large samples with inferred motivation to malinger (Binder, Villaneuva, Howieson, & Moore, 1993; Binder & Willis, 1991; Lee, Loring, & Martin, 1992; Millis, 1992).

Researchers have employed two primary test strategies for assessing malingered memory deficits (Iverson & Franzen, 1996). The first consists of examining the performance of simulators, experimental-malingerers, or participants with inferred motivation to malinger on standard assessment procedures. The second involves studying group differences on tests specifically designed to detect nonoptimal performance, such as the Memorization of 15 Items Test (Lee et al., 1992; Schretlen, Brandt, Krafft, & Van Gorp, 1991), the modified 16 Items Test (Paul, Franzen, Cohen, & Fremouw, 1992), symptom validity testing (forced-choice task based on the patients' own claimed symptoms (Bernard Houstong & Natoli, 1993), and a variety of other forced-choice test procedures. The forced-choice paradigm is the most popular methodology in malingering research (Iverson & Franzen, 1996), with a strategy that exposes the patient to a "signal," which the patient subsequently denies being able to perceive or remember. This signal is then adapted to a two-alternative, forced-choice task in which the patient is given the signal along with a distractor, and is requested to choose the stimuli that was previously exposed. The patient has a 50% probability of obtaining the correct response by chance without any knowledge of the signal; therefore, scores that fall below this percentage provide reasonable indication of deliberate exaggeration. Forced-choice procedures have involved digit spans, word lists, nonverbal tests of intellectual ability, and tests composed of information and vocabulary questions.

Findings from Malingering Studies

Wiggins and Brandt (1988) found that simulators produced different performance patterns from memory-impaired participants, characterized by better recall and worse recognition than would be expected in true amnesia. Corroborating these results, Brandt and colleagues (1985) report that malingered amnesia may be characterized by a worse recognition memory than organic amnesia. Together, these studies help define at least one pattern of simulated amnesia, consisting of exaggerated poor performance on recognition memory tasks.

However, Bernard, Houston, and Natoli (1993) note that these results were obtained using tests that were not widely employed. To address participants' ability to fake believable deficits on several widely used memory tests, Bernard et al. (1993) administered the WMS-R, the Complex Figure Test (CFT; Rey, 1941; Osterrieth, 1944), the Auditory Verbal Learning Test (AVLT; Rey, 1964), and the Rey Memory Test (RMT; Rey, 1964). The study compared performances between three groups: a malingering with incentive ($N = 30$), malingering without incentive ($N = 28$) and a controls ($N = 28$), with all groups consisting of randomly assigned undergraduate psychology students participating for partial course credit. The control group's assigned goal was to perform to the best of their ability, with the role of representing themselves accurately. The goals for the two malingering groups were (a) to approach the tests *as if* they had real memory problems, and (b) to demonstrate memory problems on the tests. The malingering groups' scenarios were similar in that both were told they had been in an auto accident with identical results in terms of injuries (head injury, unconsciousness) and consequences (e.g., several weeks hospitalization, reduced earning power, memory problems). The *difference* in scenarios was that, for the group that was malingering without an incentive, the car went out of control and hit a tree; for the group that was malingering with an incentive, the accident was caused by another person, resulting in a law suit to determine the amount of financial compensation to be obtained from the responsible party.

Malingerers performed uniformly poorly, but did not exaggerate their poor performance to the extent that they would be easily detected. In pairwise comparisons of group means, the mean scores of the two malingering groups were significantly poorer than the control group, but not significantly different from each other in 80% of the cases. Overall, there were few differences between malingerers in the incentive and nonincentive conditions, with both groups of malingerers performing more poorly than the controls. Malingering and non-malingering participants could be distinguished largely on the basis of poorer performance on recognition-versus-recall tasks, specifically on the WMS-R Figural Memory, CFT Recall, and AVLT Recognition. These findings support results obtained by Wiggins and Brandt (1988) and Brandt and colleagues (1985), who also found that malingered amnesia was characterized by poorer performance on recognition (poorer than that found in organic amnesia) than recall.

Simplicity and Task Order Effects
Rey (1941, 1964) suggests that malingerers can be prone to perform more poorly than patients with brain damage on specific simple measures. However, Bernard (1990) disagrees and concludes that the task cannot be too simple. Bernard found that the simulated malingerers did not perform significantly worse than nonmalingerers on the WMS-R Mental Control subtest, which assesses overlearned material. In contrast, on the Information and Orientation questions there was a significant difference between malingered and nonmalingered groups. However, the differences on the Information and Orientation questions were so small that they are not of clinical assistance.

Additionally, performance on the RMT, the only test included in this study that was developed specifically to detect malingering, did *not* identify malingerers. The author suggests that the task order may have been important in decreasing its sensitivity—it was the last of all measures in their protocol to be administered (Bernard, 1990).

In their subsequent study, Bernard, Houston, and Natoli (1993), re-examined the ability of memory measures to discriminate malingers and nonmalingers. They administered the WMS-R, AVLT, CFT, and the RMT, but this time they administered the RMT at the beginning of the protocol (as well as two new potential objective indicators of simulated malingering). This study compared two groups, a simulated malingering group ($N = 31$) and a control group ($N = 26$), both drawn from undergraduate students in introductory psychology classes who were participating for partial course credit. One of the new measures, Hebb's Recurring Digits, offered the most promise, as simulated malingerers appeared to demonstrate failure to learn the recurring digit sequence. Interestingly, the RMT discriminated significantly between malingerers and controls when it was placed at the beginning of the battery. However, the mean of the malingerers was above the recommended cut-off of 9, meaning that a substantial number of malingerers would be missed (false negatives) using this measure alone.

Another study examined the use of several previously studied malingering measures included in a single protocol. Iverson and Franzen (1996) evaluated five procedures used to detect malingered memory deficits by administering them to students ($N = 20$) and psychiatric subjects ($N = 20$) with instructions to malinger or try their best. They compared these groups to 20 memory-impaired participants who completed the procedures under instructions to try their best. The advantages of this study design included use of clinical participants, provision of specific experimental instructions and incentive for performance, and multiple objective assessment procedures. The study included measures that were previously examined with respect to malingering: Personal History/Orientation Questionnaire, Memorization of 16 Items Test, 21 Items Test, Digit Span, and Logical Memory with the Forced-Choice Supplement (used for the first time in this study).

Each test was able to classify correctly all of the participants who were performing their best and the actual memory-impaired patients, but correct classification rates for experimental malingerers varied from 5 to 85% on the individual tests. When the criteria for classification became considering all scores together with deficient performance (below the cut score) on one procedure, this produced a 92.5% hit rate for participants instructed to malinger and a 100% hit rate for controls and memory-impaired participants.

Qualitative Signs of Malingering

The literature describes several qualitative signs of malingering. For example, Bernard (1991) found significantly different recall patterns for controls, simulated malingerers, and patients with closed head injuries, in that simulated malingerers suppress the primary effect. One study examined both qualitative and quantitative level of performance in patients with mild head injuries who have produced questionable data, and are, therefore, thought to be malingering (Trueblood, 1994). Previous studies suggest that qualitative indicators of poor effort include excessive failures on easy items (Hunt & Older, 1943), absurd or grossly illogical responses (Anderson, Trethowan, & Kenna, 1956; Wachspress, Berenberg, & Jacobson, 1953), and approximate answers (effective in identifying individuals faking schizophrenia, as reported by Bash & Alpert, 1980). Poorly motivated individuals also produced lower FSIQ and Digit Spans in comparison to adequately motivated patients with mild head injuries (Binder & Willis, 1991; Trueblood & Schmidt, 1993). Trueblood (1994) found that it is important to consider the entire test protocol, not just one or two measures of malingering, because malingerers may "see through" particular measures designed for malingering, or selectively malinger on one test, but not another.

Expected Performance of Malingering Patients on the WMS-III

While there are no measures specifically built into the WMS-III to detect potential malingering, some signs and patterns should lead a clinician to consider invalid scores in memory as well as across a wide range of neuropsychological test performances. In general, clinicians should consider memory patterns that do not conform to studied clinical conditions as possible indicators of malingering. At the Index level, better General Memory than WAIS-III FSIQ and better General Memory than Immediate Memory Indexes are suspect. Additionally, better performances at delay than immediate recall on Logical Memory, Faces, Visual Reproduction, Verbal Paired Associates, and Family Pictures subtests can suggest malingering (although in some cases, it is possible that such patterns can reflect valid increased consolidation across delay periods). Lower scores on recognition than on delayed recall performance would also be problematic. Unusual memory patterns at either the Index or subtest level would also constitute signs of problematic motivation. WMS-III subtests with recognition paradigms may reveal the most: Atypical responding (including scores that are at chance, or less than 50% correct, for yes-no answers) is suspect. Unexpected difficulty with responses on the Information Orientation subtest may also be a flag for malingering, and, therefore, this subtest should also be included. For example, an examiner should consider carefully a person who has problems indicating the place of testing, or the date, but yet drove to the test session on the correct day. Therefore, clinicians may want to use specific subtests such as Logical Memory I and II, Word Lists I and II, Verbal Paired Associates I and II, Faces I and II, and Information and Orientation. The clinician should watch for unusual within-test performances such as failure to demonstrate a primacy or recency effect on Word Lists, or better performance on the backward conditions of Digits Span and Spatial Span. Higher Letter-Number Sequencing span than Digit Span of the WAIS-III would be atypical.

In summary, malingering performances can be characterized by inconsistencies within and across cognitive domains, inconsistencies of test performances with respect to clinical observation, and history of injury severity. Dramatic differences between day-to-day functioning and memory scores should also raise the possibility of invalid scores. Other questionable responses include better performances on harder items on a subtest, and absurd, illogical, vague, or approximate responses. Extra-test behavior, such as unwillingness to provide any response or frequent "Don't know" responses, as well as prolonged latencies for easy items may also be suspect as well. In considering a malingered test protocol, clinical judgment is very important.

Moderating Influences of Malingering

An important clinical finding in the malingering research is that warning participants about malingering may prevent malingering in the first place. Johnson and Lesniak-Karpiak (1997) found that warning prior to administration of memory and motor tests was effective in reducing exaggeration of difficulty on selected neuropsychological tests. Simulators who were not warned performed significantly worse than the control group across all memory and motor dependent measures. Additionally, simulators who were not warned performed significantly worse than simulators who were warned on Verbal Memory, General Memory, and Delayed Recall, suggesting that warning reduced exaggeration of cognitive difficulty in these areas. Simulators who were warned performed significantly slower than the control group on the motor task, but not perform differently than simulators who were not warned. However, simulators with warning and control group performances were not significantly different.

These results imply that giving a warning to patients who may be at risk for malingering will provide a more accurate cognitive profile on neuropsychological tests (see Rapid Reference 6.7 for expected findings for patients who

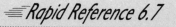

Rapid Reference 6.7

Expected Findings for Patients who are Malingering

- Performance on memory Indexes or subtests is inconsistent with that of known clinical conditions.
- Patients have better *General (Delayed) Memory Index* than *WAIS-III FSIQ*.
- Patients have better *General (Delayed) Memory Index* than *Immediate Memory Indexes*.
- Patients perform better on *delay* than *immediate* recall on *Logical Memory, Faces, Visual Reproduction, Verbal Paired Associates,* or *Family Pictures.*
- Performance on *recognition* paradigms is at chance level (or less than 50% correct for yes-no answers).
- Patients score lower on *recognition* than *delayed recall* performance.
- Patients show unexpected difficulty responding on the *Information Orientation* subtest (e.g., they have problems indicating the place or the date of testing yet drove to the test session on the correct day).
- Patients fail to demonstrate primacy or recency effects on *Word Lists.*
- Patients perform better on the backward than forward conditions of *Digit Span* and *Spatial Span.*
- Patients perform better on harder items on a subtest.
- Patients offer absurd, illogical, vague, or approximate responses.
- Patients seem unwilling to provide any response, provide frequent "Don't know" responses, or show prolonged latencies for easy items.
- Patients have dramatic differences between day-to-day functioning and memory scores.

Note: Informative subtests include *Logical Memory I and II, Word Lists I and II, Verbal Paired Associates I and II, Faces I and II,* and *Information and Orientation.* One or all of these patterns merely suggest the possibility of malingering; clinical judgment and other measures must be considered when determining whether poor performance is feigned.

are malingering). For clinicians involved in assessments for legal purposes, a straightforward warning is likely to reduce malingered responding. As Johnson and Lesniak-Karpiak (1997) point out, this places the neuropsychologist back in the role of expert examiner and interpreter of test information as opposed to the role of someone who must surreptitiously detect potentially fraudulent behavior on the part of the client. While provision of a warning alone is unlikely to suffice in eradicating malingering behavior, it can serve as an adjunct to existing techniques including pattern analysis and symptom validity testing (Johnson & Lesniak-Karpiak, 1997).

AGING AND MEMORY

Normal aging is of significant interest because older individuals represent an increasing proportion of the population. The average life span in the 1800s was 30 to 40 years of age. By the 20th century, the average life expectancy of an American increased by more than 25 years, from 47 years in 1900 to 75 years in 1980 (Kovar, 1977). In 1900, 4% of the population was over age 65, but by the end of the 1980s, 11% was over age 65. At the start of the new millennium, older individuals account for approximately 17% of the population (Albert, 1988b). Demographic changes, including basic public health measures (such as sanitation and sewage treatment), improved nutrition, and availability of antibiotics are all likely to have impacted the normal human lifespan. Differentiating between age-related cognitive changes and beginning stages of dementing illnesses is of more importance today with respect to early detection, diagnosis, and treatment of dementing illnesses.

Methodological Issues

Studies differ in defining normal age groups. Many exclude potential individuals who have existing medical conditions such as hypertension and other cardiovascular problems, diabetes, previous substance abuse, and other conditions that may adversely affect the brain; these exclusions result in study of the "healthiest" of the elderly, and thus may not represent the aging population at large. Effects of aging may interact with age-related illnesses. Many investigations reveal an education effect, such that more highly educated persons score better on standardized tests, making cross-sectional studies more difficult to interpret because older adult cohorts are almost universally less educated than younger adult cohorts (Kaufman, 2000). Matching younger and older groups by education may not yield comparable levels due to cohort changes in educational standards, but correction for educational attainment—even if not perfect—greatly facilitates the interpretation of data in aging studies. Goodman and Zarit (1994), for example, administered WMS Logical Memory and Associate Learning and other tests, to 90 healthy women at least 75 years of age (mean education = 13 years), all of whom reported some everyday memory problems. Of this group, 74 were initially categorized as having age-associated memory impairment. After controlling for education, however, only 54 were so classified; 24 were no longer classified as impaired and 4 were no longer classified as unimpaired.

Cross-sectional designs that do not include estimates of premorbid function are also problematic because older participants who have reduced memory function may not have changed over time. Longitudinal designs, while more ideal, are costly, and individuals who drop out of studies tend to perform more poorly than those who continue to participate in retesting (Kleemier, 1962). Gender effects of aging are often not directly studied, although control groups are generally selected to match on gender.

Normal Aging

Normal aging is associated with a decline in several domains of cognition, including short-term memory (Albert & Moss, 1996). Other changes include constructional capabilities, divided attention, abstraction, and naming, with initial changes detected across mid-50s to the 70s in cross-sectional studies (Albert, 1988). Certain measures prove to be sensitive to age effects, including those that use distraction and delayed free recall procedures (Craik, 1984). Conversely, studies using immediate or primary memory measures, such as Digit Span, or Remote Recall of Events, and cued recall and recognition formats tend to show smaller or insignificant effects (Albert, 1988a; Craik, Byrd, & Swanson, 1987; Kazniak, Poon, & Riege, 1986).

Horn (1989) and his colleagues (Horn & Hofer, 1992; Horn & Noll, 1997) distinguish between abilities that are *maintained* and those that are *vulnerable*. Maintained abilities increase during adulthood and peak at around the age of 50 or 60 before declining gradually, until about age 75 when the decline becomes more precipitous (Kaufman & Lichtenberger, 2001). Crystallized Intelligence, as measured by tasks such as ability to define words and range of general information are good examples of maintained abilities. In contrast, vulnerable abilities peak in early adulthood (about age 20 to 25 usually) and then decline steadily and rapidly as one ages. Illustrations of highly vulnerable abilities are measures of fluid reasoning (solving abstract matrices), visualization (WAIS-III Picture Completion), and processing speed (WAIS-III Digit-Symbol Coding). Based on Horn's (1989) research and research with Wechsler's adult scales (Kaufman & Lichtenberger, 2001) short-term memory tests like Wechsler's Digit Span are typically vulnerable abilities, but not as extremely vulnerable as measures of fluid ability, visualization, or speed.

Illustrative Memory Research on Previous Editions of the WMS

Many studies have examined the effects of aging on memory using the WMS or WMS-R. Cullum, Butters, Troster, and Salmon (1990) studied forgetting rates in normal aging by contrasting two groups of healthy individuals, ages 50 to 70 ($N = 32$) and 75 to 95 ($N = 47$) on the entire WMS-R. The older group did significantly worse on Verbal Memory, Visual Memory, General Memory, and Delayed Memory. Despite equivalent scores on the Dementia Rating Scale and total raw score on the Attention/Concentration of the WMS-R, the older group demonstrated significantly more rapid forgetting rates on the Visual Reproduction, Verbal Paired Associates, and Visual Paired Associates subtests. They did not differ on Logical Memory. While the older group demonstrated lower scores overall, both showed relatively high savings scores: The younger group obtained their highest savings score on Visual Paired Associates (97%) while the older obtained their highest on Verbal Paired Associates (88%), and the lowest score for both was on the Visual Reproduction subtest (younger group, 85%; older group 69%). The older group demonstrated difficulties with the Visual Reproduction at both immediate and delayed conditions.

Similar findings of greater age-related decrements in visual rather than verbal memory as well as greater variability among older subjects were reported using the WMS and other instruments (Bak & Greene, 1980; Kaszniak et al., 1986). The performances of the older group are distinguishable from individuals with Alzheimer's disease. Butters and colleagues (1988) reported far lower savings scores for a sample of patients with Alzheimer's disease on the Visual

Reproduction (20%) and Logical Memory (15%) subtests of the WMS-R. These results indicate that participants with Alzheimer's disease show severe forgetting for both visual and verbal material, whereas the elderly participants decline was more evident in the visual memory task.

Trahan (1992) corroborated these findings in his investigation of the Visual Reproduction subtest of the WMS with an added 30-min delay condition, in an effort to study forgetting rates in different age groups and to determine whether the forgetting rates reflected different levels of initial learning during the acquisition stage. He studied four age groups, 18 to 29 ($N = 97$), 30 to 49 ($N = 81$), 50 to 69 ($N = 51$), and 70+ ($N = 26$). Forgetting Score was defined as the raw score during acquisition minus the raw score at delayed recall. There were no differences in forgetting rate between groups, suggesting that age differences on this visual delayed-recall task may reflect differences in learning during acquisition phase rather than accelerated forgetting rates in older adults.

Because memory testing, particularly when part of a neuropsychological battery, is often used clinically to determine level of functional competence in the real world, Goldstein, McCue, Rogers, and Nussbaum (1992) examined the predictive utility of three memory tests, including the WMS, for functional capabilities in an elderly cohort, using score on the Performance Assessment of Self-Care Skills (PASS) as the criterion at two weeks and 6 months. The geriatric sample was tested at an inpatient psychiatry unit. The PASS is a performance test that requires the participant to carry out specific tasks while being observed, including using the telephone to obtain information, balancing a checkbook after writing a check, preparing an envelope for mailing the check, demonstrating management of medications, and verbalizing appropriate response to danger, among others. The study examined three groups: subsamples of individuals classified as (a) having dementia, (b) being depressed, and (c) being normal. The WMS correlated significantly with the PASS, in the expected direction, in the depressed and normal subsamples, but not in the dementia group.

Aging from Age 20 to 89 Years as measured by the WMS-III

Heaton and colleagues (Heaton, Manly, Taylor, & Tulsky, 2001; Manly, Heaton, & Taylor, 2000) analyzed the eight WMS-III Memory Indexes (and the WAIS-III scores) for ages 20 to 89 years to study age changes across the adult lifespan. Heaton and colleagues (2001) and Manly and colleagues (2000) controlled for education to permit meaningful comparison of the Memory Indexes obtained by different age groups. The two studies conducted by Heaton and his colleagues included WMS-III standardization cases and additional "education oversampling" cases, but the sample sizes differed in the two reports: $N = 885$ for Heaton's study (2001) and $N = 1089$ for Manly's study (2000). To permit age-by-age comparisons, Heaton and colleagues based all standard scores on norms for ages 20 to 34 years and, as mentioned, statistically corrected for educational differences among the age groups.

Major Results of Heaton's WMS-III Aging Study

Heaton and colleagues (2001) compared z scores for the age group obtaining the lowest education-corrected mean index (ages 85–89 in each case) and the highest mean index (usually ages 20–24), and reported this difference in SD units. The fact that the peak age is 20 to 24 years for 6 of the 8 WMS-III Indexes indicates that these abilities are vulnerable to the normal aging process (the exceptions were Auditory Delayed Recognition, which peaked at ages 30–34, and the Working Memory Index, which peaked at 25–29). The differences between high and low means in SD units (measures of effect size) were substantial, ranging from about 1.2 to 1.3 SD for Auditory Delayed Recognition, Auditory Immediate Memory, and Visual Immediate Memory to about 1.6 to 1.7 for the three measures of delayed recall: General Memory, Auditory Delayed, and Visual Delayed (Heaton et al., 2001). The magnitude of these values further illustrates that *both* the immediate and delayed recall scales on the WMS-III are quite vulnerable. Consider the values of about 1.5 SD to 1.7 SD for 5 of the 8 indexes, and compare them to differences on the WAIS-III Indexes (Heaton et al., 2001; Kaufman & Lichtenberger, 2001). The WAIS-III Processing Speed Index and Perceptual Organization Index measure the kinds of abilities that have traditionally been found to be extremely vulnerable; these Indexes produced effect sizes of 1.9 SD and 1.5 SD, respectively, across the same 20 to 89-year age range. The following five WMS-III Indexes, with the Index having the highest effect size listed first, are just as vulnerable: Auditory Delayed Memory, General Memory, Visual Delayed Memory, Immediate Memory, and Working Memory. Quite clearly, the three delayed recall Indexes are the most vulnerable to aging, commensurate with WAIS-III measures of processing speed, fluid intelligence, and visualization.

In Heaton and colleagues' (2001) study, the least vulnerable ability on the WMS-III was Auditory Delayed Recognition, followed closely by the separate auditory and visual measures of immediate memory. However, the magnitude of the effect sizes (about 1.2–1.3 SD) still reflects vulnerability; by way of contrast, the maintained ability measured by WAIS-III VCI had an effect size of 0.6 SD.

Integration of WMS-III Results with Previous Findings

Interestingly, effect sizes for visual recall tasks, both immediate and delayed, were commensurate with effect sizes for auditory recall tasks (contrary to previous findings with the WMS and WMS-R, cited earlier in this section) that found greater declines on visual tasks (Bak & Greene, 1980; Cullum et al., 1990; Kaszniak et al., 1986; Trahan, 1992). In view of the large number of participants in the data analyzed by Heaton and his colleagues and the careful exclusionary criteria that were applied in selecting the sample, far more weight should be given to the generalizability of Heaton's data than the findings of previous investigations of the WMS or WMS-R with normal adults that commonly used small samples and did not apply strict control over who was eligible for the "normal" samples. A case in point is the investigation by Howieson and colleagues (1993), who administered WMS-R Logical Memory and Visual Reproduction as part of a more thorough battery of tests to optimally healthy, elderly individuals between 65 and 74 years of age ($N = 17$) and ages 84 and older ($N = 34$). The groups averaged 14 years of education and earned above average WAIS-R Vocabulary scores. These researchers found a larger age effect for visuospatial memory than for verbal memory, but those results may have been artifacts of small sample sizes and highly educated subjects.

The age-related decreases on all WMS-III Indexes, in most cases beginning in the 20s, are noteworthy because of the extensive exclusionary criteria used by the publisher (The Psychological Corporation, 1997) when selecting the sample. Though the WMS-III standardization sample represents a "normal" sample, examiners should note the sampling techniques that were used. The Psychological Corporation (1997) excluded three categories of adults: (1) those with sensory or motor deficits (e.g., color-blindness, uncorrected hearing loss); (2) those undergoing current treatment for alcohol or drug dependency or who consumed more than three alcoholic beverages on at least three nights per week, and those currently taking certain medications (e.g., antidepressants); and (3) adults with known or possible neuropsychological disorders, those who see a doctor or other professional for memory problems or problems with thinking, and those with related problems (e.g., suffering a head injury that required hospitalization for more than 24 hours, diagnosis of epilepsy or Alzheimer's Dementia).

The WMS-III standardization sample, therefore, was *normal,* but not *typical.* Indeed, the third exclusionary category is age-related, as both the number and severity of cognitive/neurological pathologies accelerate in old age (Rabbitt, Bent, & McInnes, 1997). More older than younger individuals, therefore, would have been excluded from the WMS-III standardization sample: The sample of adults ages 75 to 79, for example, is undoubtedly higher functioning than a random sample of 75- to 79-year-olds in the population. Therefore the memory losses associated with aging are undoubtedly "lower-bound" estimates of the actual deficits within the population. The vulnerability shown for all WMS-III Indexes are probably "real" age-related declines and not artifacts of including increasing numbers of memory-impaired adults with increasing age.

The WMS-III results are consistent with the literature on memory and aging, which is often interpreted within the context of Tulving's (1983) distinction between episodic and semantic memory. Episodic memory refers to personally experienced events or episodes, whereas semantic memory reflects general world knowledge. Prototypical episodic memory tasks include immediate or delayed recall of word lists, geometric designs, text, faces, and more personally oriented tasks that require individuals to recall things that occurred to them within a specific context. Typical experimental tests of semantic memory are measures of information, naming ability, or vocabulary. All of the WMS-III tasks and scales reflect *episodic* memory.

The vulnerability of the WMS-III scales is consistent with the burgeoning literature on age changes in episodic memory that usually reports notable declines with aging on immediate recall, delayed recall, and delayed recognition of a variety of verbal and nonverbal stimuli (e.g., Colsher & Wallace, 1991; Korten et al., 1997; Souchay, Isingrini, & Espagnet, 2000; Zelinski & Burnight, 1997). Even an elite sample of elderly professors at Berkeley (ages 60–71) performed much more poorly than middle-aged professors (ages 45–59) and young professors (ages 30–44) on a verbal paired-associate learning task (Shimamura, Berry, Mangels, Rusting, & Jurica, 1995). In contrast, "the dominant pattern in the literature is that semantic memory shows little variation from early adulthood to earlier portions of the late adult life span. . . . Although significant decline in semantic memory may typically not be seen until the mid-70s, there is evidence that further decline in very old age is systematic and gradual" (Backman, Small, Wahlin, & Larsson, 2000, pp. 510–511).

In general, the experimental psychology literature on memory and aging mimics the findings of the studies of both Wechsler tests, the WMS-III and WAIS-III: Episodic memory—like the immediate and, especially, delayed recall scales on the WMS-III, as well as the fluid intelligence, processing speed, and visualization abilities assessed by the WMS-III—is quite vulnerable to the effects of aging. In contrast, semantic memory tasks and the related tests of Crystallized Intelligence on the WAIS-III (the ones that compose the Verbal Comprehension factor) are maintained abilities that do not decline appreciably until old age. Also, the elderly Berkeley professors who performed so poorly on a paired-associate memory task performed as well as young and middle-aged professors when repeating prose passages about a woman who was robbed (WMS-R Logical Memory), the elements that make up the earth's atmosphere, and the tribal cultures in the Mississipian period (Shimamura et al., 1995).

Clinical Value of the Excellent WMS-III Norms

The great clinical value of the excellent, carefully stratified standardization sample obtained for the WMS-III (and WAIS-III) across the broad age span of 16 to 89 cannot be overstated. Because many neuropsychological instruments are strongly related to age and education, clinicians are often cautioned to adjust diagnostic cutting scores and question use of conventional norms for individuals who are less educated or less intelligent than the normative group. However, many commonly used instruments lack specific guidelines for such adjustments, so that normal participants are at risk for being misclassified as impaired or brain-damaged with use of standard cut-off scores (Marcopulos, McLean, & Giuliano, 1997). In particular, clinicians are most likely to misinterpret test performances of normal elderly individuals with less than eight years of education as representing a dementia (Stern et al., 1992; cf Marcopulos et al., 1997). Additionally, some authors have observed that people with low education levels may be at greater risk of developing cognitive impairment or showing a greater decline than people with high education levels (Bornstein & Suga, 1988; Frisoni, Rozzini, Bianchetti, & Trabucchi, 1993; Yu et al., 1989), perhaps due to presence of greater risk factors over the life cycle including poorer health, nutrition, housing and working conditions (Gurland, 1981). Available normative data for most neuropsychological instruments are largely based on high-school educated, white, urban-dwelling adults (Erickson, Eimon, & Hebben, 1992; La Rue, 1992; Ivnik et al., 1992; Spreen & Strauss, 1991), and elderly norms or longitudinal studies of aging often include upper-class participants with a mean education of 14 years (Mitrushina & Satz, 1991; Schaie, 1983).

In summary, the availability of accurate norms for elderly individuals is especially crucial. Nadler, Mittenberg, DePiano, and Schneider (1994) report that psychologists specializing in neuropsychology who were provided a sample neuropsychological profile of test results for a healthy, 74-year-old individual were prone to misinterpret test results in the direction of greater impairment. Twenty-three percent of the clinicians thought the protocol reflected dementia when considering WAIS-R, WMS, and other data. Consequently, the excellent WMS-III and WAIS-III norms through old age, with appropriate representation at all levels of education, facilitates accurate diagnoses and provides a crisper picture of what is normal, permitting greater understanding of the abnormal.

⚓ TEST YOURSELF ⚓

1. **Malingering is**

   (a) a condition observed most often in children with behavioral disorders.

   (b) a behavioral observation made when an individual takes more time in completing a task than is warranted.

   (c) a phenomenon that is observed most often in individuals over the age of 60.

   (d) an attempt to appear to have a worse condition or affliction than is truly the case, based on an external incentive.

2. **Results from substance abuse studies are problematic to interpret for all the reasons except**

   (a) substance abusers often use more than one substance.

   (b) cognitive deficits can be confounded by effects of withdrawal.

   (c) effects of deficits related to substance abuse may be related to age.

   (d) studies consistently find that substance abusing individuals do not score below the Average range.

3. **The memory protocol of patients with Alzheimer's disease and Parkinson's disease can often be distinguished in the following manner:**

   (a) Patients with Parkinson's disease demonstrate less forgetting over time and are able to recognize information that was previously learned.

   (b) Patients with Alzheimer's disease demonstrate less forgetting over time and are able to recognize information that was previously learned.

   (c) Attentional problems, particularly for verbal information, are the hallmark of Parkinson's disease.

   (d) Individuals with Parkinson's disease demonstrate superior visual-versus-verbal memory, whereas individuals with Alzheimer's disease display the opposite pattern.

4. **Clinicians may mitigate malingering by giving a warning, before administering the tests, that the tests can detect motivational problems such as exaggeration.** True or False?

5. **Left temporal lobe epilepsy tends to be associated with problems in auditory/verbal immediate and delayed recall performances.** True or False?

6. **Aging is noted to affect memory performance more than any other capability.** True or False?

7. **When compared to individuals with Bipolar Disorder, individuals with schizophrenia do worse on memory tests.** True or False?

8. **There is much debate regarding whether memory is**

   (a) selective, or reflects impairment of a generalized impairment in patients with schizophrenia.

   (b) worse for younger patients with schizophrenia than older.

   (c) inversely related to intelligence in patients with schizophrenia.

   (d) valid as a construct to measure in patients with schizophrenia.

Answers: 1. d; 2. d; 3. a; 4. True; 5. True; 6. False; 7. True; 8. a

Seven

ILLUSTRATIVE CASE REPORTS

This chapter includes case studies of two adults who were referred for neuropsychological evaluations. The first case report is of Mr. Simon G., an 81-year-old man with Alzheimer's disease referred for testing to determine the progress of his disease, which was first diagnosed 5 years ago. The second case report examines the profile of Ms. Natalie L., a 47-year-old woman who recently experienced a head injury. Natalie's case was presented in chapter 4 as an example of how to progress through the steps of WMS-III interpretation. This chapter presents the culmination of her data in a complete neuropsychological case report.

Chapters 1 through 6 of this book review the key features of the WMS-III and how to administer, score, and interpret the instrument. The goal of this chapter is to bring all of these facets of the book together to illustrate how the WAIS-III may be used as a part of a comprehensive test battery. Specifically, the case reports demonstrate how hypotheses are cross-validated with multiple sources of information (behavioral observations, background information, and supplemental tests) and how all clinicians can integrate and communicate this information in an understandable format. The structure of case reports vary, of course, depending on the clinician's or clinic's style and needs. For example, psychoeducational reports tend generally to have a different format and style than neuropsychological reports. The focus of both of these cases in this chapter is neuropsychological, therefore, the cases are presented in a typical neuropsychological format. Each of the reports contains reason for referral, background information, appearance and behavioral characteristics, tests administered, test interpretations, summary, and recommendations. A tabular summary of some of the test scores is also presented within the reports. All pertinent identifying information in each of the case reports has been modified to protect the confidentiality of the clients.

SIMON G., AGE 81, ALZHEIMER'S DISEASE

Reason for Referral

Mr. Simon G. is an 81-year-old, African-American man who was referred for a neuropsychological assessment by his neurologist to evaluate progression of his Alzheimer's disease and to assess his capability to continue driving in familiar areas. Currently, his driving is restricted to the small town in which he resides, with no freeway travel. A neurologist diagnosed Mr. G. at an Alzheimer's diagnostic clinic 5 years ago, when the patient demonstrated signs of memory changes (forgetting to take money from his business to his bank, misplacement of important belongings, and mild confusion). The summary section of this report compares previous testing obtained upon his diagnosis to the current testing.

Background Information

Neither Mr. G. nor his wife were reliable sources of information. Mrs. G. indicated on several occasions that she had "a short-term memory problem" and joked that she may require an assessment as well. Mrs. G. recently had a "slight stroke," according to their son, who participated in the clinical interview by phone. The limited information in this section, which is thought to be accurate, was provided by the couple in an interview and was confirmed by their son.

Mr. G. lives in a small house with his wife, to whom he has been married for 55 years. They have owned their own retail business for over 50 years. Both Mr. and Mrs. G. retired from working full-time about 10 years ago, but are still involved with the functioning of the business. Neither Mr. G. nor his wife clean or cook anymore and they have hired support to run the household. Mr. and Mrs. G.'s adult son and daughter live at least 60 miles away. Mr. G. was an only child who grew up in a small rural town. He reported having a "typical" childhood. His hobbies currently consist of gardening and listening to music. He is actively involved in church and used to sing in the choir.

Mr. G. indicated that he completed high school and attended two years of college. He reportedly disliked math in high school and attained Cs in Algebra and Geometry, but obtained As in all other subjects, which lead to honor-roll placements. He married shortly after he left college and worked odd jobs until he and his wife began their own business.

His wife said that Mr. G.'s medical history included a removal of a malignant melanoma 15 years ago and removal of a benign mole 6 years ago. He had a detached retina 5 years ago and is nearsighted. No other medical problems were noted.

Alcohol and substance abuse are not part of his history. He does not smoke. He was not taking any medications at the time of assessment.

Behavioral Observations

The patient's housekeeper drove him to both sessions, and he arrived on time. Mr. G. was well-groomed in a casual suit for both sessions, and his hair and mustache were neatly trimmed. Eye contact was appropriate. Mr. G. participated well in social interactions and small talk before testing began. He maintained a notably elegant style of speech and social graces during casual conversation. Rapport was readily established with Mr. G. Once testing began, however, Mr. G. became quite defensive about failing basic questions, stating, "Now why would I want to remember that?" or, "Now you know, these are questions for someone with book smarts; I'm a musician." When asked how many children he had (15 minutes into the session) he stated, "You should have asked me that question at the beginning, when I was fresh." Early in the sessions, he became difficult to test in that he interrupted repeatedly, stating that he had "chronic fatigue syndrome" and was "more tired than you can ever imagine." His son indicated that it was he, not his father, who suffers from chronic fatigue syndrome.

When frustrated with his test performance, Mr. G.'s verbal output became dysarthric and he sometimes produced neologisms. When flustered, he omitted many words in a sentence. Word-finding difficulties were also evident, although when relaxed, syntax and phrase length were within normal limits. When finally asked not to interrupt the examiner during item administration, Mr. G. complied readily. Due to difficulties in testing compliance, the assessment was completed in two sessions in a total of four hours. There were no signs of suspiciousness, paranoia, or hallucinatory behavior during the evaluation. Mood was within normal limits but affect was moderately labile. Despite his frustration, he smiled readily, became engaged in social interaction, and was easily guided back to his baseline affective state by the end of each session.

These results are thought to be a valid and reliable indicator of Mr. G.'s neuropsychological functioning. The importance of working to the best of his ability was emphasized prior to the testing.

Tests Administered

- Boston Naming Test
- Boston Visuospatial Quantitative Battery: Drawings
- Finger Tapping
- Galveston Orientation Test
- Grooved Pegboard
- Kløve-Reitan Sensory Perceptual Examination
- Letter and Design Cancellation Tests
- Recursive Loops
- Trail Making Test (A and B)
- Wechsler Adult Intelligence Scale–III (WAIS-III): selected subtests
- Wechsler Memory Scale–III (WMS-III)

(Available test scores for the latter two are listed in Table 7.1)

Test Results and Interpretation

Orientation

Mr. G. was oriented to person and place, but not to time. When asked what year it was, he responded, "I cannot tell you how tired I am." When asked the month, he replied, "I know what month my birthday is."

Attention and Concentration

Mr. G.'s overall auditory attention ability was in the Low Average range (16th percentile) as he was able to repeat a span of four digits forward and three digits backward. His visual attention was assessed with the Letter and Design Cancellation Tests. Letter cancellation was moderately impaired for completion time, but was within normal limits for number of errors (3). Design cancellation was within normal limits for time, but was moderately impaired with respect to omission errors, which occurred on all quadrants of the page. Visual attention was further assessed with Trail A, on which performance was within limits for time, but moderately impaired with respect to errors (2). He made one tracking and one perceptual error. Finally, visual attention to missing de-

Table 7.1 Summary of Simon G.'s Test Scores

Panel A. Wechsler Memory Scale–Third Edition (WMS-III)

	Index Score	Percentile Rank	Confidence Interval (95%)
Primary Indexes			
Auditory Immediate	62	1	57–72
Visual Immediate	71	3	66–86
Immediate Memory	59	0.3	55–70
Auditory Delayed	71	3	66–84
Visual Delayed	81	10	74–94
Auditory Recognition Delayed	55	0.1	56–78
General Memory	66	1	61–77

	Age-Scaled Score	Percentile Rank
Primary Subtests		
Logical Memory I Recall	2	0.4
Faces I Recognition	6	9
Verbal Paired Associates I Recall	5	5
Family Pictures I Recall	5	5
Spatial Span	8	25
Logical Memory II Recall	4	2
Faces II Recognition	10	50
Verbal Paired Associates II Recall	6	9
Family Pictures II Recall	4	2
Auditory Recognition Delayed	1	0.1

tails in drawn pictures was in the Borderline range (5th percentile). On a task measuring cognitive processing speed (Digit Symbol-Coding task), where Mr. G. was asked to draw symbols rapidly below numbers according to specific pairings shown on a page, performance was also in the Borderline range (5th percentile), providing corroborating evidence that attention and concentra-

Table 7.1 Continued

Panel B. Wechsler Adult Intelligence Scale–Third Edition (WAIS-III): Selected Subtests

	Scaled Score	Percentile Rank
Verbal Scales		
Information	6	9
Digit Span	7	16
Vocabulary	12	75
Arithmetic	4	2
Similarities	9	6
Performance		
Picture Completion	5	5
Block Design	7	16
Digit Symbol	5	5

tion were at least mildly problematic, and on some measures, moderately impaired.

Executive Function, Problem-Solving Skills

Mr. G. was asked to copy a series of recursive loops. This task requires self-monitoring to inhibit perseverative errors. Using his dominant (right) hand, he was unable to produce a single figure correctly and perseverated on a loop for each production. Over productions, these became segmented, rather than connected, suggesting significant difficulty with maintaining mental set. Interestingly, the overall direction of the loops was better maintained with his left hand, although again, they became segmented and perseverated. Continuation of a line of cursive "mn's" was also increasingly segmented over productions in his dominant hand. With his left hand, the letters became more and more illegible and productions represented a possible perseveration to the first loop task. Cognitive flexibility, as measured by Trail B, was severely impaired, and he only completed half the test. Mr. G. lost track of what his next move should be several times, and appeared to have difficulty both organizing a strategy for the task demands and scanning the page efficiently. When provided with a suggestion to deduce where to go next by examining what line he had just completed, the strategy did not assist Mr. G.'s performance and he committed two stimulus-pull errors. With respect to conceptual reasoning, Mr. G.'s verbal abstraction was in the Average range (37th percentile).

Overall Intelligence

Mr. G. was administered only select subtests of the WAIS-III, so that VIQ, PIQ, and FSIQ are not available. His level of premorbid functioning is believed to be in the High Average range, given specific neuropsychological performances at the current and earlier assessment conducted 5 years ago.

Verbal/Language Abilities

Mr. G.'s fund of knowledge was in the Borderline range (9th percentile) but his ability to define words was in the High Average range (75th percentile). In contrast, on the Boston Naming test, his ability to express the correct word for a pictured object was moderately-to-severely impaired (26/60). However, phonemic cueing assisted his performance on approximately half the items he missed (9/19 times). His speech and verbal expression were notable for neologisms that were composed of transposed phonemes or similar phonemes to target words, particularly when he was frustrated. Prosodic intonation and phrase length were intact. However, Mr. G.'s use of syntax was problematic on occasion due to omission of words. Writing was smooth and legible, although inconsistent use of capitalization was noted.

Visual-Spatial Abilities

On tasks of abstract visual-spatial construction on the WAIS-III, Mr. G.'s performance was Low Average (16th percentile). On a WAIS-III task that required him to copy modeled block designs, he had difficulty rendering details of a stripe on a 4-block item and could only put two blocks together for the first 9-block item. On several paper-and-pencil drawing and copying tests, impairment in visual-spatial abilities was noted. For example, Mr. G. was unable to spontaneously draw a recognizable flower. While the components of the center, leaves, and stem were present, they were in poor proportion. In contrast to his spontaneously drawn flower, his *copy* of a flower was considerably better, with perseveration errors on the petals and sketchy overdrawing of all elements. His copy of a red-cross symbol was notable for proportional difficulties, and in his first attempt he demonstrated a perseverative error by drawing a square. His spontaneous drawing of a house was one-dimensional and the lines did not join where they should have met (corners of house and attachment to roof). His copy was significantly better and included a three-dimensional perspective, although the lines were crooked and poorly angled. A spontaneous clock drawing was impaired for placement of numbers, and the hands were almost set properly for the requested time, but did not conform to the numbers that he had produced on the face. These results suggest conceptual difficulties.

Memory

The WMS-III was administered to Mr. G. to obtain a comprehensive assessment of his memory functioning, including immediate and delayed recall for visual and verbal material. Overall, Mr. G.'s delayed memory performance was in the Extremely Low range, as evident by his General (Delayed) Memory Index of 66 (1st percentile). His performance on the Immediate Memory Index (59; 0.3rd percentile) was also in the Extremely Low range of functioning and was not significantly different from his delayed memory abilities. Careful examination of Mr. G.'s subtest scores revealed that his delayed recall scores were at or near the floor for both verbal and visual tasks, with the exception of facial recognition capabilities. There were no significant discrepancies between his immediate recall for auditory and visual material, nor delayed recall for auditory and visual domains.

Within the auditory domain, Mr. G. displayed uniformly depressed performance on tasks of immediate and delayed recall. His immediate recall of prose passages (Logical Memory) was at the 0.5th percentile and his delayed memory (60-min recall) of these passages was at the 2nd percentile. This pattern of scores suggests significant compromise for recall of one-trial, semantic information. A similar pattern of performance was evident in his recall of learned pairs (Verbal Paired Associates), which was at the 5th percentile in the immediate condition and was at the 9th percentile after a 60-min delay. The difference between his Auditory Delayed Index (71; 3rd percentile) and Auditory Recognition Delayed Index (55; 0.1st percentile) was not significant, indicating that Mr. G. does not benefit from the additional information available in recognition paradigms, over and above what he is able to recall spontaneously.

His poor performance at delay is therefore not attributed to retrieval deficit; rather, the difficulty appears to be in the encoding stage of memory processes. He became quite frustrated and somewhat oppositional during recognition testing, stating insightfully, "I don't remember anything you said; how would I recognize anything?"

In contrast to his relatively consistent performance within the auditory domain, Mr. G. showed more variability within his visual memory. Mr. G.'s ability to recognize faces that were presented earlier (Faces I Recognition) was at the 9th percentile in the immediate condition, but after a 60-min delay, his facial recognition score was in the Average range (50th percentile). This pattern of stronger delayed visual memory of faces than immediate visual memory of faces suggests increased consolidation over time (for this special class of stimuli). However, on another task of visual memory, his performances on immediate and delayed conditions were equally impaired. Mr. G. was asked to view a scene of a family and then immediately recall where people were positioned and what they were doing (Family Pictures I). The delayed condition required him to recall the same type of information after a 60-min delay. His performance on this task was at the 5th percentile for the immediate condition and at the 2nd percentile for the delayed condition.

An additional facet of memory tapped by the WMS-III was Mr. G.'s verbal learning capabilities. To assess his verbal learning over multiple trials, Mr. G. was required to learn unrelated word pairs via repeated exposure to the pairs. He performed at the 5th and 9th percentiles on the immediate and delayed conditions of this task (Verbal Paired Associates I and II), suggesting that his memory/learning ability did not profit from repeated exposure to the unrelated word-pairs.

Sensory Perception and Motor Function

Mr. G. did not demonstrate deficits in visual or tactile perception. Testing determined that his visual fields were intact. All unilateral and bilateral simultaneous stimuli were lateralized correctly. Mr. G. was not administered auditory testing, as stimulation did not reliably surpass detection threshold. Motor speed was assessed by having Mr. G. tap a lever as quickly as possible with each index finger, separately. His performance was in the Normal range for both hands (Average for right = 45.5, Average for left = 45), and notable in that there was no advantage for his dominant (right) hand.

Summary and Conclusions

Mr. G. is an African-American, 81-year-old man who was referred for neuro-psychological testing to determine the progression of Alzheimer's disease, which was diagnosed 5 years ago.

Mr. G.'s auditory attention span was in the Low Average range, but his visual attention varied between Moderately Impaired to Borderline, and errors were reduced when he took more time to complete the tasks. His visual attention to missing details in drawn pictures was in the Borderline range of functioning. His executive functioning abilities were severely impaired, as evidenced in his poor performance on making copies of simple series, in which he made several perseverative errors. Additionally, his cognitive flexibility was severely impaired. In contrast, his verbal abstraction ability was in the Average range.

His verbal and language abilities varied between Moderately Impaired and High Average. Mr. G.'s fund of general academic knowledge was in the Borderline range, suggesting at least mild retrograde amnesia, while his ability to define words remained in the High Average range. In contrast, his ability to name pictured objects was moderately to severely impaired and suggests word-finding difficulties. Although his prosodic intonation and phrase length were intact, his use of syntax was problematic on occasion due to omission of words. Writing was smooth and legible, although inconsistent use of capitalization was noted.

Mr. G.'s visual-spatial abilities were generally in the Low Average range. Problems in proportion errors in rendering three-dimensionality, and perseverations were noted on drawings.

Overall, Mr. G.'s WMS-III Immediate and General (Delayed) Memory Indexes were in the Extremely Low range of functioning, showing about equal impairment whether recalling information immediately or after a delay. Mr. G.'s subtest scores revealed significant forgetting in both verbal and visual domains. There was no advantage for encoding verbal-versus-visual material. Within the auditory domain, Mr. G.'s memory abilities were fairly consistently impaired across immediate and delayed conditions. Typically, patients benefit from the additional cues presented in recognition paradigms and evidence stronger performance through recognition than retrieval. However, Mr. G.'s Auditory Recognition Index was substantially lower than his Auditory Delayed Index. Thus, because his performance did not improve on recognition paradigms, results suggest problematic encoding of new information, as opposed to a retrieval deficit.

Mr. G.'s verbal learning over multiple trials showed that he did not profit from repeated exposure to unrelated word-pairs. Mr. G.'s verbal learning of word-pairs over multiple trials was Borderline and was better than recall of semantic information presented once.

In contrast to his verbal memory, Mr. G.'s visual memory showed some areas of relative strength. His immediate visual memory for faces appears stronger than his verbal memory, and after a 60-min delay, his facial recognition score was Average. This pattern in his immediate and delayed memory of facial stimuli suggests increased consolidation over time for this special class of visual stimuli. However, on other tasks of visual memory, his performance was impaired across the board.

Mr. G.'s sensory perception and motor function were within normal limits. Testing did not reveal deficits in unilateral or bilateral visual and tactile perception. However, detection of auditory stimulation was reduced and testing was not completed in this modality. Motor speed was in the Normal range for both hands and atypical in that there was no advantage for his dominant (right) hand.

In summary, the neuropsychological protocol as a whole reflected possible dysfunction of multiple cortical regions, including bilateral hippocampal, temporal, parietal, and frontal lobes. Overall, his performance suggests a moderate to severe stage of Alzheimer's disease.

Comparison of Current Performances to Previous Testing

Comparison of Mr. G.'s current performance to analogous results from earlier testing, done 5 years ago, revealed important changes. Mr. G. now demonstrates temporal disorientation, whereas 5 years ago he did not. Simple auditory attention is grossly the same (Digit Span of 4 forward and 3 backward). His Digit Symbol-Coding performance was normal in the previous testing and is now in the Borderline range of functioning. At the previous testing, his simple visual attention performance was normal and is now problematic for perceptual errors and tracking errors in the Trail A condition. Cognitive flexibility assessment was severely impaired at this testing and was discontinued before completed (Trail B), whereas performance on a cognitive flexibility task was slow, but intact, 5 years ago. Verbal (list) learning was in the Below Average range for unrelated word-pairs at the previous testing, and has subsequently decreased (at delay condition, at the floor of possible scores). While his auditory memory of a learned list previously demonstrated a significant advantage for information that was retrieved from recognition rather than recall, his recognition capabilities are now in the Severely Deficient range, suggesting that his current memory impairment is due predominantly to an encoding deficit rather than a retrieval problem. His naming abilities are now moderately to severely impaired, whereas they were mild to moderately impaired at the earlier testing. Abstract visual-constructional abilities, as measured by Block Design, remain in the Low Average range, as they were previously. However, drawing tasks conducted at this testing suggested significant conceptual difficulties, possible mild visual-spatial and visual-motor deficits, and moderate deficits for planning elements at spontaneous drawing conditions.

Recommendations

1. This assessment revealed decreased performances in all cognitive domains, including problem-solving capabilities and executive functioning. Specific results should be reviewed with Mr. G.'s children and his wife (as well as other individuals who will be active in decision-making and execution of his care). Mr. G.'s affairs should be put in order if this has not yet been done, and it is appropriate to consider conservatorship at this time.

2. Given overall deterioration in cognitive functions, it is strongly recommended that Mr. G. give up driving, even in areas of town that are familiar. He may still retain "automatic" or procedural aspects of driving a vehicle. However, in the context of new and sudden circumstances, he is prone to confusion and poor judgment where rapid adaptation, flexible decision-making, and appropriate response choices are needed. He is therefore at risk for causing or failing to avoid car accidents. To keep himself and others safe, he should not continue driving.

3. Despite Mr. G.'s loss of significant capabilities, he still has many cognitive areas that remain relatively functional. Areas of strengths include vocabulary, verbal abstraction, and verbatim repetition; he is still able to learn small bits of information, although long-term retention is poor. Pictorial scenes are recalled immediately, but again, there is forgetting at delay. In contrast, new facial identities are recalled after a delay. Mr. G. is still able to converse meaningfully, write down his thoughts, and, by his report, partake in leisure activities such as gardening and appreciation of music. These should be emphasized where possible in daily activities in order to maintain them as long as possible.

4. If the family decides to arrange for his care in the house, then his day should be kept to a rigid routine, and any deviations should be reviewed with him several times. Reminders should be put in writing (e.g., doctor's appointments, visits with family members, etc.) at a place that he learns to check reliably. This kind of regular prompting will help him to prepare for upcoming events sufficiently, from both an emotional and practical standpoint (i.e., handling any anticipatory anxiety about conducting a different activity, pulling together necessary items for the appointments, dressing appropriately, etc.). If he is given lead-time and knows what to expect, he is likely to function more adequately. Calm, verbal reminders of upcoming events in the daily routine will ease transitions and make them smoother. If he wants to undertake complex chores such as shopping, household maintenance and repair, or conducting errands around town, he should be accompanied by someone who can help him if he loses track or becomes confused about his targeted activities. He is likely to forget to take medications, if any should be prescribed in the future. He is not in charge of finances at this time, so no further comment about this arena of function is mentioned. Stress level should be kept to a minimum, and regular physical activity is likely to help him maintain his psychological and physical health for as long as possible.

5. Mr. G. should *not* be expected to make any rapid decisions in emergency situations. Family members should arrange a schedule of "checking in" frequently or arrange for someone to do so, especially because his wife's health is currently fragile.

6. A hearing examination is suggested, given that he could not detect unilateral finger taps reliably.

7. Retesting is recommended in a year to evaluate potential further decline, and adjustments of recommendations will be made accordingly.

NATALIE L., AGE 47, CLOSED HEAD INJURY

Reason for Referral

A comprehensive neuropsychological assessment was conducted for Ms. Natalie L. to assess her cognitive functioning after sustaining a closed head injury when her car was hit by an oncoming car. Ms. L. complained recently of memory difficulties and increased emotionality. Information for this report was obtained through clinical interview and administration of neuropsychological and psychological measures.

Background Information

History of Injury

The background information was obtained from Ms. L. and her husband. Ms. L.'s car accident occurred 3 months ago, as she was crossing an intersection. The oncoming car, which was reportedly traveling 70 to 80 mph, hit the passenger side, totaling her car. Ms. L. lost consciousness, but did not know for how long. She was taken to a trauma center where she stayed overnight. Her last memory prior to the accident was working with a client's papers and detailing an order at the office, about an hour before. She did not recall the first 2 weeks thereafter (including several doctor visits in that period). She noted that she was taking Vicodin and Valium that her doctor prescribed, so her experience of being "out of it" for the subsequent 2 weeks may have been due to a combination of her injury and medication effects. Her husband first saw her 2 hours after the accident, and he described her as confused and agitated, and having no recollection of the wreck. She had sustained cuts at her top left and right side, as well as the back of her head, due to impact with the headrest and side of the car as her body was thrown backward on impact. She also suffered an impact tear of the left rotator cuff and injured two vertebrae in her neck. The neck and shoulder injury prompted doctors to worry about her neck and shoulder injury and to keep her over night for observation. She said that nobody has evaluated or treated her for a possible head injury until this assessment. She reported she has no plans to pursue a lawsuit, as she feels that the accident was "50% my fault."

After the accident, Ms. L. experienced back, neck, and shoulder pain, but feels the pain is at a tolerable level and controllable with ibuprofen. Initially, shoulder pain woke her up or caused insomnia, but now, it only bothers her at night once in a while. She has been recuperating since but would like to return to work full-time. She is employed as a retail clothing salesperson. She said, "I love to work and take care of customers. I'd rather be doing something than sitting around wasting time." She has a staunch work ethic and is quite uncomfortable with the amount of time she has been out of work already.

Immediately after the accident, Ms. L. was confused and could not recall where her car was, despite being reminded repeatedly that it had been totaled. Her boss visited her, but when her employer spoke of her children, Ms. L. did not know how she knew her children. She needs to be reminded of doctors' appointments. Ms. L. works with numbers, places orders, and interacts with clients at her job. She also works with computer programs. She is concerned about how well she will be able to function, as she finds that she has a hard time recalling conversations she has had. For example, her friends have indicated that she asks them questions that they have already answered, and that the few conversations she has had with long-term customers have been difficult for her to recall, even when she is reminded. She loses things around the house. No changes in speech, mechanical abilities, or writing were noted. Reading comprehension is somewhat more problematic. While helping her son with his homework, she must reread the material in order to determine the answers.

Mr. L. indicated that his wife has been more emotional since the accident, stating that she is easily moved to tears when watching a sad show on TV, which rarely occurred before. He said that, since the accident, his wife periodically "flies off the handle" and has "temper tantrums." Mr. and Ms. L.'s son confided in his father that "Mom's a grump, now." Since the accident, Ms. L. does not like being around people, whereas before, she was quite sociable. Insignificant things "set her off," but with her husband's assistance, she has learned to recognize when it happens. She gets upset at other drivers while on the road and swears much more frequently. She has not become physically violent, however. Initially after the accident, she began spending hundreds of dollars on things that they did not need, such as furniture, or would buy more than one of an item, which limited her debit card. Both she and her husband reported that her sexual drive is also much higher, and she has less control of her inhibitions. No changes in weight or eating patterns were observed. Ms. L.

is still able to enjoy some activities. She likes to water ski and cook, as well as garden.

Personal History

Ms. L. was born and raised in a major metropolitan area. She has four siblings, and they all live nearby. Ms. L. resides in a house with her husband, 9-year-old son, and 15-year-old daughter. Neither of the children have learning difficulties, and they have done well academically. Her husband works as an administrator in a hospital. Ms. L. completed high school and one year of college. Her grades in high school and college were primarily Bs. She indicated that the easiest courses for her were Math, Art, and Science. She denied having had symptoms of a learning disability or Attention-deficit Disorder. She has never repeated a grade and was not placed in special education classes.

Medical History

Ms. L. did not have any serious illnesses during childhood. She underwent surgery for uterine fibroids at the age of 36. Ms. L. has never received psychiatric or psychological care. Substance abuse and dependence are not part of her history as she does not like to be "under the influence" of any substance. She experimented with marijuana once or twice while in college, and estimated that she drinks socially approximately four times a year, but never until intoxicated.

Behavioral Observations

Ms. L. was able to schedule appointments, but she required reminders from her husband. She was timely for the test session. Her attire was casual and neat, and her grooming was appropriate. Ms. L.'s demeanor was initially nervous and constrained but rapport was readily established, and she appeared to be relaxed within a half-hour. Her mood was within normal limits. During test procedures, she appeared to try her best, but became visibly frustrated about her performance on memory procedures. No difficulty was demonstrated in comprehending questions and directions. Her language output was within normal limits for phrase length, prosody, and volume, and she did not appear to have any word-finding problems. Occasionally, the content of her speech was mildly circuitous and tangential. However, her verbalizations were spontaneous and generally reality-oriented. Hallucinatory behavior was not demonstrated during the evaluation. Due to her apparent level of motivation and understanding of the task demands, the results of this evaluation are thought to be a valid indicator of Ms. L.'s cognitive functions. The nature and purpose of the testing were explained to Ms. L. The importance of working to the best of her ability was emphasized prior to the testing. The consistency of the neuropsychological test results did not suggest malingering. Personality test data showed that Ms. L. was mildly defensive in her approach but not enough to be clinically important.

Tests Administered

Background information and history
- Clinical Interview

Neuropsychological Data
- Benton Controlled Oral Word Association
- Block Span
- Finger Tapping
- Galveston Orientation and Amnesia Test
- Grooved Pegboard
- Kløve-Reitan Sensory Perceptual Examination
- Rey-Osterrieth Complex Figure Test
- Ruff Language Screening Examination
- Ruff Spatial Screening Exam
- Ruff Two and Seven Selective Attention Test
- Selective Reminding Test
- Stroop Color Word Naming
- Trail Making Test (A and B)
- Wechsler Adult Intelligence Scale–Third Edition (WAIS-III)
- Wechsler Memory Scale–Third Edition (WMS-III)
- Wisconsin Card Sorting Test (WCST)

Personality/Emotional Functioning
- Minnesota Multiphasic Personality Inventory-2 (MMPI-2)

(Test scores are listed in Table 7.2)

Table 7.2 Summary of Natalie L.'s Test Scores

Panel A. Wechsler Memory Scale–Third Edition (WMS-III)

	Index Score	Percentile Rank	Confidence Interval (95%)
Primary Indexes			
Auditory Immediate	89	23	83–97
Visual Immediate	112	79	100–120
Immediate Memory	100	50	92–108
Auditory Delayed	77	6	71–89
Visual Delayed	112	79	100–120
Auditory Recognition Delayed	75	5	70–93
General Memory	87	19	80–96
Working Memory	88	21	80–99

	Age-Scaled Score	Percentile Rank
Primary Subtests		
Logical Memory I Total Recall	8	25
Faces I Recognition Total	11	63
Verbal Paired Associates I Recall Total	8	25
Family Pictures I Recall Total	13	84
Letter-Number Sequencing Total	7	16
Spatial Span Total	9	37
Logical Memory II Recall Total	4	2
Faces II Recognition Total	10	50
Verbal Paired Associates II Recall Total	8	25
Family Pictures II Recall Total	14	91
Auditory Recognition Delayed Total	5	5

(continued)

Table 7.2 Continued

Panel B. Wechsler Adult Intelligence Scale–Third Edition (WAIS-III)

	IQ/Index	Confidence Interval	Percentile Rank	Descriptive Category
Scale/Index				
Verbal	99	94–014	47	Average
Performance	111	104–117	77	High Average
Full Scale	104	100–108	61	Average
Verbal Comprehension	105	99–110	63	Average
Perceptual Organization	116	108–122	86	High Average
Working Memory	86	80–94	18	Low Average
Processing Speed	88	80–98	21	Low Average
Verbal Scale				
Information		10		50
Digit Span		8		25
Vocabulary		11		65
Arithmetic		8		25
Comprehension		11		65
Similarities		12		75
Letter-Number Sequencing		7		16
Performance Scale				
Picture Completion		11		65
Picture Arrangement		13		84
Matrix Reasoning		14		91
Block Design		13		84
Object Assembly		11		63
Digit Symbol-Coding		8		25
Symbol Search		8		25

Test Results and Interpretation

Cognitive Functioning

Results of the Galveston Orientation and Amnesia Test revealed that Ms. L. was oriented to person and place. There were no overt indications of delirium or psychotic processes. To assess her overall level of intellectual ability and cognitive strengths and weaknesses, Ms. L. was administered the Wechsler Adult Intelligence Test–Third Edition (WAIS-III). The WAIS-III is composed of 14 separate subtests and measures both verbal skills and specific nonverbal abilities such as constructing designs with blocks. Ms. L.'s scores were in the Average range for Verbal IQ (VIQ), High Average range for Performance IQ (PIQ), and Average range for Full Scale IQ (FSIQ). Because of significant discrepancies between her scores on the factor indexes, neither her VIQ of 100 or PIQ of 111 are meaningful representations of her global verbal and nonverbal abilities. Similarly, her FSIQ represents nothing more than the average of several diverse skills. Her separate Index scores provide a clearer understanding of her global cognitive abilities. She obtained a Verbal Comprehension Index Score of 105 (63rd percentile, Average range), which was significantly lower than her Perceptual Organization Index of 116 (86th percentile, High Average range). Her Working Memory Index was 86 (18th percentile, Low Average range) and her Processing Speed Index was 88 (21st percentile, Low Average range). Thus, her visual-spatial reasoning capabilities were significantly better than her speed of processing, attentional, and verbal capabilities. Ms. L.'s premorbid functioning is estimated to have been in the Average range, considering specific test results and educational and occupational background.

The pattern of attention and concentration abilities evident in the WAIS-III Indexes was also evident in Ms. L.'s individual subtest scores, as well as on supplemental tests of neuropsychological abilities. For example, her performance on simple attentional tasks was mildly reduced. Ms. L.'s span of auditory immediate attention (Digit Span) and ability to complete mental arithmetic problems were at the 25th percentile, and her ability to mentally hold and manipulate numbers and letters (Letter-Number Sequencing) was at the 16th percentile. In addition, her arithmetic was deficient on the language screen exam and was notable for attentional errors in mental calculations and a division problem done on paper. Ms. L.'s capacity to attend to visuospatial material was in the Low Average range (Block Span). She replicated a pattern of 5 locations from a sequence of spatially configured blocks (24th percentile). In addition, Ms. L.'s visuospatial selective attention varied, as speed was mildly sacrificed for accuracy. She was asked to cross out the target numbers 2 and 7 embedded among rows of either other digits or alphabetical letters. In the latter condition, parallel processing is possible. During a 5-min period, Ms. L.'s performance was in the Low Average range for total items in both the digit and letter condition, but in the High Average range for suppression of errors in the digit condition and in the Average range for the letter condition. The test compared serial (digit-to-digit) and parallel processing (letter-to-digit), and her pattern was typical, as the results were better in the parallel mode (Total Letters = 106, Total Digits = 94).

Ms. L.'s low-average performance on the Processing Speed Index was evident during the two tasks that comprise this Index. During these tasks, her graphomotoric speed was evaluated by having her rapidly draw symbols below numbers according to specific pairings shown on the page (Digit Symbol-Coding, 25th percentile), and, on a separate task by requiring her to scan a row of symbols and mark whether target symbols were present in the row (Symbol Search, 25th percentile). These tasks required both target identification and evaluation of multiple codes efficiently. Ms. L.'s Low Average processing speed was significantly lower than her High Average overall visual-spatial skills.

Motor speed was further assessed by having Ms. L. tap a lever as quickly as possible with her index finger. For each hand, speed performances were averaged across five alternating intervals of 10 seconds each. Results were in the High Average range bilaterally. Eye-hand coordination was measured by having Ms. L. insert metal pegs into randomly rotated slots as quickly as possible. Ms. L.'s fine-motor dexterity was in the Average range bilaterally. There were no deficiencies detected in motor speed or dexterity. Ms. L. did not demonstrate deficits in visual, auditory, or tactile perception. Testing revealed that visual fields were intact. All unilateral and bilateral simultaneous stimuli were lateralized correctly. Upon light touch, no suppression of stimuli was noted for the right or left hand or for the right and left side of the face.

Susceptibility to interference was evaluated by the Stroop Color Word Naming Test, a timed task in which Ms. L. was asked to identify different colors while suppressing interfering stimuli. Ms. L.'s performance was Low Average for completion time on all conditions, including the final condition, which had difficult suppression demands. However, she made two errors on the last condition, placing her performance in the Borderline range for accuracy. She completed sequencing of an ascending series of numbered dots (Trails A) in a Low Average amount of time and without errors. Completion time for a subsequent task requiring alternate sequencing of numbered and lettered dots (Trails B) was also Low Average, and, again, without error. Overall, she had mild difficulties on cognitive flexibility and suppression of prepotent responding tasks.

In contrast to her Low Average attentional capabilities and speed of processing, Ms. L. obtained scores that were almost all in the Average range or above across several problem-solving tasks. For verbal reasoning using practical judgment and social conventions (WAIS-III Comprehension), her performance was Average (65th percentile), although her solutions to emergency situations were mildly impulsive. On a task of verbal abstraction (Similarities), her performance was in the High Average range (75th percentile). On a separate task requiring verbal fluency in generating different words beginning with a specific letter of the alphabet, she performed in the Low Average range and made no perseverative errors. On an analogous nonverbal task, her total production and suppression of perseverative errors were Average. Her nonverbal reasoning skills were a relative strength, as was evident by her High Average to Superior performance on two WAIS-III Perceptual Organization tasks. She scored at the 91st percentile on a task requiring her to use reasoning to complete a gridded pattern, and she scored at the 84th percentile on a task that required her to rearrange a set of mixed-up pictures and put them into a logical order. On the Wisconsin Card Sorting Test, Ms. L. was able to obtain six categories on a task in which she was required to generate hypotheses, maintain set, and switch rules in response to verbal feedback, and she did not make a preponderance of perseverative errors. Two instances of loss of set were noted, however.

Variable results were obtained on tasks measuring verbal abilities. Ms. L. repeated multisyllabic words presented individually without difficulty but made two omission errors in a 13-word sentence. After reading a short passage, she was able to answer questions about it and had no problems recalling information. When reading out loud, verbal production was clear and fluent. She did not have problems labeling items upon confrontational naming. Spelling was in the Borderline range for commonly used words, and she indicated she could spell one word on paper, but not aloud. Her ability to provide word definitions was in the Average range (65th percentile). Verbal expression was intact. There was no evidence of paraphasias or neologisms. Syntax was employed appropriately, but mild tangentiality was heard. Ms. L.'s mathematical ability was in the Borderline range (due to an attentional error) on the Language Screening Exam but was in the Low Average range on the WAIS-III, which assesses mental mathematical skills through everyday word problems (Arithmetic, 25th percentile).

Ms. L.'s visual-spatial abilities were generally in the Average range. Ms. L. did not show difficulty orienting to personal space. Identifying left and right locations on objects in front of her was intact. Graphomotorically, Ms. L.'s handwriting was legible, and no unusual tremor or pressure was noted. Copies of simple objects were grossly intact, with very mild impulsivity noted on her clock drawing. Her copy of a complex geometric design (Rey-Osterrieth) was in the Low Average range with respect to the number of elements present and in the Average range with respect to placement. Mild impulsivity was noted for three details on the drawing, which she attempted to self-correct. The drawing was also slightly disproportionate in length. The time required to complete the task was in the Average range.

On a visual-perceptual measure, Ms. L. was asked to examine pictures and identify omitted details. Her performance was in the Average range of functioning (WAIS-III Picture Completion, 65th percentile). On an abstract spatial construction task, Ms. L. was asked to arrange a number of colored blocks to matched modeled designs. Her performance was in the High Average range (Block Design, 84th percentile), and she assembled all items correctly. On a concrete spatial construction task, where Ms. L. was given puzzles to put together, performance was Average (Object Assembly, 63rd percentile). Again, she was able to assemble them all successfully within the time limits.

Learning and Memory Functioning

A verbal learning test required Ms. L. to learn 12 words across a number of trials (Selective Reminding). Ms. L. was unable to reach criterion by the 12th trial and total correct was low-average. Her ability to store and recall the words from memory continuously was average, but total long-term retrieval and storage were deficient. Ms. L. made two intrusion errors. She appeared to "lock-up" on this task, as she perceived she was not performing well. She became tearful and upset and required a moment to collect herself before proceeding.

On a task of visuospatial learning (Trail Learning), Ms. L. was required to learn a complex trail within a spatial configuration of multiple possible pathways. She demonstrated a rapid learning curve and obtained the trail by the 8th trial (10-trial criterion). Ms. L. was able to respond to feedback and learn from her errors (total errors and step errors were average). Visual learning was a relative strength in comparison to verbal learning.

Ms. L.'s overall memory abilities, including long- and short-term, verbal and nonverbal, were assessed with the Wechsler Memory Scale–Third Edition (WMS-III). There was a significant discrepancy between her Low Average Auditory Immediate Index score (89; 23rd percentile) and High Average Visual Immediate Index score (112; 79th percentile), which indicates that (a) her recall was better for visual material, and that (b) the Immediate Memory Index does not meaningfully represent her global immediate memory abilities. There was also a significant discrepancy between her Borderline Auditory Delayed Index score (77; 6th percentile) and High Average Visual Delayed Index score (112, 79th percentile), suggesting that her delayed recall was better for visual material as well. There was no significant difference between her Auditory Delayed and Auditory Recognition Delayed Indexes, which were both in the Borderline range, suggesting that a recognition format does not improve memory scores over and above what she could retrieve spontaneously. Her auditory memory difficulties are therefore likely due to an encoding, rather than a retrieval, deficit.

In analyzing her WMS-III subtest profile, Ms. L. appeared to have relative strengths in her associative memory as well as her spatial relations. Her strong associative memory and spatial relations were especially evident in her performance on a task that required her to remember the location and activity of people depicted in a scene together (91st percentile). Her strong spatial relations were commensurate with her high-average performance on the WAIS-III Perceptual Organization Index. In contrast, her weakest performance was on a test requiring her to recall a story heard 60-min earlier (2nd percentile). These individual subtest scores were consistent with her overall stronger visual (rather than verbal) memory abilities. Across all auditory immediate and delayed subtests, her mean subtest scaled score was in the Low Average range, while her mean subtest scaled score across visual immediate and delayed subtests was in the Average range.

Similar memory results were found in additional visual memory tests. At 3-

and 60-min delays, Ms. L. was asked to draw a complex figure copied earlier. Her renditions included an Average number of details, and her placement was also Average at both 3- and 60-min delays. The overall configuration was preserved, but some details were omitted, and others were slightly distorted. However, when compared to the target, her productions were quite recognizable. In addition, the 60-min delayed recall of a previously learned trail was Average, as were the number of errors.

Psychological and Personality Functioning

Validity Scales. The MMPI-2 validity scale configuration was within normal limits, and suggested mild defensiveness at subclinical levels. The results are likely to be a valid reflection of current psychological and personality functioning.

Clinical Results. The clinical scale configuration revealed that Ms. L. feels angry and resentful about her circumstances. She described difficulties making sound judgments and decisions, and she may exhibit disturbed thinking. She is likely to be sensitive and overly responsive to opinions of others; she may also take a suspicious and guarded stance toward others. She tends to be moralistic and rigid in her opinions and attitudes and may overemphasize rationality. She also exhibits some features of rebelliousness toward authority, as well as a tendency toward impulsive actions and immediate gratification of impulses. When dissatisfied with her own behavior, she tends to use projection as a defense mechanism. She reported interpersonal difficulties and significant social discomfort. Hostility, argumentativeness, and emotional lability make a negative impact on her interpersonal interactions. Consequently, she tends to withdraw from and avoid others, thereby becoming socially alienated.

Ms. L. is experiencing some dysphoria and anxiety (including an elevation on a post-traumatic stress symptom scale) and becomes agitated in response to these feelings. She is not comfortable with depending upon others. Marital distress is noted. In the protocol, she reports emotional dyscontrol, and she becomes tearful and angry quickly and often, without much cause. Despite her outbursts and attempts to control her circumstances, she is unable to take an effectively dominant, assertive role in dealing with others. Ego strength and competitive drive are deflated as she is encumbered by health concerns. Neurological symptoms were acknowledged in the form of difficulties with attention, concentration, and memory, and these largely drive clinical scale elevations. These results are consistent with clinical observation during interview and testing.

Summary

Ms. L. is a 47-year-old Caucasian woman who was referred for neuropsychological consultation to delineate her cognitive and emotional status after a closed head injury that she suffered 3 months ago.

Notable difficulties in cognitive functioning were observed in the following areas:

1. *Intellectual functioning.* When compared to individuals in her age group, there is a discrepancy between Ms. L.'s visual-spatial abilities (High Average range) and her verbal conceptualization skills (Average range). An advantage for visual-processing may have been present premorbidly, given Ms. L.'s reported history. In addition, her global Index scales reveal significantly weaker attention/concentration and verbal memory abilities (Low Average range) than her overall verbal conceptualization skills. Her processing speed is also an area of deficit (Low Average range).

2. *Simple Attention.* This was variable, resulting in low-average performance on some measures for both auditory and visual attention. For example, attentional errors were made in a verbal repetition task, and performance was likely to be reduced on a prose passage task due to attentional problems. Also, Ms. L. sacrificed speed for accuracy on a visual attention task. Performance on a task of rapid graphomotor function represented the lowest subtest on intellectual testing and was low-average. Her performance on an arithmetic task was deficient on the language screen exam, and was notable for attentional errors in mental calculations and a division problem done on paper.

3. *Executive Functioning.* This may be slightly compromised, in that she had some difficulty inhibiting prepotent responding (Stroop) and there were two instances of loss of set on a measure of hypothesis testing and set maintenance (Wisconsin Card Sort). Mild impulsivity was observed on a verbal problem-solving task, and verbal fluency was also low-average. However, cognitive flexibility and figural fluency were intact. Problem solving and social reasoning were average to superior.

4. *Learning and Memory.* Learning was deficient for verbal material, but it should be noted that Ms. L. became anxious and upset during this test (Selective Reminding). In contrast, she was able to learn a complex trail within a spatial configuration of multiple possible pathways, demon-

strating a more rapid learning curve, and she obtained the trail by the 8th trial (10-trial criterion). Ms. L. was able to respond to feedback and learn from her errors (total errors and step errors were average).

Her visual learning was a relative strength in comparison to verbal learning. A significant discrepancy between her Low Average Auditory Immediate and High Average Visual Immediate Index scores suggested that attentional capabilities are stronger in the visual domain. There was also a significant discrepancy between her Borderline Auditory Delayed Index and High Average Visual Delayed Index, suggesting that delayed recall was better for visual material, as expected from immediate recall performances. Her Auditory Delayed and Auditory Recognition Delayed Indexes were both in the Borderline range, suggesting that a recognition format does not improve memory scores over and above what she could retrieve spontaneously. Her auditory memory difficulties are therefore likely due to an encoding, rather than a retrieval, deficit.

In contrast, relatively strong visual memory observed on the WMS-III was corroborated by production of a complex figure, which was average at both immediate and 60-min recall conditions for presence and placement of elements. Occasional details were omitted in these productions. The 60-min delayed recall of a previously learned trail was average, as were the number of errors.

5. *Sensory/Motor.* Sensory testing was within normal limits for visual, auditory, and tactile modalities. Motor dexterity was deficient in the nondominant hand (injured in the accident) with respect to time.

6. *Psychological functioning.* Objective personality assessment showed that Ms. L. approached the test in a mildly defensive manner, although validity scales were within normal limits. The clinical scale configuration revealed that she feels angry about her circumstances. She is likely to be sensitive and overly responsive to opinions of others and to take a suspicious and guarded stance toward others. She reported interpersonal difficulties and significant social discomfort. Hostility, argumentativeness, and emotional lability make a negative impact on her interpersonal interactions and result in social alienation. Ms. L. is experiencing some dysphoria and anxiety (including an elevation on a post-traumatic stress symptom scale), and she becomes agitated in response to these feelings. She is not comfortable with depending upon others. Marital distress is

noted. In the protocol, she reports emotional dyscontrol, and she becomes tearful and angry quickly and often, without much cause. Neurological symptoms were acknowledged in the form of difficulties with attention, concentration, and memory, and these largely drive clinical scale elevations. She described difficulties making sound judgments and decisions, and she may exhibit disturbed thinking. She tends to be moralistic and rigid in her opinions and attitudes, and she tends to overemphasize rationality; however, she also demonstrates some features of rebelliousness, as well as a tendency toward impulsive actions and immediate gratification of impulses. When she is dissatisfied with her actions, she uses projection as a defense mechanism. These results are consistent with clinical observations during interview and testing.

Diagnostic Impressions

1. Post-concussion Syndrome with mild neurocognitive and social/emotional sequelae.
2. Mood and Anxiety Disorders due to medical condition.

Conclusions

Ms. L. was referred for a comprehensive neuropsychological evaluation after suffering a closed head injury 3 months ago in an automobile collision accident. Neck and shoulder injury as well as cognitive and emotional changes were a result of this accident. Ms. L. stated that she was an adequately functioning individual prior to her injuries and is struggling to maintain her previous level of functioning subsequent to the accident.

This assessment revealed a pattern of significant findings that are likely the result of a mild nervous system disorder. Ms. L. reported a brief loss of consciousness, and post-traumatic amnesia and confusion. The impact injured her neck and shoulder, and she sustained cuts on her head. Cognitive difficulties observed in this assessment included variable attentional problems, decreased cognitive efficiency, mild executive system dysfunction (in the form of problems in self-organization, difficulty in set-maintenance, and inhibition of prepotent responding), and an additional verbal learning and memory deficit. Additional behavioral changes including impulsivity, irritability, increased spending, and decreased inhibition were reported. Taken together, these changes probably reflect mild residual sequelae from the car accident in the form of mild diffuse brainstem changes, and focal prefrontal, lateral, and mesial temporal dominant hemisphere (presumably left) dysfunction. Biparietal, occipital, and nondominant mesial temporal structures appear to be relatively spared. Objective personality assessment demonstrated clinical levels of introversion and distrust of others, perhaps in reaction to her sense of increased vulnerability. Ms. L. appears to be experiencing both effects of a mild traumatic brain injury and a subsequent anxious and depressive reaction to these cognitive difficulties. Ms. L. has a rather staunch work ethic and high expectations for her own cognitive performance. These standards may cause an additional hardship in adjusting to the mild changes she is experiencing. Collectively, these are causing significant distress and impairment in occupational and social functioning. A review of medical, academic, and employment records would further assist in the determination of causation.

With treatment, the prognosis is fair to good that she will return to pre-injury functioning, considering the degree of dysfunction reflected by test findings, her age, and her medical condition. Spontaneous recovery, in all likelihood, has not yet fully occurred, because only 3 months have passed since the injury.

Recommendations

1. A course of cognitive remediation (15–20 sessions) is recommended to assist Ms. L. in developing strategies to improve her attention and learning efficiency for auditory/verbal information and to help her inhibit prepotent responding where contingencies dictate alternate courses of action.

2. Supportive psychotherapy (15–20 sessions) is highly recommended to help Ms. L. better cope with her mild changes in cognitive dysfunction and significant emotional lability. Finding healthier outlets for emotional expression will improve interpersonal relationships with her family members. Strategies for handling overwhelming frustration will undoubtedly assist her performance both in the workplace and in the social sphere. Additionally, post-traumatic stress symptomology should be addressed in this context. Finally, her rigid personality features that underlie unreasonably high standards for personal performance are detrimental to the prognosis. Rapport is an important issue from the standpoint that she is likely to be guarded and distrustful. If rapport is established, however, assistance in modifying her self-expectations to a realistic level will, in itself, be therapeutic.

Ideally, for the sake of efficiency, a single clinician (preferably a neuropsychologist) would be capable of meeting the first two recommendations of cognitive remediation and supportive psychotherapy. A clinician who is knowledgeable and empathic about the consequences of a mild traumatic brain injury can be of greatest assistance to Ms. L.

3. Ms. L. is experiencing significant distress regarding work performance, but she expressly does not want to cut back on work hours to help alleviate the pressure. She most likely wants to prove that she can do the job, as she has only been at this job for a short time. Because cutting her back on hours at work may be counterproductive for her self-image (and therefore, recovery) a suggestion is that she does not take any job-related trips out of town, where she must work intensively for several days in a new environment. This is likely to overwhelm her.

4. A psychopharmacologic evaluation by a psychiatrist is also strongly suggested to help control Ms. L.'s anxiety, depression, and irritability. She is exerting a great deal of effort to keep her emotions controlled. As she is generally against taking substances of any kind, Ms. L. should be gently educated that medication usage is not a sign of weakness, that usage is temporary, and that the side effects can be closely monitored. Also, psychotropic medications must be taken regularly to provide optimal results. With progress in cognitive rehabilitation/psychotherapy, Ms. L. can discontinue these medications when she has learned better coping skills.

5. Ms. L. should continue her medical care for treatment of her neck and shoulder injuries.

Appendix A

Administrative Checklist for the WMS-III

Developed by Joseph J. Ryan, Thomas L. Weaver, and Shane J. Lopez

Name of examiner: _____

Name of examinee: _____

Name of observer: _____

Date: _____

(Note: If an item is not applicable, mark NA to the right of the answer area.)

Information and Orientation

Circle One

1. Reads questions clearly, exactly as presented in the Instruction *Manual*.	Yes	No
2. Records responses verbatim.	Yes	No
3. Asks for clarification when necessary.	Yes	No
4. Avoids leading questions.	Yes	No
5. Allows examinee ample time to respond to each question.	Yes	No
6. If the examinee doesn't know mother's name, (Item 5) asks, "Then what is your father's name?"	Yes	No
7. Provides clarification to Item 11, such as "What is the name of this facility?"	Yes	No
8. On item 14, prohibits examinee's use of watch or clock.	Yes	No
9. Records actual time, the examinee's response, and the difference in minutes between the two.	Yes	No
10. If examinee answers "Yes" for Item 16, queries extent of hearing impairment (if any).	Yes	No
11. Insures that examinee's hearing is sufficient for completing auditory portions of the scale by having him/her repeat a complex sentence (e.g., "The lawyer's closing argument convinced him").	Yes	No

12. If the examinee answers "Yes" to Item 17, queries extent of visual impairment. The examiner may ask the examinee to describe a standard picture (e.g., cookie theft picture from Boston Diagnostic Aphasia Exam) to ensure visual functions are adequate for completing the visual subtests.	Yes	No
13. Queries extent of color blindness (if any) on Item 18.	Yes	No
14. Records 0 or 1 point for Items 1–18.	Yes	No
15. Adds points correctly.	Yes	No

Comments:_____

_____

_____

Logical Memory I

	Circle One	
1. Reads directions verbatim.	Yes	No
2. Reads directions clearly.	Yes	No
3. If a tape recorder is used, informs the examinee, "I am going to use a tape recorder so that I can write down your exact words later on."	Yes	No
4. Reads stories verbatim.	Yes	No
5. Reads stories clearly.	Yes	No
6. Paces stories appropriately. Story A requires between 27 and 30 s to present and Story B requires between 33 and 40 s to present.	Yes	No
7. Prompts correctly if examinee is hesitant or freezes up when asked to recall the stories (e.g., "Tell me what you can remember," or "What happened first?" or "What happened next?").	Yes	No
8. If a prompt is given, does not include prompted information in the score.	Yes	No
9. Avoids leading questions.	Yes	No
10. Places check mark next to story units recalled verbatim.	Yes	No
11. Writes examinee's words next to story units not recalled verbatim.	Yes	No
12. Places check mark next to each correctly recalled thematic unit.	Yes	No

13. Prompts examinee to remember the stories for later ("I want you to remember as much of these stories as you can because I will ask you to tell me the stories again later").   Yes   No
14. Allows 1 point for each correct story unit.   Yes   No
15. Allows 1 point for each correct thematic unit.   Yes   No

Comments:_____

_____

_____

Faces I   *Circle One*

1. Reads directions verbatim.   Yes   No
2. Reads directions clearly.   Yes   No
3. Centers stimulus booklet in front of and close to examinee   Yes   No
4. Exposes each photograph for 2 s.   Yes   No
5. Says, "Remember this one" after exposing each photo.   Yes   No
6. Repeats and paraphrases directions if they are not understood by the examinee.   Yes   No
7. Circles *Y* or *N* on the record form to record examinee's response.   Yes   No
8. Allows 1 point credit for each correct response.   Yes   No
9. Adds points correctly.   Yes   No
10. States, "I want you to try to remember the first group of faces I asked you to remember because later on I'm going to ask you to pick them out of another group of faces," after completing the initial recall trial.   Yes   No

Comments:_____

_____

_____

Verbal Paired Associates I   *Circle One*

1. Reads directions verbatim.   Yes   No
2. Reads direction clearly.   Yes   No
3. Pauses where instructed in initial directions.   Yes   No
4. Repeats and paraphrases directions, if necessary.   Yes   No
5. If examinee begins to repeat word pairs prematurely, instructs him or her to wait until entire list is presented.
6. Speaks words about 1 s apart.   Yes   No
7. Separates word pairs by 2 s interval.   Yes   No

8.	Pronounces word pairs clearly.	Yes	No
9.	Pauses 5 s after reading each list and before prompting examinee for responses.	Yes	No
10.	Says, "Which word goes with _____?" after initially presenting the target word list.	Yes	No
11.	States, "That's right" after the examinee gives correct responses.	Yes	No
12.	Says, "No_____ goes with _____" upon eliciting incorrect responses from the examinee.	Yes	No
13.	Provides correct response if examinee does not respond within 5 s or if the examinee gives an incorrect response.	Yes	No
14.	Records all responses verbatim.	Yes	No
15.	Allows 1 point for each correct response.	Yes	No
16.	After completing List A, states, "Now I will read the same list again, except with the word pairs in a different order. Listen carefully."	Yes	No
17.	Uses same recall procedures as above with Lists B, C, and D.	Yes	No
18.	Presents all four lists, regardless of number of failures.	Yes	No
19.	After completing List D, says, "Later on I will ask you to recall these word pairs again, so try to remember them."	Yes	No
20.	Totals points correctly.	Yes	No

Comments:_____

_____

_____

Family Pictures I   *Circle One*

1.	Reads directions verbatim.	Yes	No
2.	Reads directions clearly.	Yes	No
3.	Centers stimulus booklet in front of and close to examinee.	Yes	No
4.	Points to each character as it is introduced.	Yes	No
5.	Uses stopwatch when timing scene exposure.	Yes	No
6.	States, "Now I am going to show you the _____ scene. I want you to remember as much about the scene as you can" after each picture presentation.	Yes	No
7.	Exposes each scene for 10 s.	Yes	No
8.	For each query following presentation of all pictures, states, "Who was in the _____ scene?"	Yes	No

9.	States, "Pretend this is the _____ scene. You said the _____ was in the _____ scene. On this card, point to where that character was in the picture."	Yes	No
10.	Says, "Now tell me what _____ was doing."	Yes	No
11.	Asks, "Were there any other characters in the _____ scene?"	Yes	No
12.	Names and queries all characters identified by the examinee.	Yes	No
13.	Queries location and action of all characters identified by the examinee.	Yes	No
14.	If examinee says there were additional characters in the scenes, queries for location and activity for each character named.	Yes	No
15.	Records examinee's responses verbatim.	Yes	No
16.	Avoids leading questions.	Yes	No
17.	Appropriately records examinee's response on the record form.	Yes	No
18.	After completing the questioning for all four scenes, states "Later on I will ask you questions about these scenes again, so try to remember them."	Yes	No
19.	Uses Scoring Criteria in Appendix B when scoring the "Activity" category.	Yes	No
20.	Allows 0, 1, or 2 points where appropriate.	Yes	No
21.	Calculates Recall Total Score correctly.	Yes	No

Comments:_____
_____
_____

Word Lists I   *Circle One*

1.	Reads directions verbatim.	Yes	No
2.	Reads directions clearly.	Yes	No
3.	Reads target words at approximately 1 word per 1.5 s.	Yes	No
4.	Pronounces target words clearly.	Yes	No
5.	Places a check mark next to each word recalled (some examiners prefer to place a number next to each word to signify the order in which it was recalled).	Yes	No
6.	Records intrusions verbatim.	Yes	No

7. Records preservations verbatim.	Yes	No
8. Allows 1 point for each correct response.	Yes	No
9. Administers all four Word List trials, Short Delay recall, and List B.	Yes	No
10. Adds points correctly.	Yes	No
11. Prompts the examinee to remember the word list for the delayed recall trial by stating, "I want you to remember the first list of words that we did four times because I'm going to ask you to tell them to me again later on."	Yes	No

Comments:_____

_____

_____

Visual Reproduction I   *Circle One*

1. Records examiner's and examinee's name and date on the front of the Visual Reproduction Response Booklet.	Yes	No
2. Reads directions verbatim.	Yes	No
3. Reads directions clearly.	Yes	No
4. Provides two #2 pencils with erasers.	Yes	No
5. Records hand examinee used (right vs. left).	Yes	No
6. Uses stopwatch in timing design exposure.	Yes	No
7. Places stimulus booklet in front of and close to examinee.	Yes	No
8. Exposes each design for 10 s.	Yes	No
9. Provides general encouragement when necessary (e.g., "Don't worry about your artistic ability; just draw it as well as you remember").	Yes	No
10. If examinee says, "I don't remember," examiner says "Well, just draw it as well as you remember."	Yes	No
11. Allows examinee enough time to draw and erase, if necessary.	Yes	No
12. On Design D, explains increasing difficulty level and points to left and right side of response booklet.	Yes	No
13. On Design E, points to left and right side of response booklet.	Yes	No
14. States, "Later on I will ask you to draw all the designs again, from memory, so try to remember them."	Yes	No
15. Refers to Appendix C for scoring criteria.	Yes	No

16. Calculates Recall Total Score correctly.   Yes   No

Comments:_____

_____

_____

Letter-Number Sequencing   *Circle One*

1. Reads directions verbatim.   Yes   No
2. Reads directions clearly.   Yes   No
3. Administers all practice trials.   Yes   No
4. Allows examinee ample time to respond.   Yes   No
5. Corrects examinee if he or she makes an error on   Yes   No
    any practice item and then repeats instructions, as necessary.
6. Continues with subtest even if the examinee fails all   Yes   No
    practice items.
7. Begins with Item 1.   Yes   No
8. Administers all three trials of each item.   Yes   No
9. Pronounces letters and digits singly, distinctly, and at the   Yes   No
    rate of 1 digit/letter per s, without chunking.
10. Drops voice inflection slightly on last letter or digit.   Yes   No
11. Pauses after each sequence to allow examinee time to   Yes   No
    respond.
12. Discontinues after failure of all three trials within an item.   Yes   No
13. Records examinees response to each trial verbatim.   Yes   No
14. Allows credit if the examinee says the letters before the   Yes   No
    numbers, as long as the numbers and letters are in the
    correct sequence.
15. Assigns 1 point for each trial passed.   Yes   No
16. Adds points correctly.   Yes   No

Comments:_____

_____

_____

Spatial Span   *Circle One*

1. Places Spatial Span board with cube numbers facing   Yes   No
    examiner and the board centered at the examinee's midline.
2. Reads directions verbatim.   Yes   No
3. Reads directions clearly.   Yes   No
4. Taps out sequences at the rate of 1 cube per s.   Yes   No

5.	Pauses after each sequence to allow ample time for responding	Yes	No
6.	Administers both trials of each item.	Yes	No
7.	Records the actual numbers tapped by the examinee.	Yes	No
8.	If the examinee responds using both hands, examiner instructs the examinee to use one hand only.	Yes	No
9.	Discontinues after failure on both trials of an item.	Yes	No
10.	Assigns score of 0 if the examinee does not tap all of the specified cubes or makes an error in the tapping sequence.	Yes	No
11.	Administers Spatial Span Backward even if examinee obtains a score of 0 on Spatial Span Forward.	Yes	No
12.	Gives the examinee a sample item for Spatial Span Backward.	Yes	No
13.	Gives the examinee the correct answer to the sample item if the examinee fails the sample on Spatial Span Backward.	Yes	No
14.	Administers second sample item if examinee fails the first example.	Yes	No
15.	Proceeds with Item 1 even if examinee fails second sample item.	Yes	No
16.	Records the number of each cube in the order in which it is tapped.	Yes	No
17.	Assigns 1 point for each trial passed.	Yes	No
18.	Adds points correctly.	Yes	No

Comments:_____

_____

_____

Mental Control

Circle One

1.	Reads directions verbatim.	Yes	No
2.	Reads directions clearly.	Yes	No
3.	Repeats and paraphrases directions, if necessary.	Yes	No
4.	Crosses any element the examinee omits and writes any elements that the examinee says in the wrong sequence.	Yes	No
5.	On Item 8 sample, pauses and gestures after "12" to allow examinee a chance to respond.	Yes	No
6.	Uses stopwatch to record exact response time.	Yes	No
7.	Stops timing immediately after examinee completes his or her response.	Yes	No

	Yes	No
8. Circles accuracy score (0, 1, or 2) as appropriate.	Yes	No
9. Assigns appropriate bonus points, as necessary.	Yes	No
10. Adds points correctly.	Yes	No

Comments:_____

_____

_____

Digit Span   *Circle One*

1. Reads directions verbatim.	Yes	No
2. Reads directions clearly.	Yes	No
3. Begins with Item 1.	Yes	No
4. Administers both trials of each item.	Yes	No
5. Pronounces digits singly, distinctly, and at the rate of 1 digit per s, without chunking.	Yes	No
6. Drops voice inflection slightly on the last digit.	Yes	No
7. Pauses after each sequence to allow examinee time to respond.	Yes	No
8. Administers Digits Backward even if examinee obtains a score of 0 on Digits Forward.	Yes	No
9. Gives sample item for Digits Backward.	Yes	No
10. Gives the examinee the correct answer to sample item if the examinee fails the item on Digits Backward.	Yes	No
11. Discontinues Digits Forward after failure of both trials of any item.	Yes	No
12. Discontinues Digits Backward after failure of both trials of any item.	Yes	No
13. Assigns 1 point for each trial passed.	Yes	No
14. Records successes and failures on Record Form.	Yes	No
15. Adds points correctly.	Yes	No

Comments:_____

_____

_____

Logical Memory II   *Circle One*

1. Administers subtest 25 to 35 min after Logical Memory I.	Yes	No
2. Reads directions verbatim.	Yes	No
3. Reads directions clearly.	Yes	No

	Circle One	
4. If using a tape recorder, indicates this to the examinee as directed in the examination booklet ("For this task I am going to use a tape recorder so that I can write down your exact words later on").	Yes	No
5. Provides prompts if necessary (e.g., "The story was about a woman who was robbed," or "The story was about a weather bulletin").	Yes	No
6. Notes on the record form if prompts are used.	Yes	No
7. States, "Take your best guess" if examinee does not provide a response.	Yes	No
8. Provides no help other than general encouragement.	Yes	No
9. Places check mark next to story units that are recalled verbatim.	Yes	No
10. Writes examinee's words next to story units not recalled verbatim.	Yes	No
11. Places check mark next to each correctly recalled thematic unit.	Yes	No
12. Totals points correctly.	Yes	No

Comments:_____

_____

Logical Memory II-Recognition

	Circle One	
1. Reads directions verbatim.	Yes	No
2. Reads directions clearly.	Yes	No
3. Reads each question clearly.	Yes	No
4. Avoids leading questions.	Yes	No
5. Says, "Take your best guess" if examinee does not provide an answer.	Yes	No
6. Circles *Y* or *N* on the response sheet.	Yes	No
7. Adds points correctly.	Yes	No

Comments:_____

_____

Faces II

	Circle One	
1. Administers subtest 25 to 35 min after Faces I.	Yes	No
2. Reads directions verbatim.	Yes	No

3. Reads directions clearly. Yes No
4. Centers stimulus booklet close to and in front of examinee. Yes No
5. Repeats and paraphrases directions if not understood by the examinee. Yes No
6. Says, "Take your best guess" if examinee does not provide an answer. Yes No
7. Circles Y or N on the record form to record examinee's response. Yes No
8. Allows 1 point credit for each correct response. Yes No
9. Adds points correctly. Yes No
Comments:_____

_____
_____

Verbal Paired Associates II   *Circle One*
1. Administers subtest 25 to 35 min after VPA I. Yes No
2. Reads directions verbatim. Yes No
3. Reads directions clearly. Yes No
4. Repeats and paraphrases directions, where necessary. Yes No
5. Queries, "Which word goes with _____?" on each trial. Yes No
6. Pronounces words clearly. Yes No
7. Allows examinee approximately 10 s to respond. Yes No
8. Says, "Take your best guess" if examinee does not provide an answer. Yes No
9. Records all responses verbatim. Yes No
10. Does not provide a correct response if examinee fails to respond or if an incorrect response is elicited. Yes No
11. Records 0 or 1 point as appropriate. Yes No
12. Adds points correctly. Yes No
Comments:_____

_____
_____

Verbal Paired Associates II-Recognition   *Circle One*
1. Reads directions verbatim. Yes No
2. Reads directions clearly. Yes No

3. Repeats and paraphrases directions, where necessary.   Yes   No
4. Speaks words about 1 s apart.   Yes   No
5. Separates word pairs by an interval of 2 s.   Yes   No
6. Pronounces word pairs clearly.   Yes   No
7. Circles *Y* or *N* on the record form to indicate examinee's   Yes   No
   response.
8. States, "Take your best guess" if examinee does not provide   Yes   No
   a response.
9. Allows 1 point credit for each correct response.   Yes   No
10. Adds points correctly.   Yes   No

Comments:_____

_____

_____

Family Pictures II   *Circle One*

1. Administers subtest 25 to 35 min after Family Pictures I.   Yes   No
2. Reads directions clearly.   Yes   No
3. Reads directions verbatim.   Yes   No
4. Centers stimulus booklet in front of and close to examinee.   Yes   No
5. Repeats and paraphrases directions when necessary.   Yes   No
6. Reads queries for each scene clearly.   Yes   No
7. Reads queries for each scene verbatim.   Yes   No
8. Names and queries all characters identified by the examinee.   Yes   No
9. Queries location and action of all characters identified by   Yes   No
   the examinees.
10. For each scene, asks examinee, "Were there any other   Yes   No
    characters in the _____ scene?"
11. Records examinee's responses verbatim.   Yes   No
12. Avoids leading questions.   Yes   No
13. Appropriately records examinee's responses on the   Yes   No
    response sheet.
14. Uses Scoring Criteria in Appendix B when scoring the   Yes   No
    "Activity" Category.

Comments:_____

_____

_____

Word Lists II

		Circle One	
1.	Administers subtest 25 to 35 mins after Word Lists I.	Yes	No
2.	Reads directions clearly.	Yes	No
3.	Reads directions verbatim.	Yes	No
4.	Repeats and paraphrases directions, where necessary.	Yes	No
5.	Allows ample time for examinee to recall as many words as possible.	Yes	No
6.	Places a check mark next to each word correctly recalled (some examiners prefer to place a number next to each word to signify the order in which it was recalled).	Yes	No
7.	Records intrusions verbatim.	Yes	No
8.	Records all perseverations verbatim.	Yes	No
9.	Allows 1 point for each correct response.	Yes	No
10.	Adds points correctly.	Yes	No

Comments:_____

_____

_____

Word Lists II-Recognition

		Circle One	
1.	Reads directions clearly.	Yes	No
2.	Reads directions verbatim.	Yes	No
3.	Repeats and paraphrases directions, as necessary.	Yes	No
4.	Reads words clearly.	Yes	No
5.	Allows ample time for examinee to respond.	Yes	No
6.	States, "Take your best guess" if the examinee does not provide a response.	Yes	No
7.	Circles *Y* or *N* on the record form to record examinee's response.	Yes	No
8.	Allows 1 point credit for each correct response.	Yes	No
9.	Adds points correctly.	Yes	No

Comments:_____

_____

_____

Visual Reproduction II

		Circle One	
1.	Administers subtest 25 to 35 mins after Visual Reproduction I.	Yes	No
2.	Reads directions verbatim.	Yes	No

3. Reads directions clearly.	Yes	No
4. Places Stimulus Booklet II in front of and close to examinee.	Yes	No
5. Repeats and paraphrases directions, where necessary.	Yes	No
6. Provides two #2 pencils with erasers.	Yes	No
7. Records hand examinee uses (right vs. left).	Yes	No
8. Provides general encouragement when appropriate (e.g., "Each page had one or more designs on it," or "Just try to remember one of them").	Yes	No
9. Avoids leading comments.	Yes	No
10. Refers to Scoring Criteria in Appendix C.	Yes	No
11. Records observations where appropriate.	Yes	No
12. Calculates Recall Total Score correctly.	Yes	No

Comments:_____

_____

_____

Visual Reproduction II-Recognition   *Circle One*

1. Reads directions verbatim.	Yes	No
2. Reads directions clearly.	Yes	No
3. Places stimulus booklet in front of and close to examinee.	Yes	No
4. Repeats and paraphrases directions, when necessary.	Yes	No
5. Provides ample time for examinee to respond.	Yes	No
6. States, "Take your best guess" if the examinee does not provide a response.	Yes	No
7. Circles Y or N on the record form to indicate examinee's response.	Yes	No
8. Allows 1 point credit for each correct response.	Yes	No
9. Calculates Recognition Total Score correctly.	Yes	No

Comments:_____

_____

_____

Visual Reproduction II-Copy   *Circle One*

1. Reads directions clearly.	Yes	No
2. Reads directions verbatim.	Yes	No
3. Records hand examinee used (right vs. left).	Yes	No
4. Places stimulus booklet in front of and close to examinee.	Yes	No
5. Repeats and paraphrases directions, when necessary.	Yes	No

6. Provides ample time for examinee to complete each copy.   Yes   No
7. Provides general encouragement when appropriate.   Yes   No
8. Records observations when appropriate.   Yes   No
9. Refers to Scoring Criteria in Appendix C.   Yes   No
10. Calculates Copy Total Score correctly.   Yes   No

Comments:_____

_____

_____

Visual Reproduction II-Discrimination   *Circle One*

1. Reads directions verbatim.   Yes   No
2. Reads directions clearly.   Yes   No
3. Places stimulus booklet in front of and close to examinee. Yes   No
4. Repeats and paraphrases directions, when necessary.   Yes   No
5. Provides ample time for examinee to respond.   Yes   No

Comments:_____

_____

_____

Other Aspects of Test Administration   *Circle One*

1. Establishes rapport before testing.   Yes   No
2. Encourages effort and offers appropriate feedback.   Yes   No
3. Is well-organized.   Yes   No
4. Has needed material readily available.   Yes   No
5. Has extra paper and pencils.   Yes   No
6. Adheres to standardized instructions.   Yes   No
7. Is fluid with the administration of the test.   Yes   No
8. Has test materials and protocol out of examinee's view.   Yes   No
9. Makes smooth transition from subtest to subtest.   Yes   No
10. Provides support between subtests, if needed.   Yes   No
11. Focuses examinee's attention on tasks.   Yes   No
12. Allows breaks when appropriate.   Yes   No
13. Manages minor levels of anxiety and other behavior   Yes   No
    appropriately.
14. Makes the testing experience a positive one.   Yes   No

Comments:_____

_____

_____

General Scoring

Information and Orientation   *Circle One*
1. Calculates total score correctly.   Yes   No

Logical Memory I
1. Calculates Story A Recall Unit Score correctly.   Yes   No
2. Calculates Story A Thematic Unit Score correctly.   Yes   No
3. Calculates Story B Recall Unit Score correctly.   Yes   No
4. Calculates Story B Thematic Unit Score correctly.   Yes   No
5. Calculates first Recall Total Score correctly.   Yes   No
6. Calculates Story B, second Recall Unit Score correctly. Yes   No
7. Calculates Story B, second Recall Thematic Unit Score Yes   No
   correctly.
8. Calculates Recall Total Score correctly.   Yes   No
9. Calculates Thematic Total Score correctly.   Yes   No
10. Calculates Learning Slope correctly.   Yes   No

Faces I
1. Calculates Recognition Total Score correctly.   Yes   No

Verbal Paired Associates I
1. Calculates Lists A, B, C, and D Recall Scores correctly. Yes No
2. Calculates first Recall Total Score correctly.   Yes   No
3. Calculates Recall Total Score correctly.   Yes   No
4. Calculates Learning Slope correctly.   Yes   No

Family Pictures I
1. Allows appropriate credit for examinee's Activity   Yes   No
   responses.
2. Calculates all Character-Based Scores correctly.   Yes   No
3. Calculates Recall Total Score correctly.   Yes   No

Word Lists I
1. Calculates Trials 1, 2, 3, and 4 Recall Scores correctly. Yes No
2. Calculates first Recall Total Score correctly.   Yes   No
3. Calculates Recall Total Score correctly.   Yes   No
4. Calculates List B Recall Score correctly.   Yes   No
5. Calculates Short-Delay Recall Score correctly.   Yes   No
6. Calculates Contrast 1 correctly.   Yes   No

7. Calculates Learning Slope correctly.   Yes   No
8. Calculates Contrast 2 correctly.   Yes   No

Visual Reproduction I

1. Calculates scores for Designs A, B, C, D, and E correctly.   Yes   No
2. Calculates Recall Total Score correctly.   Yes   No

Letter-Number Sequencing

1. Calculates Total Score correctly.   Yes   No

Spatial Span

1. Calculates Forward Total Score correctly.   Yes   No
2. Calculates Backward Total Score correctly.   Yes   No
3. Calculates Total Score correctly.   Yes   No

Mental Control

1. Calculates Total Score correctly.   Yes   No

Digit Span

1. Calculates Forward Total Score correctly.   Yes   No
2. Calculates Backward Total Score correctly.   Yes   No
3. Calculates Total Score correctly.   Yes   No

Logical Memory II

1. Calculates Story A Recall Unit Score correctly.   Yes   No
2. Calculates Story A Thematic Unit Score correctly.   Yes   No
3. Calculates Story B Recall Unit Score correctly.   Yes   No
4. Calculates Story B Thematic Unit Score correctly.   Yes   No
5. Calculates Recall Total Score correctly.   Yes   No
6. Calculates Thematic Total Score correctly.   Yes   No
7. Calculates Percent Retention correctly.   Yes   No

Logical Memory II-Recognition

1. Calculates Recognition Total Score correctly.   Yes   No

Faces II

1. Calculates Recognition Total Score correctly.   Yes   No
2. Calculates Percent Retention correctly.   Yes   No

Verbal Paired Associates II

1. Calculates Recall Total Score correctly.   Yes   No
2. Calculates Percent Retention correctly.   Yes   No

Verbal Paired Associates II-Recognition
1. Calculates Recognition Total Score correctly.   Yes   No

Family Pictures II
1. Allows appropriate credit for examinee's Activity responses. Yes   No
2. Calculates all Character-Based Scores correctly.   Yes   No
3. Calculates Recall Total Score correctly.   Yes   No
4. Calculates Percent Retention correctly.   Yes   No

Word Lists II
1. Calculates Recall Total Score correctly.   Yes   No
2. Calculates Percent Retention score correctly.   Yes   No

Word Lists II-Recognition
1. Calculates Recognition Total Score correctly.   Yes   No

Visual Reproduction II
1. Calculates scores for Designs A, B, C, D, and E correctly.   Yes   No
2. Calculates Recall Total Score correctly.   Yes   No
3. Calculates Recognition Total Score correctly.   Yes   No
4. Calculates Copy Total Score correctly.   Yes   No
5. Calculates Discrimination Total Score correctly.   Yes   No
6. Calculates Percent Retention correctly.   Yes   No
7. Accurately transfers all scores to the Visual Reproduction   Yes   No
   Scoring Page.
8. Accurately calculates Visual Reproduction I Recall Total   Yes   No
   Score.
9. Accurately calculates Visual Reproduction II Recall Total   Yes   No
   Score.
10. Accurately calculates Visual Reproduction II Copy Total   Yes   No
    Score.

Score Conversion Page of Record Form   *Circle One*
1. Transfers Primary Subtest raw scores to Conversion Page   Yes   No
   correctly.
2. Uses Table D.1 correctly.   Yes   No
3. Converts raw scores to scaled scores for each subtest   Yes   No
   correctly.
4. Adds scaled scores correctly for Auditory Immediate Index.   Yes   No
5. Adds scaled scores correctly for Visual Immediate Index.   Yes   No

6. Adds scaled scores correctly for Immediate Memory Index.   Yes   No
7. Adds scaled scores correctly for Auditory Delayed Index.   Yes   No
8. Adds scaled scores correctly for Visual Delayed Index.   Yes   No
9. Adds scaled scores correctly for Auditory Recognition   Yes   No
Delayed Index.
10. Adds scaled scores correctly for General Memory Index.   Yes   No
11. Adds scaled scores correctly for Working Memory Index.   Yes   No
12. Calculates Auditory Recognition Delayed Total Score   Yes   No
correctly.
13. Transfers correct Reference Group scaled scores.   Yes   No

Comments:_____

_____

_____

Profile Page   *Circle One*

1. Transfers all Index Sums of scaled scores to Profile Page   Yes   No
correctly.

2. Uses Table E.1 correctly.   Yes   No

Appendix B

WMS-III Interpretation Worksheet

Step 1: Compare and Interpret Immediate and Delayed Memory within each Modality.

Auditory Immediate Index	Auditory Delayed Index	Difference	Is there a significant difference?		
			Significant ($p < .01$)	Significant ($p < .05$)	Not Significant
			18 or more	13–17	4–12

⇩

Visual Immediate Index	Visual Delayed Index	Difference	Is there a significant difference?		
			Significant ($p < .01$)	Significant ($p < .05$)	Not Significant
			23 or more	17–22	0–16

⇩

Auditory Delayed Index	Auditory Recognition Delayed Index	Difference	Is there a significant difference?		
			Significant ($p < .01$)	Significant ($p < .05$)	Not Significant
			24 or more	18–23	0–17

⇩

Step 2: Compare and Interpret Memory between Auditory and Visual Modalities.

Auditory Immediate Index	Visual Immediate Index	Difference	Is there a significant difference?		
			Significant ($p < .01$)	Significant ($p < .05$)	Not Significant
			19 or more	15–18	0–14

⇩

(continued)

Step 2: Continued

Auditory Delayed Index	Visual Delayed Index	Difference	Is there a significant difference?		
			Significant ($p < .01$)	Significant ($p < .05$)	Not Significant
			22 or more	16–21	0–15

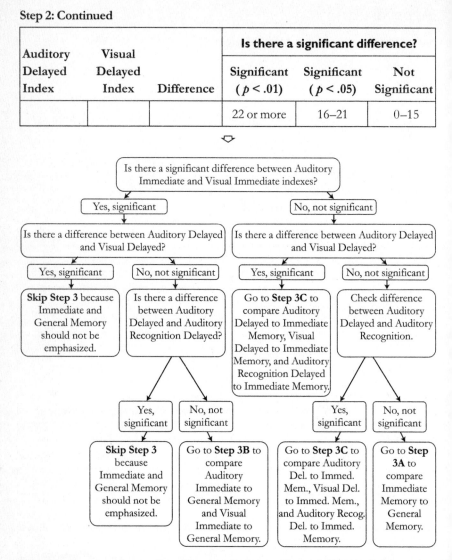

Step 3A: Compare Immediate Memory Index to General (Delayed) Memory Index.

Immediate Memory Index	General Memory Index	Difference	Is there a significant difference?		
			Significant ($p < .01$)	Significant ($p < .05$)	Not Significant
			16 or more	12–15	0–11

Step 3B: Compare Auditory Immediate and Visual Immediate Indexes to General (Delayed) Memory Index.

Auditory Immediate Index	General Memory Index	Difference	Is there a significant difference?		
			Significant ($p < .01$)	Significant ($p < .05$)	Not Significant
			15 or more	11–14	0–10
Visual Immediate Index	General Memory Index	Difference	Is there a significant difference?		
			Significant ($p < .01$)	Significant ($p < .05$)	Not Significant
			20 or more	15–19	0–14

Step 3C: Compare Auditory Delayed, Visual Delayed, and Auditory Recognition Delayed Indexes to Immediate Memory Index.

Auditory Delayed Index	Immediate Memory Index	Difference	Is there a significant difference?		
			Significant ($p < .01$)	Significant ($p < .05$)	Not Significant
			18 or more	14–17	0–13
Visual Delayed Index	Immediate Memory Index	Difference	Is there a significant difference?		
			Significant ($p < .01$)	Significant ($p < .05$)	Not Significant
			20 or more	15–19	0–14
Auditory Recognition Delayed Index	Immediate Memory Index	Difference	Is there a significant difference?		
			Significant ($p < .01$)	Significant ($p < .05$)	Not Significant
			22 or more	17–21	0–16

⇨

(continued)

Step 4: Compare and Interpret Working Memory with Immediate and General (Delayed) Memory, as well as Auditory and Visual Immediate Indexes.

Working Memory Index	Immediate Memory Index	Difference	Is there a significant difference?		
			Significant ($p < .01$)	Significant ($p < .05$)	Not Significant
			19 or more	14–18	0–13

⇩

Working Memory Index	General Memory Index	Difference	Is there a significant difference?		
			Significant ($p < .01$)	Significant ($p < .05$)	Not Significant
			18 or more	14–17	0–13

⇩

Working Memory Index	Auditory Immediate Index	Difference	Is there a significant difference?		
			Significant ($p < .01$)	Significant ($p < .05$)	Not Significant
			18 or more	13–17	0–12

⇩

Working Memory Index	Visual Immediate Index	Difference	Is there a significant difference?		
			Significant ($p < .01$)	Significant ($p < .05$)	Not Significant
			22 or more	17–21	0–16

⇩

Step 5: Interpret Significant Strengths and Weaknesses of the WMS-III Sub-test Profile.

A. Determine which mean one should use to calculate strengths and weaknesses.

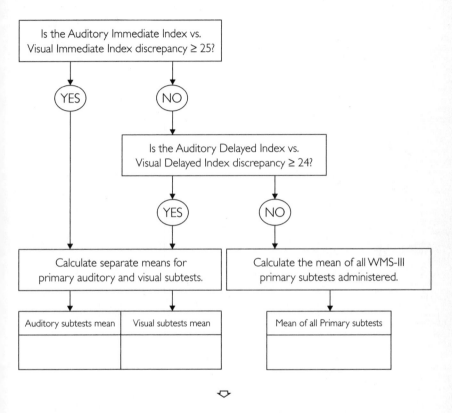

B. Use appropriate *rounded* mean in calculating the "Scaled Score – Mean Difference."

C. Compare the "Size Difference Needed for Significance" to the "Scaled Score – Mean Difference" by looking at the value under the appropriate column (Overall = size discrepancy needed when overall mean was used; Auditory/Visual = size difference needed when comparing auditory subtest scaled scores to mean of auditory subtests and when comparing visual subtests to mean of visual subtests).

(continued)

Step 5: Continued

Subtests	Scaled Score	Rounded Mean	Scaled Score vs. Mean Difference	Size Difference Needed for Significance		Strength or Weakness (S or W)	Percentile Rank (*See Table 4.6*)
				Overall	Auditory/ Visual		
Auditory							
Auditory Logical Memory I				±3	±3		
Verbal Paired Associates I				±2	±2		
Letter-Number Sequencing				±4	±3		
Logical Memory II				±4	±3		
Verbal Paired Associates II				±3	±3		
Auditory Recognition Delayed				±4	±4		
Visual							
Faces I				±4	±4		
Family Pictures I				±4	±4		
Spatial Span				±4	±4		
Faces II				±4	±4		
Family Pictures II				±3	±3		

⇨

Step 6: Generate Hypotheses about the Fluctuations in the WMS-III Profile.

See pages 99–108 and Rapid Reference 4.7.

⇩

Step 7: Follow Up Hypotheses with Supplementary WMS-III Scores.

A. Examine hypotheses with supplemental subtests (see Rapid Reference 4.8).

B. Examine supplemental subtests that are at least 1 SD above or below the normative mean of 10 or that are significantly above or below the client's own subtest mean.

C. Convert Auditory Process Composite Percentiles (Single-Trial Learning, Learning Slope, Retention, and Retrieval) to Standard Scores for comparison to each other using the table below.

Standard Scores Corresponding to National Percentile Ranks

Percentile Rank	Standard Score	Percentile Rank	Standard Score	Percentile Rank	Standard Score	Percentile Rank	Standard Score
99.9	145	88	118	56–54	102	18–17	86
99.8	143	87	117	53–52	101	16–15	85
99.7	141	86	116	51–49	100	14–13	84
99.6	140	85–84	115	48–46	99	12–11	82
99.5	139	83–82	114	45–43	98	10	81
99	135	81	113	42–40	97	9	80
98	130	80–79	112	39–38	96	8	79
97	128	78–77	111	37–35	95	7	78
96	126	76–75	110	34–33	94	6	77
95	125	74–73	109	32–31	93	5	76
94	123	72–70	108	30–29	92	4	74
93	122	69–68	107	28–27	91	3	72
92	121	67–66	106	26–25	90	2	70
91	120	65–63	105	24–23	89	1	65
90	119	62–60	104	22–21	88	0.4	60
89	118	59–57	103	20–19	87	0.1	55

(continued)

Step 7: Continued

D. Follow-Up Auditory Immediate Index by Comparing Single-Trial Learning and Learning Slope.

Single-Trial Learning Percentile Rank	Learning Slope Percentile Rank		
Single-Trial Learning Standard Score	Learning Slope Standard Score	Standard Score Difference	Is there a notable difference?
			20 points or more

E. Follow-Up Auditory Immediate Index with Retention Composite.

Retention Composite Percentile Rank	Auditory Delayed Index		
Retention Composite Standard Score	Auditory Delayed Index	Standard Score Difference	Is there a notable difference?
			20 points or more

F. Compare Auditory Delayed Index and Auditory Recognition Delayed Index.

Auditory Delayed Index	Auditory Recognition Delayed Index	Difference	Is there a significant difference?		
			Significant ($p < .01$)	Significant ($p < .05$)	Not Significant
			24 or more	18–23	0–17

References

Acker, C. (1986). Neuropsychological deficits in alcoholics. The relative contributions of gender and drinking history. *British Journal of Addiction, 81,* 223–233.

Adams, K. M., Rennik, P., Schooff, K., & Keegan, J. (1975). Neuropsychological measurement of drug effects: Polydrug research. *Journal of Psychodelic Drugs, 7,* 151–160.

Albert, M. S. (1988a). Cognitive Function. In M. S. Albert & M. B. Moss (Eds.), *Geriatric Neuropsychology* (pp. 33–53). New York: Guilford Press.

Albert, M. S. (1988b). General issues in geriatric neuropsychology. In M. S. Albert & M. B. Moss (Eds.), *Geriatric Neuropsychology* (pp. 3–10). New York: Guilford Press.

Albert, M. S., & Moss, M. B. (1996). Neuropsychology of aging: Findings in humans and monkeys. In E. L. Schneider & J. W. Rowe (Eds.), *Handbook of the Biology of Aging* (4th ed., pp. 217–233). San Diego, CA: Academic Press.

American Psychiatric Association (1994). *Diagnostic and statistical manual of mental disorders* (4th ed.). Washington, DC: American Psychiatric Association.

Anastasi, A., & Urbina, S. (1997). *Psychological testing* (7th ed.). Upper Saddle River, NJ: Prentice-Hall.

Anderson, E. W., Trethowan, W. H., & Kenna, J. C. (1956). An experimental approach to the problem of simulation in mental disorder. *Proceedings of the Royal Society of Medicine, 49,* 513–520.

Andreasen, N. C., & Carpenter, W. T., Jr. (1993). Diagnosis and classification of schizophrenia. *Schizophrenia Bulletin, 19,* 199–214.

Ardila, A., Rosselli, M., & Strumwasser, S. (1991). Neuropsychological effects of cocaine abuse. *International Journal of Neuroscience, 57,* 73–79.

Augustine, E. A., & Novelly, R. A. (1981). Memory and IQ correlates of seizure control following anterior temporal lobectomy. *Epilepsia, 22,* 233.

Backman, L., Small, B. J., Wahlin, A., & Larsson, M. (2000). Cognitive functioning in very old age. In F. I. M. Craik & T. A. Salthouse (Eds.), *The handbook of aging and cognition* (2nd ed., pp. 499–558). Mahwah, NJ: Erlbaum.

Baddeley, A. D. (1986). *Working memory.* Oxford, England: Oxford University Press.

Bagby, R. M., Gillis, J. R., Toner, B. B., & Goldberg, J. (1991). Detecting fake-good and fake-bad responding on the Millon Clinical Multiaxial Inventory-II. *Psychological Assessment, 3,* 496–498.

Bak, J. S., & Greene, R. L. (1980). Changes in neuropsychological functioning in an aging population. *Journal of Consulting and Clinical Psychology, 3,* 395–399.

Bash, I. Y., & Alpert, M. (1980). The determination of malingering. *Annals of the New York Academy of Sciences, 347,* 86–99.

Beatty, W. W., Hames, K. A., Blanco, C. R., Nixon, S. J., & Tivis, L. J. (1996). Visuospatial perception, construction, and memory of alcoholism. *Journal of Studies on Alcohol, 57,* 136–143.

Becker, J. T., Boller, F., Saxton, J., & McGonigle-Gibson, K. L. (1987) Normal rates of forgetting of verbal and non-verbal material in Alzheimer's disease. *Cortex, 23,* 59–72.

Benton, A. L., & Spreen, O. (1961). Visual Memory Test. *Archives of General Psychiatry, 4,* 79–83.

Bernal, B., Ardila, A., & Bateman, J. R. (1994). Cognitive impairments in adolescent drug-abusers. *International Journal of Neuroscience, 75,* 203–212.

Bernard, L. C. (1990). Prospects for faking believable memory deficits on neuropsychological tests and the use of incentives in simulation research. *Journal of Clinical and Experimental Neuropsychology, 12,* 715–728.

Bernard, L. C. (1991). The detection of faked deficits on the Rey Auditory Verbal Learning Test: The effect of serial position. *Archives of Clinical Neuropsychology, 6,* 81–88.

Bernard, L. C., Houston, W., & Natoli, L. (1993). Malingering on neuropsychological memory tests: Potential objective indicators. *Journal of Clinical Psychology, 49,* 45–53.

Bernard, L. C., McGrath, M. J., & Houston, W. (1993). Discriminating between simulated malingering and closed head injury on the Wechsler Memory Scale-Revised. *Archives of Clinical Neuropsychology, 8,* 539–551.

Binder, L. M. (1992). Forced-choice testing provides evidence of malingering. *Archives of Physical Medicine, 73,* 377–380.

Binder, L. M., & Willis, S. C. (1991). Assessment of motivation after financially compensable minor head trauma. *Psychological Assessment, 3,* 175–181.

Binder, L. M., Villaneuva, M. R., Howieson, D., & Moore, R. T. (1993). The Rey AVLT recognition memory task measures motivational impairment after mild head trauma. *Archives of Clinical Neuropsychology, 8,* 137–148.

Blanchard, J. J., & Neale, J. M. (1994). The neuropsychological signature of schizophrenia: Generalized or differential deficit? *American Journal of Psychiatry, 151,* 40–48.

Bornstein, R. A., Chelune, G. J., & Prifitera, A. (1989). IQ-memory discrepancies in normal and clinical samples. *Psychological Assessment, 1,* 203–206.

Bornstein, R. A., & Suga, L. J. (1988). Educational level and neuropsychological performance in healthy elderly subjects. *Developmental Neuropsychology, 4,* 17–22.

Brandt, J. (1988). Malingered amnesia. In R. Rogers (Ed.), *Clinical assessment of Malingering and Deception* (pp. 65–83). New York: Guilford Press.

Brandt, J., Rubinksy, E., & Lassen, G. (1985). Uncovering malingered amnesia. *Annals of the New York Academy of Sciences, 444,* 502–503.

Brebion, G., Amador, X., Smith, M. J., & Gorman, J. M. (1998). Memory impairment and schizophrenia: The role of processing speed. *Schizophrenia Research, 30,* 31–39.

Brewer, W. J., Edwards, J., Anderson, V., Robinson, T., & Pantelis, C. (1996). Neuropsychological, olfactory, and hygiene deficits in men with negative symptom schizophrenia. *Biological Psychiatry, 40,* 1021–1031.

Brinkman, S. D., Largen, J. W., Gerganoff, S., & Pomara, N. (1983). Russell's revised Wechsler Memory Scale in the evaluation of dementia. *Journal of Clinical Psychology, 39,* 989–993.

Brooker, A. E. (1997). Performance on the Wechsler Memory Scale-Revised for patients with mild traumatic brain injury and mild dementia. *Perceptual and Motor Skills, 84,* 131–138.

Brown, R. G., & Marsden, C. D. (1988). "Subcortical dementia": The neuropsychological evidence. *Neuroscience, 25,* 363–387.

Butters, N., Cermak, L. S., Montgomery, K., and Adinolfi, A. (1977). Some comparisons of the memory and visuo-perceptive deficits in chronic alcoholics and patients with Korsakoff's disease. *Alcoholism: Clinical and Experimental Research, 1,* 73–80.

Butters, N., & Granholm, E. (1987). The continuity hypothesis: Some conclusions and their implications for the etiology and neuropathology of alcoholic Korsakoff's syndrome. In O. A. Parsons, N. Butters, & P. Nathan (Eds.), *Neuropsychology of Alcoholism: Implications for Diagnosis and Treatment* (pp. 176–206). New York: Wiley.

Butters, N., Salmon, D. P., Cullum, C. M., Cairns, P., Tröster, A. I., Jacobs, D., Moss, M., & Cermak, L. S. (1988). Differentiation of amnesic and demented patients with the Wechsler Memory Scale–Revised. *Clinical Neuropsychologist, 2,* 133–148.

Cabeza, R., & Nyberg, L. (1997). Imaging cognition: An empirical review of PET studies with normal studies. *Journal of Cognitive Neuroscience, 9,* 1–26.

Cala, L. A., Jones, B., Mastaglia, F. L., & Wiley, B. (1978). Brain atrophy and intellectual impairment in heavy drinkers: A clinical, psychometric, and computerized tomography study. *Australian and New Zealand Journal of Medicine, 8,* 147–153.

Carlin, A. S. (1986). Neuropsychological consequences of drug abuse. In I. Grant & K. M. Adams (Eds.), *Neuropsychological Assessment of Neuropsychiatric Disorders* (pp. 478–598). New York: Oxford University Press.

Carlin, A. S., Strauss, F. F., Grant, I., & Adams, K. M. (1978). Prediction of neuropsychological impairment in polydrug abuse patients. *Addictive Behaviors, 5,* 229–234.

Carlin, A. S., & Trupin, E. (1977). The effects of long-term chronic cannabis use on neuropsychological functioning. *International Journal of Addiction, 12,* 617–624.

Carroll, J. B. (1993). *Human cognitive abilities: A survey of factor analytic studies.* New York: Cambridge University Press.

Cattell, R. B. (1941). Some theoretical issues in adult intelligence testing. *Psychological Bulletin,* 38, 592.

Cattell, R. B. (1957). *Personality and motivation structure and measurement.* New York: World Book.

Chapman, L. L., White, D. A., & Storandt, M. (1997). Prose recall in dementia. *Archives of Neurology, 54,* 1501–1504.

Chlopan, B. E., Hagen, R. L., & Russell, E. W. (1990). Lateralized anterior and posterior lesions and performance on Digit Span and Russell's revision of the Wechsler Memory Scale. *Journal of Consulting & Clinical Psychology, 58,* 855–861.

Cicerone, K. D. (1997). Clinical sensitivity of four measures of attention to mild traumatic brain injury. *Clinical Neuropsychologist, 11,* 266–272.

Civil, R. H., Whitehouse, P. J., Lanska, D. J., & Mayeux, R. (1993). Degenerative dementias. In P. J. Whitehouse (Ed.), *Dementia* (pp. 167–214). Philadelphia: F. A. Davis.

Cole, J. C., Lopez, B. L., & McLeod, J. S. (2001). *Comprehensive Tables for determination of strengths and weaknesses on the WMS-III.* Manuscript submitted for publication.

Colsher, P. L., & Wallace, R. B. (1991). Longitudinal application of cognitive function measures in a defined population of community-dwelling elders. *Annals of Epidemiology, 1,* 215–230.

Conner, R., & Woodall, F. E. (1983). The effects of experience and structured feedback on WISC-R error rates made by student-examiners. *Psychology in the Schools, 20,* 376–379.

Craik, F. I. M. (1984). Age differences in remembering. In L. R. Squire & N. Butters (Eds.), *Neuropsychology of Memory* (pp. 3–12). New York: Guilford Press.

Craik, F. I. M., Byrd, M., & Swanson, J. M. (1987). Patterns of memory loss in three elderly samples. *Psychology and Aging, 2,* 79–86.

Cullum, C. M., Butters, N., Troster, A. I., & Salmon, D. P. (1990). Normal aging and forgetting rates on the Wechsler Memory Scale-Revised. *Archives of Clinical Neuropsychology, 5,* 23–30.

Cummings, J. L. (1986). Subcortical dementia: Neuropsychology, neuropsychiatry, and pathophysiology. *British Journal of Psychiatry, 159,* 682–697.

Cummings, J. L., & Benson, D. F. (1992). *Dementia: A Clinical Approach* (2nd ed.). Boston: Butterworth-Henemann.

Davidson, H., Suffield, B., Orenczuk, S., Nantau, K., & Mandel, A. (1991, February). *Screening for malingering using the Memory for Fifteen Items Test (MFIT).* Poster presentation. International Neuropsychological Society nineteenth annual meeting. San Antonio.

Delis, D., Direnfeld, L., Alexander, M., & Kaplan, E. (1982). Cognitive fluctuations associated with the on-off phenomenon in Parkinson's disease. *Neurology, 3,* 1049–1052.

Dubois, B., Boller, F., Pillon, B., & Agid, Y. (1991). Cognitive deficits in Parkinson's disease. In R. Boller & J. Grafman (Eds.), *Handbook of Neuropsychology, V* (pp. 195–240). Amsterdam: Elsevier Science Publishers.

Ellis, R. J., & Oscar Berman, M. (1989). Alcoholism, aging, and functional cerebral asymmetries. *Psychological Bulletin, 106,* 128–147.

Elwood, R. W. (1991). The Wechsler Memory Scale-Revised: Psychometric characteristics and clinical application. *Neuropsychology Review, 2,* 179–201.

Erickson, R. C., Eimon, P., & Hebben, N. (1992). A bibliography of normative articles on cognitive tests for older adults. *Clinical Neuropsychologist, 6,* 98–102.

Evans, D., Funkenstein, H., Albert, M., Scherr, P. A., Cook, N. R., Chown, M. J., Hebert, L. E., Hennekens, C. H., & Taylor, J. O. (1989). Clinically diagnosed Alzheimer's disease and other conditions causing cognitive impairment in a community-based population of older persons. *Journal of American Medical Association, 262,* 2551–2556.

Flanagan, D. P., & McGrew, K. S., & Ortiz, S. O. (2000). *The Wechsler intelligence scales and Gf-Gc theory.* Boston: Allyn & Bacon.

Flowers, K., Pearce, I., & Pearce, J. (1984). Recognition memory in Parkinson's disease. *Journal of Neurology, Neurosurgery, and Psychiatry, 4,* 1174–1181.

Folstein, S. E. (1989). *Huntington's disease: A disorder of families.* Baltimore: Johns Hopkins University Press.

Franzen, M. D., & Iverson, G. L. (2000). The Wechsler Memory Scales. In G. Groth-Marnat (Ed.), *Neuropsychological assessment in clinical practice: A guide to test interpretation and integration* (pp. 195–222). New York: Wiley.

Freed, D. M., Corkin, S., Growdon, J. H., & Nissen, M. J. (1989). Selective attention in Alzheimer's disease: Characterizing cognitive subgroups of patients. *Neuropsychologia, 27,* 325–339.

Frisoni, G. B., Rozzini, R., Bianchetti, A., & Trabucchi, M. (1993). Principal lifetime occupation and MMSE score in elderly persons. *Journal of Gerontology, 48,* S310–S314.

Fuld, P. A., Masur, D. M., Blau, A. D., Crystal, H., & Aronson, M. K. (1990). Object memory evaluation for prospective detection of dementia of normal functioning elderly: Predictive and normative data. *Journal of Clinical & Experimental Neuropsychology, 12,* 520–528.

Gass, C. S., Russell, E. W., & Hamilton, R. A. (1990). Accuracy of MMPI-based inferences regarding memory and concentration in closed-head-trauma patients. *Psychological Assessment, 2,* 175–178.

Gold, J. M., Randolph, C., Carpenter, C. J., Goldberg, T. E., & Weinberger, D. R. (1992). The performance of patients with schizophrenia on the Wechsler Memory Scale-Revised. *Clinical Neuropsychologist, 6,* 367–373.

Goldman, M. S. (1995). Recovery of cognitive functioning in alcoholics: The relationship to treatment. *Alcohol, Health & Research World, 19,* 148–154.

Goldstein, G., McCue, M., Rogers, J., & Nussbaum, P. D. (1992). Diagnostic differences in memory test based predictions of functional capacity in the elderly. *Neuropsychological Rehabilitation, 2,* 307–317.

Goodman, C. R., & Zarit, S. H. (1994). Effects of education on assessment of age-associated memory impairment. *American Journal of Geriatric Psychiatry, 2,* 118–123.

Gotham, A. M., Brown, R. G., & Marsden, C. D. (1988). "Frontal" cognitive function in patients with Parkinson's disease "on" and "off" levodopa. *Brain, 111,* 299–321.

Grant, I. & Judd, L. L. (1976). Neuropsychological and EEG disturbances in polydrug users. *American Journal of Psychiatry, 133,* 1039–1042.

Grant, I., Mohns, L., Miller, M., & Reitan, K. M. (1976). A neuropsychological study of polydrug users. *Archives of General Psychiatry, 33,* 973–978.

Gregory, R. J. (1987). *Adult intellectual assessment.* Boston: Allyn & Bacon.

Groth-Marnat, G. (ed.) (2000). *Neuropsychological assessment in clinical practice: A guide to test interpretation and integration.* New York: Wiley.

Gurland, B. J. (1981). The borderlands of dementia: The influence of sociocultural characteristics on rates of dementia occurring in the senium. In N. E. Miller & G. D. Cohen (Eds.), *Clinical aspects of Alzheimer's disease and senile dementia* (pp. 61–84). New York: Raven Press.

Halgin, R., Riklan, M., & Misiak, H. (1977). Levodopa, parkinsonism, and recent memory. *Journal of Nervous & Mental Disease, 164,* 268–272.

Hartman, D. E. (1988). *Neuropsychological Toxicology.* New York: Pergamon Press.

Hasegawa, I., Fukuishma, T., Ihara, T., & Miyashita, Y. (1998). Callosal window between prefrontal cortices: Cognitive interaction to retrieve long-term memory. *Science, 281,* 814–818.

Haut, M. W., Petros, T. V., & Frank, R. G. (1991). Semantic sensitivity in the acute phase of recovery from moderate and severe closed head injury. *Neuropsychology, 5,* 81–88.

Haut, M. W., Weber, A. M., Demarest, D., Keefover, R. W., & Rankin, E. D. (1996). Controlling for constructional dysfunction with the visual reproduction subtest of the Wechsler Memory Scale-Revised in Alzheimer's disease. *Clinical Neuropsychologist, 10,* 309–312.

Haut, M. W., Weber, A. M., Wilhellm, K. L., Keefover, R. W., & Rankin, E. D. (1994). The visual reproduction subtest as a measure of visual perceptual/constructional functioning in dementia of the Alzheimer's type. *Clinical Neuropsychologist, 8,* 187–192.

Hawkins, K. A. (1998). Indicators of brain dysfunction derived from graphic representation of the WAIS-III/WMS-III Technical Manual clinical samples data: A preliminary approach to clinical utility. *Clinical Neuropsychologist, 12,* 535–551.

Hawkins, K. A., Hoffman, R. E., Quinlan, D. M., Rakfeldt, J., Docherty, N. M., & Sledge, W. H. (1997). Cognition, negative symptoms, and diagnosis: A comparison of schizophrenic, bipolar, and control samples. *Journal of Neuropsychology, 9,* 81–89.

Hawkins, K. A., Sullivan, T. E., & Choi, E. J. (1997). Memory deficits in schizophrenia: Inadequate assimilation or true amnesia? Findings from the Wechsler Memory Scale-Revised. *Journal of Psychiatry & Neuroscience, 22,* 169–179.

Heaton, R. K., Manly, J. J., Taylor, M. J., & Tulsky, D. S. (2001). Association between demographic characteristics on WAIS-III and WMS-III. Manuscript in Preparation.

Heilbronner, R. L., Buck, P., & Adams, R. L. (1990). Discrepancies between Wechsler's FSIQs and MQs in brain damaged and nonbrain damaged adults. *International Journal of Clinical Neuropsychology, 12,* 24–28.

Helkala, E. L., Laulumaa, V., Soininen, H., & Riekkinen, P. J. (1989). Different error pattern of episodic and semantic memory in Alzheimer's disease and Parkinson's disease with dementia. *Neuropsychologia, 2,* 1241–1248.

Hightower, M. G., & Anderson, A. P. (1986). Memory evaluation of alcoholics with Russell's Revised Wechsler Memory Scale. *Journal of Clinical Psychology, 42,* 1000–1005.

Hiscock, M., & Hiscock, C. (1989). Refining the forced-choice method for the detection of malingering. *Journal of Clinical and Experimental Neuropsychology, 11,* 967–974.

Hobart, M. P., Goldberg, R., Bartko, J. J., & Gold, J. M. (1999). Repeatable battery for the Assessment of Neuropsychological Status as a Screening Test in Schizophrenia, II: Convergent/Discriminant validity and diagnostic group comparisons. *American Journal of Psychiatry, 156,* 1951–1957.

Horn, J. L. (1965). Fluid and crystallized intelligence: A factor analytic and developmental study of the structure among primary mental abilities. University of Illinois, Urbana-Champaign. Unpublished doctoral dissertation.

Horn, J. L. (1989). Cognitive diversity: A framework of learning. In P. L. Ackerman, R. J. Sternberg, & R. Glaser (Eds.), *Learning and individual differences* (pp. 61–116). New York: Freeman.

Horn, J. L., & Cattell, R. B. (1966). Refinement and test of the theory of fluid and crystallized intelligence. *Journal of Educational Psychology, 57,* 253–270.

Horn, J. L., & Cattell, R. B. (1967). Age differences in fluid and crystallized intelligence. *Acta Psychologica, 26,* 107–129.

Horn, J. L., & Hofer, S. M. (1992). Major abilities and development in the adult period. In R. J. Sternberg & C. A. Berg (Eds.), *Intellectual development* (pp. 44–99). Boston: Cambridge University Press.

Horn, J. L., & Noll, J. G. (1997). Human cognitive capabilities: Gf-Gc theory. In D. P. Flanagan, J. L. Genshaft, & P. A. Harrison (Eds.), *Contemporary intellectual assessment: Theories, tests and issues* (pp. 53–91). New York: Guilford.

Horn, S. (1974). Some psychological factors in Parkinsonism. *Journal of Neurology, Neurosurgery, & Psychiatry, 3,* 27–31.

Hunt, W. A., & Older, H. J. (1943). Detection of malingering through psychometric tests. *Naval Medical Bulletin, 41,* 1318–1323.

Iverson, G. L., & Franzen, M. D. (1994). The Recognition Memory Test, Digit Span, and Knox Cube Test as markers of malingered memory impairment. *Assessment, 1,* 323–334.

Iverson, G. L., & Franzen, M. D. (1996). Using multiple objective memory procedures to detect simulated malingering. *Journal of Clinical & Experimental Neuropsychology, 18,* 38–51.

Iverson, G. L., Franzen, M. D., & McCracken, L. M. (1991). Evaluation of an objective assessment technique for the detection of malingered memory deficits. *Law & Human Behavior, 15,* 667–676.

Ivnik, R. J., Malec, J. F., Smith, G. E., Tangalos, E. G., Petersen, R. C., Kokmen, E., & Kurland, L. T. (1992). Mayo's older Americans normative studies: WMS-R norms for ages 56 to 94. *Clinical Neuropsychologist, 6,* 49–82.

Jacobs, D., Troster, A. I., Butters, N., Salmon, D. P., & Cermak, L. S. (1990). Intrusion errors on the visual reproduction test of the Wechsler Memory Scale-Revised: An analysis of demented and amnesic patients. *Clinical Neuropsychologist, 4,* 177–191.

Johnson, J. L., & Lesniak-Karpiak, K. (1997). The effect of warning on malingering on memory and motor tasks in college samples. *Archives of Clinical Neuropsychology, 12,* 231–238.

Katzman, R. (1976). The prevalence and malignancy of Alzheimer's Disease. *Archives of Neurology, 33,* 217–218.

Katzman, R. (1986). Alzheimer's Disease. *New England Journal of Medicine, 314,* 964–973.

Kaufman, A. S. (1990). *Assessing adolescent and adult intelligence.* Boston, MA: Allyn & Bacon.

Kaufman, A. S. (1994). *Intelligent testing with the WISC-III.* New York: Wiley.

Kaufman, A. S., & Kaufman, N. L. (1993). *Kaufman Adolescent and Adult Intelligence Test (KAIT) manual.* Circle Pines, MN: American Guidance Service.

Kaufman, A. S. (2000). Seven questions about the WAIS-III regarding differences in abilities across the 16 to 89 year life span. *School Psychology Quarterly, 15,* 3–29.

Kaufman, A. S., & Lichtenberger, E. O. (1999). *Essentials of WAIS-III Assessment.* New York: Wiley.

Kaufman, A. S., & Lichtenberger, E. O. (2001). *Assessing adolescent and adult intelligence* (2nd ed.). Needham Heights, MA: Allyn & Bacon.

Kaufman, A. S., Lichtenberger, E. O., & McLean, J. E. (2001). Two-and three-factor solutions of the WAIS-III. *Assessment, 8,* 267–279.

Kazniak, A. W., Poon, L. W., & Riege, W. R. (1986). Assessing memory deficits: An information-processing approach. In L. W. Poon, T. Crook, B. J. Gurland, K. Davis, A. W. Kazniak, C. Eisdorfer, & L. W. Thompson (Eds.). *Handbook for Clinical Memory Assessment of Older Adults* (pp. 168–188). Washington, DC: American Psychological Association.

Keefe, R. S. E., Roitman, S. E., Harvey, P. D., Blum, C. S., Dupre, R. L., Prieto, D. M., Davidson, M., & Davis, K. L. (1995). A pen-and-paper human analogue of a monkey prefrontal cortex activation task: Spatial working memory in patients with schizophrenia. *Schizophrenia Research, 17,* 25–33.

Kessler, H. (1972). Epidemiological studies of Parkinson's disease. III: A Community based study. *American Journal of Epidemiology, 96,* 242–254.

King, D. J. (1994). Psychomotor impairment and cognitive disturbances induced by neuroleptics. *Acta Psychiatrica Scandinavica, 89 (Suppl. 380),* 53–58.

Kleemier, R. W. (1962). Intellectual change in the senium. *Proceedings of the Social Statistics Section of the American Statistical Association,* 290–295.

Klingberg, T., O'Sullivan, B. T., & Roland, P. E. (1997). Bilateral activation of frontoparietal network by incrementing demands in a working memory task. *Cerebral Cortex, 7,* 465–471.

Kopelman, M. D. (1985). Rates of forgetting in Alzheimer-type dementia and Korsakoff's syndrome. *Neuropsychologia, 23,* 623–638.

Korten, A. E., Henderson, A. S., Christensen, H., Jorm, A. F., Rodgers, B., Jacomb, P., &

MacKinnon, A. J. (1997). A prospective study of cognitive function in the elderly. *Psychological Medicine, 27,* 919–930.

Kovar, M. G. (1977). Elderly People: The population 65 years and over. *DHEW Publications No. (HRA)* 77–1232.

Kyllonen, P. C. (1993). Aptitude testing based on information processing: A test of the four-sources model. *Journal of General Psychology, 120,* 375–405.

Kyllonen, P. C. (in press). 'g:' Knowledge, speed strategies, or working-memory capacity? A systems perspective. In R. J. Sternberg & E. L. Grigorenko (Eds.), *The general factor of intelligence: How general is it?* Mahwah, NJ: Erlbaum.

Kyllonen, P. C., & Christal, R. E. (1990). Reasoning ability is (little more than) working memory capacity?! *Intelligence, 14,* 389–433.

La Rue, A. (1992). *Aging and neuropsychological assessment.* New York: Plenum Press.

Lanska, D. J., & Whitehouse, P. J. (1989). Huntington's disease. *Neurology Neurosurgery Update Series 8,* 1–8.

Lee, G. P., Loring, D. W., & Martin, R. C. (1992). Rey's 15-item visual memory test for the detection of malingering: Normative observations on patients with neurological disorders. *Psychological Assessment, 4,* 43–46.

Lee, G. P., Loring, D. W., & Thormpson, J. L. (1989). Construct validity of material-specific memory measures following unilateral temporal lobe ablations. *Psychological Assessment, 3,* 192–197.

Lencz, T., McCarthy, G., Bronen, R. A., Scott, T. M., Inserni, J. A., Sass, K. J., Novelly, R. A., Kim, J. H., & Spencer, D. D. (1992). Quantitative magnetic resonance imaging in temporal lobe epilepsy: Relationship to neuropathology and neuropsychological function. *Annals of Neurology, 31,* 629–637.

Lezak, M. Z. (1995). *Neuropsychological assessment* (3rd ed.). New York: Oxford University Press.

Loberg, T. (1980). Alcohol misuse and neuropsychological deficits in men. *Journal of Studies on Alcohol, 41,* 119–128.

Logie, R. H. (1996). *Visuo-spatial working memory.* Hove, East Sussex, UK: Erlbaum.

Logie, R. H. (1996). The seven ages of working memory. In J. T. E. Richardson, R. W. Engle, L. Hasher, R. H. Logie, E. R. Stoltzfus, & R. T. Zacks (Eds.), *Working memory and human cognition* (pp. 31–65). New York: Oxford University Press.

Loring, D. W. (1989). The Wechsler Memory Scale-Revised or the Wechsler Memory Scale-revisited? *Clinical Neuropsychologist, 3,* 59–69.

Mahler, M. E., & Cummings, J. L. (1990). Alzheimer's disease and the dementia of PD: Comparative investigations. *Alzheimer Disease & Associated Disorders, 4,* 133–149.

Manly, J. J., Heaton, R. K., & Taylor, M. J. (2000, August). The effects of demographic variables and the development of demographically adjusted norms for the WAIS-III and WMS-III. In D. S. Tulsky & D. Saklofske (Chairs), *The Clinical Interpretation of the WAIS-III and WMS-III: New Research findings.* Symposium conducted at the 108th Annual Convention of the American Psychological Association, Washington, DC.

Mann, K., Gunther, A., Stetter, F., & Achermann, K. (1999). Rapid recovery from cognitive deficits in abstinent alcoholics: A controlled test-retest study. *Alcohol & Alcoholism, 34,* 567–574.

Manschreck, T. C., Laughery, J. A., Weinstein, C. C., Allen, D., Humbelstone, B., Neville, M., Podlewski, H., & Mitra, N. (1988). Characteristics of freebase cocaine psychosis. *Yale Journal of Biological Medicine, 61,* 115–122.

Marcopulos, B. A., McLain, C. A., & Giuliano, A. J. (1997). Cognitive impairment or inadequate norms: A study of healthy, rural, older adults with limited education. *Clinical Neuropsychologist, 11,* 111–131.

Masur, D. M., Fuld, P. A., Blau, A. D., Crystal, H., & Aronson, M. K. (1990). Predicting development of dementia in the elderly with the selective reminding test. *Journal of Clinical Experimental Neuropsychology, 12,* 529–538.

Masur, D. M., Sliwinski, M., Lipton, R. B., Blau, A. D., & Crystal, H. A. (1994). Neuropsychological prediction of dementia and the absence of dementia in healthy elderly persons. *Neurology, 44,* 1427–1432.

Mayeux, R., Denero, J., Hemenegildo, N., Marder, K., Tang, M. X., Cote, L. J., & Stern, Y. (1992). A population-based investigation of Parkinson's disease with and without dementia: Relationship to age and gender. *Archives of Neurology, 49,* 492–497.

McIntosh, G. C. (1992). Neurological conceptualization of epilepsy. In T. L. Bennett (Ed.), *The neuropsychology of epilepsy: Critical issues in neuropsychology* (pp. 17–37). New York: Plenum Press.

McKetin, R., & Mattick, R. P. (1998). Attention and memory in illicit amphetamine users: Comparison with non-drug-using controls. *Drug & Alcohol Dependence, 50,* 181–184.

McMahon, E. A., & Satz, P. (1981). Clinical neuropsychology: Some forensic applications. In S. B. Filskov & T. J. Boll, (Eds.), *Handbook of Clinical Neuropsychology* (pp. 686–701). New York: Wiley.

McMillan, T. M., Powell, G. E., Janota, I., & Polkey, C. E. (1987). Relationships between neuropathology and cognitive functioning in temporal lobectomy patients. *Journal of Neurology, Neurosurgery, & Psychiatry, 50,* 167–176.

Millis, S. R. (1992). The Recognition Memory Test in the detection of malingered and exaggerated memory deficits. *Clinical Neuropsychologist, 6,* 406–414.

Millis, S. R., Malina, A. C., Bowers, D. A., & Ricker, J. H. (1999). Confirmatory factor analysis of the Wechsler Memory Scale-III. *Journal of Clinical & Experimental Neuropsychology, 21,* 87–93.

Mitrushina, M. N., Boone, K. B., & D'Elia, L. F. (1999). *Handbook of normative data for neuropsychological assessment.* New York: Oxford University Press.

Mitrushina, M. N., & Satz, P. (1991a). Changes in cognitive functioning associated with normal aging. *Archives of Clinical Neuropsychology, 6,* 49–60.

Mitrushina, M. N., & Satz, P. (1991b). Effect of repeated administration of a neuropsychological battery in the elderly. *Journal of Clinical Psychology, 47,* 790–801.

Mittenberg, W., & Motta, S. (1993). Effects of chronic cocaine abuse on memory and learning. *Archives of Clinical Neuropsychology, 8,* 477–483.

Money, E. A., Kirk, R. C., & McNaughton, N. (1992). Alzheimer's dementia produces a loss of discrimination but no increase in rate of memory decay in delayed matching to sample. *Neuropsychologia, 30,* 133–143.

Morice, R., & Delahunty, A. (1996). Frontal/executive impairments in schizophrenia. *Schizophrenia Bulletin, 22,* 125–137.

Morse, P. A., & Montgomery, C. E. (1992). Neuropsychological evaluation of traumatic brain injury. In R. F. White (Ed.), *Clinical syndromes in adult neuropsychology: The practitioner's handbook* (pp. 254–296). Amsterdam: Elsevier Science Publishers.

Mortimer, J. A., Pirozzolo, F., Hansch, E., & Webster, D. (1982). Relationship of motor symptoms to intellectual deficits in Parkinson's disease. *Neurology, 3,* 133–137.

Mortimer, J. A., Schuman, L. M., & French, L. R. (1981). Epidemiology of dementing illness. In J. A. Mortimer and L. M. Schuman (Eds.), *Epidemiology of Dementia* (pp. 3–23). New York: Oxford University Press.

Moss, M. B., & Albert, M. S. (1992). Neuropsychology of Alzheimer's disease. In R. F. White (Ed.), *Clinical syndromes in adult neuropsychology: The practitioner's handbook* (pp. 305–343). Amsterdam: Elsevier Science Publishers.

Moss, M. B., Albert, M. S., Butters, N., & Payne, M. (1986). Differential patterns of memory loss among patients with Alzheimer's disease, Huntington's disease, and alcoholic Korsakoff's syndrome. *Archives of Neurology, 43,* 401–414.

Murray, R. M., Greene, J. G., & Adams, J. H. (1971). Analgesic abuse and dementia. *Lancet, 2,* 242–245.

Nadler, J. D., Mittenberg, W., DePiano, F. A., & Schneider, B. A. (1994). Effects of patient age on neuropsychological test interpretation. *Professional Psychology 25,* 288–295.

Naugle, R. I., Chelune, G. J., Cheek, R., Luders, H., Awad, I. A. (1993). Detection of changes in material-specific memory following temporal lobectomy using the Wechsler Memory Scale-Revised. *Archives of Clinical Neuropsychology, 8,* 381–395.

Nestor, P. G., Shenton, M. E., McCarley, R. W., Haimson, J., Smith, R. S., O'Donnell, B., Kimble, M., Kikinis, R., & Jolesz, F. A. (1993). Neuropsychological correlates of MRI temporal lobe abnormalities in schizophrenia. *American Journal of Psychiatry, 150,* 1849–1855.

Nixon, S. J. (1996a). Alzheimer's disease and vascular dementia. In R. L. Adams, O. A. Parsons, J. L. Culbertson, & S. J. Nixon (Eds.), *Neuropsychology for clinical practice: Etiology, assessment, and treatment of common neurological disorders* (pp. 65–105). Washington, DC: American Psychological Association.

Nixon, S. J. (1996b). Secondary dementias: Reversible dementias and pseudodementia. In R. L. Adams, O. A. Parsons, J. L. Culbertson, & S. J. Nixon (Eds.), *Neuropsychology for clinical practice: Etiology, assessment, and treatment of common neurological disorders* (pp. 107–130). Washington, DC: American Psychological Association.

Nixon, S. J., & Bowlby, D. (1996). Evidence of alcohol-related efficiency deficits in an episodic learning task. *Alcoholism 20,* 21–24.

Nixon, S. J., Kujawski, A., Parsons, O. A., and Yohman, J. R. (1987). Semantic (verbal) and figural memory impairment in alcoholics. *Journal of Clinical and Experimental Neuropsychology, 9,* 311–322.

Nyberg, L., Cabeza, R., & Tulving, E. (1996). PET studies of encoding and retrieval: The HERA model. *Psychonomic Bulletin & Review, 3,* 135–148.

O'Mahony, J. F., & Doherty, B. (1993). Patterns of intellectual performance among recently abstinent alcohol abusers on WAIS-R and WMS-R subtests. *Archives of Clinical Neuropsychology, 8,* 373–380.

O'Mahony, J. F., & Doherty, B. (1996). Intellectual impairment among recently abstinent alcohol abusers. *British Journal of Clinical Psychology, 35,* 77–83.

Osterrieth, P. A. (1944). Le test de copie d'une figure complexe. *Archives de Psychologie, 30,* 206–356.

Pankratz, L., Binder, L., & Wilcox, L. (1987). Assessment of an exaggerated somatosensory deficit with Symptom Validity Assessment. *Archives of Neurology, 44,* 798.

Pankratz, L., Fausti, S. A., & Peed, S. (1975). A forced-choice technique to evaluate deafness in a hysterical or malingering patient. *Journal of Consulting & Clinical Psychology, 43,* 421–422.

Park, S., & Holzman, P. S. (1992). Schizophrenics show spatial working memory deficits. *Archives of General Psychiatry, 49,* 975–982.

Parsons, O. A. (1977). Psychological deficits in alcoholics: Facts and fancies. *Alcoholism, 11,* 51–56.

Parsons, O. A. (1996). Alcohol abuse and alcoholism. In R. L. Adams, O. A. Parsons, J. L. Culbertson, & S. J. Nixon (Eds.), *Neuropsychology for clinical practice: Etiology, assessment, and treatment of common neurological disorders* (pp. 175–202). Washington, DC: American Psychological Association.

Parsons, O. A., & Farr, S. P. (1981). The neuropsychology of alcohol and drug use. In S. B. Filskov & T. S. Boll (Eds.), *Handbook of Clinical Neuropsychology* (pp. 320–365). New York: Wiley.

Parsons, O. A., & Prigatano, G. P. (1977). Memory functioning in alcoholics. In I. M. Birnbaum & E. S. Parker (Eds.), *Handbook of Clinical Neuropsychology* (pp. 185–194). Hillsdale, NJ: Erlbaum.

Paul, D. S., Franzen, M. D., Cohen, S. H., & Fremouw, W. (1992). An investigation into the reliability and validity of two tests used in the detection of dissimulation. *International Journal of Clinical Neuropsychology, 14,* 1–9.

Penfield, W., & Mathieson, G. (1974). Memory, autopsy findings, and comments on the role of the hippocampus in experiential recall. *Archives of Neurology, 31,* 145–154.

Piotrowski, C., & Keller, J. W. (1989). Psychological testing in outpatient mental health facilities: A national study. *Professional Psychology, 20,* 423–425.

Piotrowski, C., & Lubin, B. (1989). Assessment practices of Division 38 practitioners. *Health Psychologist, 11,* 1–2.

Pope, H. G., & Yurgelun-Todd, D. (1996). The residual cognitive effects of heavy marijuana use in college students. *Journal of the American Medical Association, 275,* 521–527.

Press, R. J. (1983). The neuropsychological effects of cocaine and opiate use. Ann Arbor, MI: University Microfilms International.

Prull, M. W., Gabrieli, J. D. E., & Bunge, S. A. (2000). Aging of the brain and its impact on cognitive performance: Integration of structural and functional findings. In F. I. M. Craik & T. A. Salthouse (Eds.), *The handbook of aging and cognition* (2nd ed., pp. 91–154). Mahwah, NJ: Erlbaum.

Psychological Corporation (1997). *WAIS-III and WMS-III technical manual.* San Antonio, TX: Author.

Purves, D., Augustine, G. J., Fitzpatrick, D., Katz, L. C., LaMantia, A. S., McNamara, J. O. (Eds.). (1997). *Neuroscience.* Sunderland, MA: Sinauer.

Rabbitt, P., Bent, N., & McInnes, L. (1997). Health, age, and mental ability. *Irish Journal of Psychology, 18,* 104–131.

Rausch, R., & Babb, T. L. (1993). Hippocampal neuron loss and memory scores before and after temporal lobe surgery for epilepsy. *Archives of Neurology, 50,* 812–817.

Raz, N. (2000). Aging of the brain and its impact on cognitive performance: Integration of structural and functional findings. In F. I. M. Craik & T. A. Salthouse (Eds.), *The handbook of aging and cognition* (2nd ed., pp. 1–90). Mahwah, NJ: Erlbaum.

Reid, D. B., & Kelly, M. P. (1993). Wechsler Memory Scale-Revised in closed head injury. *Journal of Clinical Psychology, 49,* 245–254.

Rey, A. (1941). L'examen psychologigique dans le cas d'encephalopathie traumatique. *Archives de Psychologie, 37,* 126–139.

Rey, A. (1964). *L'examen Clinique en Psychologie.* Paris: Presses Universitaires de France.

Richardson, J. T. E. (1996). Evolving concepts of working memory. In J. T. E. Richardson, R. W. Engle, L. Hasher, R. H. Logie, E. R. Stoltzfus, & R. T. Zacks (Eds.), *Working memory and human cognition* (pp. 3–30). New York: Oxford University Press.

Robinson-Whelen, S., & Storandt, M. (1992). Immediate and delayed prose recall among normal and demented adults. *Archives of Neurology, 49,* 32–34.

Rossel, S. L., & David, A. S. (1997). The neuropsychology of schizophrenia: Recent trends. *Current Opinion in Psychiatry, 10,* 26–29.

Rosseli, M., & Ardila, A. (1996). Cognitive effects of cocaine and polydrug abuse. *Journal of Clinical & Experimental Neuropsychology, 18,* 122–135.

Russell, E. W. (1975). A multiple scoring method for the assessment of complex memory functions. *Journal of Consulting & Clinical Psychology, 43,* 800–809.

Russell, E. W. (1988). Renorming Russell's version of the Wechsler Memory Scale. *Journal of Clinical and Experimental Neuropsychology, 10,* 235–249.

Salmon, D. P., Granholm, E., McCullough, D., Butters, N., & Grant, I. (1989). Recognition memory span in mildly and moderately demented patients with Alzheimer's disease. *Journal of Clinical and Experimental Neuropsychology, 11,* 429–443.

Sass, K. J., Sass, A., Westerveld, M., Lencz, T., Novelly, R. A., Kim, J. H., & Spencer, D. D. (1992). Specificity in the correlation of verbal memory and hippocampal neuron loss: Dissociation of memory, language, and verbal intellectual ability. *Journal of Clinical & Experimental Neuropsychology, 14,* 662–672.

Saykin, A. J., Gur, R. C., Gur, R. E. (1991). Neuropsychological function in schizophrenia: Selective impairment in memory and learning. *Archives of General Psychiatry, 48,* 618–624.

Saykin, A. J., Shtasel, D. L., Gur, R. E., Kester, D. B., Mozley, L. H., & Gur, R. C. (1992). *Neuropsychology in schizophrenia: State of trait.* Paper presented at the 145 Annual Meeting of the American Psychiatric Association, Washington, DC.

Saykin, A. J., Shtasel, D. L., Gur, R. E., Kester, D. B., Mozley, L. H., Stafiniak, P., & Gur, R. C. (1994). Neuropsychological deficits in neuroleptic naive patients with first-episode schizophrenia. *Archives of General Psychiatry, 51,* 124–131.

Schaie, K. W. (1983). *Longitudinal studies of adult psychological development.* New York: Guilford Press.

Schretlen, D., Brandt, J., Krafft, L., & Van Gorp, W. (1991). Some caveats in using the Rey 15-Item memory test to detect malingered amnesia. *Psychological Assessment, 3,* 667–672.

Seidman, L. J., Cassens, G. P., Kremen, W. S., & Pepple, J. R. (1992). Neuropsychologicy of schizophrenia. In R. F. White (Ed.), *Clinical syndromes in adult neuropsychology: The practitioner's handbook* (pp. 381–449). Amsterdam: Elsevier Science Publishers.

Shelton, M. D., & Parsons, O. A. (1987). Alcoholics' self-assessment of their neuropsychological functioning in everyday life. *Journal of Clinical Psychology, 43,* 395–403.

Sherer, M., Nixon, S. J., Anderson, B. L., & Adams, R. L. (1992). Differential sensitivity of the WMS to the effects of IQ and brain damage. *Archives of Clinical Neuropsychology, 7,* 505–514.

Shimamura, A. P., Berry, J. M., Mangels, J. A., Rusting, C. L., & Jurica, P. J. (1995). Memory and cognitive abilities in university professors: Evidence for successful aging. *Psychological Science, 6,* 271–277.

Souchay, C., Isingrini, M., & Espagnet, L. (2000). Aging, episodic memory feeling-of-knowing, and frontal functioning. *Neuropsychology, 14,* 299–309.

Spreen, O., & Strauss, E. (1991). *A compendium of neuropsychological tests.* New York: Oxford University Press.

Spreen, O., & Strauss, E. (1998). *A compendium of neuropsychological tests* (2nd ed.). New York: Oxford University Press.

Squire, L. R. (1987). *Memory and brain.* New York: Oxford University Press.

Squire, L. R. (1992). Mechanisms of memory. In S. M. Kosslyn & R. A. Andersen (Eds.), *Frontiers in cognitive neuroscience* (pp. 500–515). Cambridge, MA: MIT Press.

Squire, L. R., & Butters, N. (Eds.). (1992). *Neuropsychology of memory.* New York: Guilford Press.

Stern, Y., Andrews, H., Pittman, J., Sano, M., Tatemichi, T., Lantigua, R., & Mayeux, R. (1992). Diagnosis of dementia in a heterogeneous population. *Archives of Neurology, 49,* 453–460.

Stern, Y., Richards, M., Sano, M., & Mayeux, R. (1993). Comparison of cognitive changes in patients with Alzheimer's and Parkinson's disease. *Archives of Neurology, 50,* 1040–1045.

Stirling, J. D., Hellewell, J. S. E., & Hewitt, J. (1997). Verbal memory impairment in schizophrenia: No sparing of short-term recall. *Schizophrenia Research, 25,* 217–225.

Storandt, M., & Hill, R. D. (1989). Very mild senile dementia of the Alzheimer type II: Psychometric test performance. *Archives of Neurology, 46,* 383–386.

Sullivan, E. V. & Sagar, H. J. (1988). Nonverbal short-term memory impairment in Parkinson's disease. *Journal of Clinical & Experimental Neuropsychology, 1,* 34.

Sullivan, E. V., Sagar, H. J., Gabrieli, J. D. E., Corkin, S., & Growdon, J. H. (1989). Different cognitive profiles on standard behavioral tests in Parkinson's disease and Alzheimer's disease. *Journal of Clinical & Experimental Neuropsychology, 11,* 799–820.

Tarter, R. E. (1980). Brain damage in chronic alcoholics: A review of the psychological evidence. In D. Richter, (Ed.), *Addiction & Brain Damage.* London: Croom Helm.

Tivis, R., Beatty, W. W., Nixon, S. J., and Parson, O. A. (1995). Patterns of cognitive impairment among alcoholics: are there subtypes? *Alcoholism: Clinical and Experimental Research, 19,* 496–500.

Trahan, D. E. (1992). Analysis of learning and rate of forgetting in age-associated memory differences. *Clinical Neuropsychologist, 6,* 241–246.

Tremont, G., Hoffman, R. G., Scott, J. G., Adams, R. L., & Nadolne, M. J. (1997). Clinical utility of Wechsler Memory Scale-Revised and predicted IQ discrepancies in closed head injury. *Archives of Clinical Neuropsychology, 12,* 757–762.

Troster, A. I., Butters, N., Salmon, D. P., Cullum, C. M., Jacobs, D., Brandt, J., & White, R. F. (1993). The diagnostic utility of savings scores: Differentiating Alzheimer's and Huntington's diseases with the logical memory and visual reproduction tests. *Journal of Clinical & Experimental Neuropsychology, 15,* 773–788.

Trueblood, W. (1994). Qualitative and quantitative characteristics of malingered and other invalid WAIS-R and clinical memory data. *Journal of Clinical & Experimental Neuropsychology, 16,* 597–607.

Trueblood, W., & Schmidt, M. (1993). Malingering and other validity considerations in the neuropsychological evaluation of mild head injury. *Journal of Clinical & Experimental Neuropsychology, 15,* 578–590.

Tulsky, D. S., & Ledbetter, M. F. (2000). Updating to the WAIS-III and WMS-III: Considerations for research and clinical practice. *Psychological Assessment, 12,* 253–262.

Tulving, E. (1983). *Elements of episodic memory.* New York: Oxford University Press.

Tulving, E. (2000). Concepts of memory. In E. Tulving & F. I. M. Craik (Eds.), *The Oxford handbook of memory* (pp. 33–43). New York: Oxford University Press.

Tweedy, J., Langer, K., & McDowell, F. (1982). The effect of semantic relations on the memory deficit associated with Parkinson's disease. *Journal of Clinical Neuropsychology, 4,* 235–247.

Vakil, E., Arbell, N., Gozlan, M., Hoofien, D., & Blachstein, H. (1992). Relative importance of informational units and their role in long-term recall by closed-head-injured patients and control groups. *Journal of Consulting & Clinical Psychology, 60,* 802–803.

Vakil, E., Hoofien, D., & Blachstein, H. (1992). Total amount learned versus learning rate of verbal and nonverbal information, in differentiating left-from right-brain injured patients. *Archives of Clinical Neuropsychology, 7,* 111–120.

van der Hurk, P. R., & Hodges, J. R. (1995). Episodic and semantic memory in Alzheimer's disease and progressive supranuclear palsy: A comparative study. *Journal of Clinical & Experimental Neuropsychology, 17,* 459–471.

Victor, M., & Adams, D. R. (1985). The alcoholic dementias. In J. A. M. Frederiks (Ed.), *Handbook of clinical neurology. Vol 46. Clinical Neuropsychology* (pp. 335–350). Amsterdam: Elsevier Science Publishers.

Wachspress, M., Berenberg, A. N., & Jacobson, A. (1953). Simulation of psychosis. *Psychiatric Quarterly, 27,* 463–476.

Washton, A. M., & Gold, M. S. (1984). Chronic cocaine abuse: Evidence and adverse effects on health and functioning. *Psychiatric Annals, 17,* 733–743.

Wechsler, D. (1945). A standardized memory scale for clinical use. *Journal of Psychology, 19,* 87–95.

Wechsler, D. (1955). *Manual for the Wechsler Adult Intelligence Scale (WAIS).* San Antonio, TX: The Psychological Corporation.

Wechsler, D. (1987). *Manual for the Wechsler Memory Scale–Revised (WAIS-R).* San Antonio, TX: The Psychological Corporation.

Wechsler, D. (1997). *Wechsler Memory Scale–Third Edition (WMS-III) administration and scoring manual.* San Antonio, TX: The Psychological Corporation.

Welsh, K., Butters, N., Hughes, J., Mohs, R., & Heyman, A. (1991). Detection of abnormal memory decline in mild cases of Alzheimer's disease using CERAD neuropsychological measures. *Archives of Neurology, 48,* 278–281.

Welsh, K., Butters, N., Hughes, J., Mohs, R., & Heyman, A. (1992). Detection and staging of dementia in Alzheimer's disease: Use of the neuropsychological measures developed for the Consortium to Establish a Registry for Alzheimer's Disease. *Archives of Neurology, 49,* 448–452.

White, R. F. (Ed.). (1992). *Clinical syndromes in adult neuropsychology: The practitioner's handbook*. Amsterdam: Elsevier Science Publishers.

White, R. F., Vasterling, J. J., Koroshetz, W., & Myers, R. (1992). Neuropsychological function in Parkinson's disease. In R. F. White (Ed.), *Clinical Syndromes in Adult Neuropsychology: The Practitioner's Handbook* (pp. 254–296). Amsterdam: Elsevier Science Publishers.

Whitehouse, P. J. (1986). Development of neurotransmitter-specific therapeutic approaches in Alzheimer's disease. In T. Crook & R. T. Bartus (Eds.), *Treatment development strategies for Alzheimer's disease* (pp. 483–498). Madison, CT: Mark Powley Associates.

Wiggins, E. C., & Brandt, J. (1988). The detection of simulated amnesia. *Law & Human Behavior, 12,* 57–78.

Wilkinson, A. (1987). CT scan and neuropsychological assessments of alcoholics. In O. Parsons, N. Butters, & P. Nathan (Eds.), *Neuropsychology of alcoholism: Implications for diagnosis and treatment* (pp. 76–98). New York: Guilford Press.

Wilson, R. S., Bacon, L. D., Fox, J. H., & Kaszniak, A. W. (1983). Primary and secondary memory in dementia of the Alzheimer type. *Journal of Clinical Neuropsychology, 5,* 337–344.

Woodcock, R. W., McGrew, K. S., & Mather, N. (2000). *Woodcock-Johnson Psycho-Educational Battery Third Edition (WJ-3)*. Chicago: Riverside.

Wyatt, R. J., Alexander, R. C., Egan, M. F., & Kirch, D. G. (1988). Schizophrenia, just the facts: What do we know, how well do we know it? *Schizophrenia Research, 1,* 3–18.

Yu, E. S., Liu, W. T., Levy, P., Zhang, M-Y., Katzman, R., Lung, C.-T., Wong, S.-C., Wang, Z-Y., & Qu, G-Y. (1989). Cognitive impairment among elderly adults in Shanghai, China. *Journal of Gerontology, 44,* S97–106.

Zakzanis, K. K. (1998). Quantitative evidence for neuroanatomic and neuropsychological markers in dementia of the Alzheimer's type. *Journal of Clinical & Experimental Neuropsychology, 20,* 259–269.

Zelinski, E. M., & Burnight, K. P. (1997). Sixteen-year longitudinal and time-lag changes in memory and cognition in older adults. *Psychology & Aging, 12,* 503–513.

Annotated Bibliography

Flanagan, D. P., McGrew, K. S., & Ortiz, S. O. (2000). *The Wechsler intelligence scales and Gf-Gc theory: A contemporary approach to interpretation*. Needham Heights, MA: Allyn and Bacon.

This book provides a theory-driven approach to interpreting the Wechsler scales including the adult tests, WAIS-III, and WMS-III. The authors apply the CHC theory to cross-battery interpretation and focus on the Wechsler scales. They provide visual guides, summary pages, and worksheets to apply their interpretive approach.

Franzen, M. D., & Iverson, G. L. (2000). The Wechsler Memory Scales. In G. Groth-Marnat (Ed.), *Neuropsychological assessment in clinical practice: A guide to test interpretation and integration* (pp. 195–222). New York: Wiley.

This chapter provides a review of the history of the Wechsler Memory Scales, the assets and limitations of each of the test's versions, and case examples using the tests.

Hawkins, K. A. (1998). Indicators of brain dysfunction derived from graphic representations of the WAIS-III/WMS-III Technical Manual clinical samples data: A preliminary approach to clinical utility. *Clinical Neuropsychologist, 12,* 535–551.

This article analyzes the index scores for clinical samples reported in the WAIS-III/WMS-III Technical Manual. Based on the graphic presentation of the data, the author draws conclusions about the usefulness of specific WMS-III Indexes in detecting brain compromise.

Mitrushina, M. N., Boone, K. B., & D'Elia, L. F. (1999). *Handbook of normative data for neuropsychological assessment*. New York: Oxford University Press.

This chapter provides excellent reviews and critiques of the research on the various normative and clinical studies for the WMS, WMS-R, and WMS-III. In addition to this review, a brief history of the WMS is given.

The Psychological Corporation (1997). *WAIS-III and WMS-III technical manual*. San Antonio, TX: Author.

This manual comes as part of the WMS-III kit. It provides introductory information on the WMS-III and WAIS-III and details development of the norms and the standardization procedures. It also presents reliability and validity studies. The WMS-III is compared to other measures of memory functioning, cognitive ability, and related abilities. It reviews studies on groups with brain dysfunction such as dementia, traumatic brain injury, temporal lobe epilepsy and others. It provides global information on interpretation along with a plethora of statistical tables for clinicians and researchers.

Tulsky, D. S., & Ledbetter, M. F. (2000). Updating to the WAIS-III and WMS-III: Considerations for research and clinical practice. *Psychological Assessment, 12,* 253–262.

This article reviews the substantive revisions of the WMS-III and the WAIS-III. The authors recognize that clinicians are often reluctant to switch to new versions of a test because of the extensive use of earlier versions in research and clinical practice. Thus, they present several points to consider when switching from the WMS-R to the WMS-III.

Wechsler, D. (1997). *Wechsler Memory Scale-Third Edition (WMS-III) administration and scoring manual.* San Antonio, TX: The Psychological Corporation.

This manual comes as part of the WMS-III kit. It provides a basic description of the WMS-III Indexes and subtests. It reviews revisions from the WMS-R to WMS-III in a subtest-by-subtest manner. WMS-III examiners can gather important information about administration and scoring from the manual. For each WMS-III subtest, the majority of the specific administration instructions are found in the stimulus booklet and record form, but this manual provides additional information on administration, recording, and scoring responses. Specific scoring criteria are provided in Appendixes for Logical Memory, Family Pictures, and Visual Reproduction. Subtest, index, and composite norms tables are provided at the end of the manual. It also provides supplementary data for determining significant and abnormal discrepancies between indexes and subtests.

Index